CW00347645

MILLER'S
POCKET
DICTIONARY
OF
ANTIQUES

MILLER'S
P O C K E T
DICTIONARY
$\overline{OF}$
ANTIQUES

AN AUTHORITATIVE A-Z FOR
COLLECTORS, DEALERS AND ENTHUSIASTS

General Editors:
JUDITH and MARTIN MILLER

MITCHELL BEAZLEY

MILLER'S POCKET DICTIONARY OF ANTIQUES

Edited and designed by Mitchell Beazley
International Ltd
Artists House 14-15 Manette Street
London W1V 5LB

General Editors: Judith and Martin Miller
Contributors: Christopher Catling and Steven Goss
Editor: Alan Folly
Art Editor: Nigel O'Gorman
Designer: Christopher Howson
Production: Barbara Hind
Artwork by: John Hutchinson

Typeset by Bookworm Typesetting, Manchester
Reproduction by M. and E. Reproductions, England
Produced by Mandarin Offset
Printed and bound in Malaysia
Set in Univers

INTRODUCTION

When we produced the first *Miller's Antiques Price Guide* in 1979, the world of antiques was still regarded as the domain of the élite few – the professional dealer, the experienced, often wealthy, collector, and the dedicated academic. Over the last ten years this has certainly changed. Now it seems that everyone is collecting antiques. People are scouring the countryside for interesting finds, searching through attics and rummaging among jumble. The media are full of stories about deceptively insignificant-looking items fetching enormous sums.

This groundswell of interest has generated a real need for information on antiques and collectables. Our series of *Miller's Antiques Price Guides* has illustrated, identified and priced some 100,000 antiques to date. Other books of ours, in particular *Understanding Antiques*, take an in-depth look at typical pieces in all major collecting categories. We have also just produced a new guide to *Collectables* which deals with more recent and, on the whole, less expensive areas of collecting – although when a 20th-century Steiff teddy bear sells at Sotheby's for £55,000, as was recently the case, it makes one look again at those childhood toys lying crumpled in a forgotten corner.

We decided to produce the *Dictionary of Antiques* because we feel that one of the most important and difficult challenges for collectors is that of understanding the vocabulary. With all sorts of items being collected all over the world, a whole distinctive terminology has been created, with many foreign and technical words, and it can be extremely confusing and even embarrassing not to understand them. This is as true for the experienced collector as for novice, because the enormous range of antiques means that even experts may be unsure of terms from another discipline. The aim of this book is to convey a basic understanding of these terms and how they are used.

The Dictionary has been arranged in A-Z order so that you can easily find the word you are seeking, even if you don't know to which category of antiques it belongs. More than 5,000 terms from all areas of collecting are simply and clearly defined, with cross-references to other useful definitions.

Getting to grips with terminology is only the first step to understanding antiques; the collector must also educate his or her eye by looking at collections in museums and attending as many auctions as possible, especially at well-established auction houses which produce thorough and accurate captions, and may supply background information. Good reference books will also furnish information about style, period, and what to look for when buying.

If all this sounds like hard work, remember that learning about antiques and collecting them can be very absorbing and tremendous fun. I do hope this pocket guide may be a useful tool to you in discovering the joys of this fascinating subject.

Judith H. Miller

PERIODS AND STYLES

Dates	British Monarch	British Period	French Period
1558-1603	Elizabeth I	Elizabethan	Renaissance
1603-1625	James I	Jacobean	
1625-1649	Charles I	Carolean	Louis XIII (1610-1643)
1649-1660	Commonwealth	Cromwellian	Louis XIV (1643-1715)
1660-1685	Charles II	Restoration	
1685-1689	James II	Restoration	
1689-1694	William & Mary	William & Mary	
1694-1702	William III	William III	
1702-1714	Anne	Queen Anne	
1714-1727	George I	Early Georgian	Régence (1715-1723)
1727-1760	George II	Early Georgian	Louis XV (1723-1774)
1760-1811	George III	Late Georgian	Louis XVI (1774-1793)
			Directoire (1793-1799)
			Empire (1799-1815)
1812-1820	George III	Regency	Restauration (1815-1830)
1820-1830	George IV	Regency	
1830-1837	William IV	William IV	Louis Philippe (1830-1848)
1837-1901	Victoria	Victorian	2nd Empire (1848-1870)
			3rd Republic (1871-1940)
1901-1910	Edward VII	Edwardian	

German Period	U.S. Period	Style	Woods
Renaissance (c1650)	Early Colonial	Gothic	Oak Period (to c1670)
		Baroque (c1620-1700)	
Renaissance/ Baroque (c1650-1700)			Walnut period (c1670-1735)
	William & Mary		
	Dutch Colonial	Rococo (c1695-1760)	
Baroque (c1700-1730)	Queen Anne		
Rococo (c1730-1760)	Chippendale (from 1750)		Early mahogany period (c1735-1770)
Neo-classicism (c1760-1800)		Neo-classical (c1755-1805)	Late mahogany period (c1770-1810)
	Early Federal (1790-1810)		
Empire (c1800-1815)	American Directoire (1798-1804)	Empire (c1799-1815)	
	American Empire (1804-1815)		
Biedermeier (c1815-1848)	Later Federal (1810-1830)	Regency (c1812-1830)	
Revivale (c1830-1880)		Eclectic (c1830-1880)	
	Victorian		
Jugendstil (c1880-1920)		Arts & Crafts (c1880-1900)	
	Art Nouveau (c1900-1920)	Art Nouveau (c1900-1920)	

A

Aalto, Alvar (1898-1976):
Finnish Art Deco architect and furniture designer, noted especially for his bentwood chairs, made from the 1930s onwards.

abadeh: Persian carpets from southern Iran, brightly coloured, often incorporating a stylized tree of life, lozenge patterns and stick-like animal and human figures.

ABC: Usually of pottery, but also of glass, vessels made for children and often ornamented with the alphabet.

abrash: Colour variations in oriental carpets, caused by using wool from different batches of vegetable-based dye.

abrisham: Persian for silk and therefore of Persian carpets made of silk.

Abstbessingen: German faience produced in that town, C18.

acacia: Very hard whitish yellow wood with brown veins. Used for inlay and banding. Also known as robinia.

acanthus leaf: Stylized version of the thistle-like leaf of the acanthus plant, commonly carved on brackets and Corinthian capitals. Often used as a motif in furniture design.

acid engraving: Technique of decorating glass by coating it in resin, incising a design and exposing the revealed areas to hydrochloric acid fumes.

acid-gilding: C19 technique for decorating pottery whereby the surface is etched with hydrofluoric acid and the low-relief pattern gilded.

acorn: Often found in garden statuary, a stone finial or pinnacle carved in the shape of an acorn.

acorn clock: Early C19 New England mantel clock in a shape suggesting an acorn.

acorn knop: Wine-glass stem moulding in the shape of an upturned acorn – the cup uppermost.

acroterion: Plinth on which a statue stands, or a small shelf at the edges of a pediment.

Act of Parliament clock: C18 wall-hung clock with a large dial, no glass, and a trunk below, which houses the weights driving the mechanism. So called because all privately owned time-pieces were taxed by an Act of Parliament passed in 1797. Thereafter, only the wealthy could afford clocks and most people relied on public clocks, usually hung in taverns.

Adam, Robert (1728-1792): A Scottish born architect who created a neo-classical architectural and decorative style of furniture.

Adam and Eve: Motif frequently found on C17 glazed earthenwares.

Adam sisters: New York doll makers noted for "Columbian" and other rag dolls.

Adams: Family of English potters who owned factories in Staffordshire (e.g. Greengales, Hanley) in the C18 and C19. Famous for parian ware busts of famous (or infamous) people in the C19.

Adams, Nathan: Boston clock-maker, active 1796-1825.

Adams, Robert and James: Leading London gunsmiths, mid C19.

Adige chest: Another name for a Cyprus chest.

Admiral jug: Toby jug depicting an admiral; originally to commemorate Lord Howe's victory over the French in 1794.

adze-surfaced wood: Pleasant irregular surface patterned with ridges, found on some medieval and Tudor chests. It is created by the wood having been faced with an adze.

aedicule: Originally the frame around a niche made for a statue. Now any classical frame to a door, window or plaque.

aegis: Originally the shield of Zeus; used to describe defensive armour depicted on classical sculpture.

aerograph decoration: Late C19 invention for applying patterns onto pottery using a mechanical air brush.

aeronautica: Objects relating to the development of flight, including balloon decorations on decorative objects from c1783, to aircraft propellers and flying suits, helmets, goggles.

Affenkapelle: German for monkey orchestra; porcelain figures first made mid C18 at Meissen and much copied by other manufacturers.

Affleck, Thomas (d.1795): Cabinet maker, born in Aberdeen. Learned his trade in London before moving to

Philadelphia where he produced furniture to the designs of Chippendale.

affronted: Used to describe a pair of figures that face each other, such as on a gatepost, rather than facing in the same direction.

Afshar: Persian nomadic tribe of the Shiraz-Kerman area producing brightly coloured woollen rugs, typically of blue, ivory and red, with stylized flower designs and diamond patterns.

after-cast: Statuary cast from the original moulds but some time after the moulds were first created.

agata: Mottled decoration in glass resembling the mineral agate, achieved by sprinkling alcohol on the molten surface. First used by New England Glass Co., late C19, and much copied.

agate ware: C18 pottery, veined or marbled to resemble the mineral agate.

Agra: Town in India, site of the Taj Mahal, producing very large carpets, usually with floral patterns in green, blue and brown.

AH: Anno Hegitae; the year of the Hegira – Mohammed's flight from Mecca – which marks the beginning of the Islamic calendar: AD 622.

Ahikaga: Also known as Muromachi era, the period of Japanese history AD 1338-1573.

Ahlspiess: German spear for foot combat with a long spike, and a disc-shaped hand guard, C15/C16.

aigrette: In jewellery, a hair-ornament consisting of precious stones arranged in a floral pattern.

air-beaded: Glass containing bubbles of air, like strings of beads.

airguns: Made from the late C17 onwards, these use compressed air to propel the bullet which is usually much smaller than those of firearms. Early examples rely on manual pumping to build up the pressure; later ones have a detachable spherical reservoir of compressed air located beneath the breech.

air-twist: Helical decoration in the stem of wine glasses, developed 1740-70, in which an air bubble in the glass is drawn out and twisted to form

complex spirals, e.g. lace twist, multiple spiral, spiral gauze, corkscrew, multi-ply, cable, etc.

alabaster: Artificial material made of lime or gypsum coloured white, yellow or red to resemble marble and used since antiquity for statuary and architectural ornament.

alabaster ware: Usually porcelain, but also glass, made to resemble alabaster.

alabastron: Ancient glass vessel with pointed base and two lug handles used for storing perfumes, ointments or unguents.

alarm mechanism: Predecessor of the alarm clock, made in great quantity mid C19, with a dial marked 1 to 12 – the pointer is set to the number of hours hence you want the alarm to go off.

Albany slip: Reddish brown glaze used to make stoneware vessels watertight, on the interior of C19 American pottery, using clays from Albany, New York.

albarello: A pottery vessel of hour-glass shape, used for storing pharmaceutical ingredients.

albata: Term used to describe silver made in Germany.

alcora ware: Maiolica produced in Alcora, Spain, mid C18, decorated with blue and white, purple and yellow figures and grotesques.

alcove: Recess in a wall, originally for a bed, often with an ornate vaulted hood and moulded frame.

alder: A pinkish brown wood with a knotty grain. Good for turning and used in country furniture.

ale glass: Drinking glass with tall stem and tall narrow bowl, capacity 3-4 fluid ounces, used for strong beer, sometimes decorated with barley ears and hops, C18.

alidade: Navigational instrument for calculating latitude and longitude consisting of a telescope sight mounted on a rotating arm marked with degrees of a circle. Often an integral part of an astrolabe.

alkanet: Plant juice which was mixed with linseed oil and used to enrich the colour of mahogany.

all-bisque doll: One with body and limbs as well as head of biscuit-fired ceramic.

Allen pepperbox: American, early C19 pistol with six revolving barrels made by leading gunsmith, Ethan Allen of Massachusetts.

Allgeyer: German manufacturer of flat cast toy soldiers, 1790-1896.

allover: Decorative motif on carpet repeated at regular intervals.

alloy: Combination of two or more metals, such as brass (copper and zinc) or pewter (tin and lead).

almorrata: Sometimes "almorratra", Spanish glass vessel with numerous spouts, often hung from a chain, used for sprinkling holy water.

Alt, Beck & Gottschalk: German maker of bisque head dolls from 1854.

Altai: The oldest surviving rug, dating to c 500BC, and copies of it.

Altare glass: Renaissance Italian glass made in Altare, Genoa and similar to contemporary Venetian glass.

aluminia: Art Nouveau range of faience wares produced by the Royal Copenhagen porcelain factory at the end of the C19, decorated with air-brushed colours and stencils showing Japanese influence.

aluminium: Abundant metal used pure or in alloys from the mid C19 for medallions, plaques and figure groups; mass-produced after 1914.

amazonite: Hard opaque green semi-precious stone used in jewellery from ancient Egypt to present day.

amboyna: Yellowish brown burred wood imported from the West Indies and used as a veneer.

American flint: Glass produced in quantity in Boston, U.S.A., mid C19; not true flint glass.

American Lowestoft: Chinese pottery imported into America in C18 and mistaken for Lowestoft wares.

American stove: General term for early C19 stoves collected for their ornate cast-iron decoration and nickel trim. Superseded by the electric oven in the early C20.

amorini: Cupids or cherubs used in decoration.

amphora: The ancient Greek amphora is often decorated with black or red figure work, and is a large oil or wine-storing vessel with a bulbous body and large strap handles from the shoulder to the neck. Later, and far more common, Roman examples consist of tall coarse wine jars with a pointed base, to push into the earth floor of cellars; often stamped with a maker's trademark.

Amstel ware: Late C18 pottery from factories along the Amstel river, Amsterdam, similar to Meissen.

Amsterdam School: Group of idealistic architects, who built much housing and designed furnishings, in a simplified Art Nouveau style in the first two decades of C20.

anabori: Form of netsuke with deeply recessed interior carving.

Anatolia: Region of Turkey noted for its prayer rugs of loosely woven wool.

anchor escapement: Invented c1760, and named after the anchor-shaped clock linkage and pallets that controlled the escape wheel.

Andersen, David: Founder of Oslo-based firm, in 1876, noted for Art Nouveau and Deco furniture and metal work.

andirons: Two large iron supports designed to support logs over an open fire. Made from C17 in wrought iron; ornamented with brass finials from C18. See firedogs and firecats.

aneroid barometer: One which measures air pressure by

means of a vacuum chamber with an elastic lid linked to the indicator needle.

angle barometer: One with the upper part of the tube bent nearly at right angles so that the mercury moves further than in a vertical column, enabling a bigger scale to be used and more accurate measurements to be taken.

Anglo-Japanese style: Style in vogue during the 1870s and 1880s which showed a Japanese influence on Victorian designs. Examples are Japanese motifs, bamboo legs, fretwork and lacquering.

Angoulême faience: Late C18 figures, often rather large.

an hua: So-called "secret" designs in shallow moulded relief below the glaze in Ming porcelain, visible when held to the light.

aniline dye: Chemical dye introduced into carpet making *c*1870; lacks the warmth of tone of vegetable dye.

animalier: A sculptor of animal forms.

ankus: Highly decorative Indian blade used for goading elephants.

annual rings: The series of concentric circles displayed in a piece of cut timber. They are formed as the tree creates a new layer of growth each year.

annulated: Ringed; often used to describe the stem of a glass.

anodized: Metalwork given a final tough protective coating by means of electrolysis.

Ansbach: Factory specializing in large, colourful faience ornaments from the 1730s, and porcelain tableware late C18 and C19.

anthemion: Stylized classical design based on the honeysuckle flower, often found on wood panelling, oak furniture and plaster friezes.

anthropoid: The term used to describe any ancient or ethnographical sculpture that represents a figure of vaguely human form.

antimacassar: Textile covering for upholstered furniture, designed to protect the head-rest from being stained by macassar hair-oil; C19.

antique: A word which cannot safely be described, but as a guide, and for some tax purposes, an item is said to be an antique if it is one hundred years old or more.

antiquities: Generally accepted to mean objects made before AD 600 in Europe, and of ancient Egyptian, Greek or Roman origin. Also used to cover the pre-Columbian era in the Americas and the products of civilizations now extinct.

aogai: A Japanese technique whereby mother-of-pearl is inlaid into lacquered wood.

ao Kutani: Japanese stoneware with patterns in green, yellow and purple glaze, made at Kutani in Kaga province, C17.

apache pistol: Deadly combination weapon combining a pistol, knuckle duster and knife used by infamous Parisian gang in late C19.

Aphrodite: In Greek mythology, the goddess of love and beauty, called Venus by the Romans.

Apis: An ancient Egyptian deity, frequently depicted in their art, in the form of a bull; said to contain the soul of Osiris.

Apollo: The Greek and Roman god of the sun, patron of music and poetry, often portrayed with a lyre. Depicted in early Christian art as a symbol of virtue.

Apostle spoon: Has a finial in the shape of one of the Twelve Apostles, common until early C17.

apple: A light reddish brown fruitwood with an irregular grain which is sometimes quite knotty.

apple corer: Implement for removing the core of an apple or other fruit, with a short handle and a scoop, of bone, ivory, base metal or silver, from early C18.

applied: Decoration which is added onto a surface is said to be "applied".

applied relief: Used of decoration on pottery made separately and fixed to the body, rather than modelled from the fabric of the vessel itself.

appliqué: Used principally of silver or needlework, but any form of applied ornamentation, made separately and then attached to the object.

Aprey: French factory, founded mid C18, producing faience wares decorated with birds and flowers.

apron: Lower front edge of a piece of furniture.

aquamanile: Medieval pottery vessel, also made in bronze or silver, in the shape of an animal whose mouth forms the spout.

aquatint: C18 engravings taken from etched copper plates and printed using resinous gums so as to imitate the subtle gradations of true water-colour or Indian ink drawings.

arabesque: Intricate decoration of branches, leaves, geometrical patterns and scroll work combined into a flowing frieze. The more stylized and fantastical forms are known as Mooresque. Also the floral motif of Islamic origin found on many carpets, characterized by complex patterns of linking tendrils.

arbalest: Early medieval crossbow fitted with a mechanism for drawing back and releasing the bow. Used to project stones as well as bolts.

arbelette: Term used to describe a double curved shape similar to an archer's bow.

arbor (1): Any spindle within a clockwork mechanism especially that to which the mainspring is attached — sometimes this spindle has a squared end for winding up the spring.

arbor (2): The axle on which a wheel is mounted in a clock movement.

arbrush: Alternative name for abrash, variation in colour tone seen on carpets made from vegetable-dyed fibre.

arcading: Carved decoration in the form of a row of arches.

arch: Found above the dial in long-case clocks, common after C17.

archaic: Early Greek art dating to the C7 BC and earlier, before the beginning of Greek colonisation of the Mediterranean region.

architect's table: Table or desk, the top of which rises at the back to provide an angled working area.

architrave: Moulded frame surrounding a door or window. Also, in classical architecture, the horizontal mouldings above a series of capitals.

Ardebil: Town in northern Iran noted for densely woven carpets, often of reds and blue with a central medallion.

Ardus: French factory, founded C18, specializing in faience wares decorated with fruit, flowers and portraits.

Argentine silver: White metal alloy of nickel, copper and zinc, more durable than copper, and used in preference to it for silver plate from the C19.

argonaut: A drinking vessel made from the shell of a nautilus, mounted in silver to resemble a sailing ship.

argyll/argyle: Silver gravy-warmer shaped like a coffee pot with a central well for the gravy and an outer casing for hot water, said to have been invented by one of the Dukes of Argyll and made c1750 to c1830.

Argy-Rousseau, Gabriel (b. 1885): French Art Nouveau glassmaker, specializing in pâte-de-verre.

arita (1): Blue and white Japanese pottery imported from the mid C17 and much imitated by European makers.

arita (2): Japanese C18 porcelain, typically with flower-basket pattern in blue, red and gold, also called Imari ware after the port from which it was exported.

ark: Generally used to describe a gabled chest.

armada chest: Name given to the German iron-bound chests used in the C17 and C18 as a fore-runner of the more modern "safe" which appeared in C19.

armada jug: Claret jug or wine ewer made from c1860 with a long slender neck, scrolling handle and pedestal foot in silver, or cut glass with silver mounting.

Armenia: Now one of the republics of the USSR; carpet making region noted for geometric patterned rugs; especially those made before 1917.

armet: Globular iron helmet with visor, beaver and gorget which superseded the basinet in C15 armour.

armillary sphere: Globe which demonstrates the movements of the planets and constellations in relation to each other.

arming chest: A chest designed for housing weapons and armour.

Armitage Sheffield: American silver-plated wares made in Philadelphia c1800 by the Armitage brothers, originally from Sheffield.

armoire: A large French cupboard or wardrobe, usually of monumental character.

armorial: A full coat of arms. Also, a term used of any object decorated with the owner's coat of arms, especially silver or silver plate.

armour: A protective, usually metal, outfit or covering.

armourer's mark: Trade mark of an armourer, found on armour plate from C17.

Arnold, John: One of two London clockmakers of the same name noted for fine work, one active 1760-95, the other, his son John Roger, 1800-30.

arquebus: Early musket, made from late C15, with a match-lock mechanism, and a projection that could be hooked over a tripod or wall to aid accuracy in firing and absorb recoil.

arrow back: An American term for Windsor chairs with arrow shaped spindles in their backs.

Art Deco: The style that succeeded Art Nouveau in the 1920s, inheriting from the latter high standards of craftmanship and an interest in new materials, but developing a more linear style, based on the shapes of the square and rectangle, in reaction against the extreme curvaceousness of Art Nouveau.

articulated: In classical sculpture, describes a portrait bust with the pupils of the eyes fully sculpted as opposed to unarticulated (blank eyes) or drilled (originally filled with glass).

Art Nouveau: Style of decorative arts named after a shop opened in Paris in 1895 by Samuel Bing to sell objects in the new style. The name soon became that of the style generally, characterized by the use of dynamic curves based on the shape of flowers and flames, and opalescent colours. The dominant style in European and American fine and applied art from 1895 to 1905, and after that in commercial design until superseded by Art Deco in the 1920s.

Arts and Crafts Movement: The general term given to the work of English artists and designers working in late C19 and early C20, who rejected mass production and sought to keep alive centuries-old crafts that were threatened by machine production particularly furniture. The Cotswold school of Gimson and the Barnsley brothers was the most influential, but many other local groups flourished.

aryballos: Ancient Greek or Roman round-botttomed flask for storing perfumes and ointments, made of glass or ceramic with two handles.

13

as bought: Trade term for antiques of uncertain date or provenance, meaning that the seller takes no responsibility for the accuracy of the description.

as found: Trade term for antiques with some flaw or damage, usually unspecified. Buyer purchases on this basis, the price reflecting condition. Often abbreviated to AF.

ash: Close grained whitish grey wood used mainly in country furniture, particularly the hooped backs of Windsor chairs, and for drawer linings. Also used as a burred veneer.

Ashbee, Charles Robert (1863-1942): Architect and craftsman who founded the Guild of Handicraft in 1888 in London, moving to Chipping Campden in 1902. Noted for fine Arts and Crafts jewellery and metalwork, and for hand-printed books published by the Essex House Press.

asparagus tongs: Similar to sugar tongs, but with a number of small concave ridges along the inner face for holding asparagus spears, from c1750 to c1830.

assay mark: Mark stamped on silver and gold by one of the assay offices (e.g. London, Birmingham, Chester, Exeter, Sheffield, Newcastle, York, Glasgow, Edinburgh, Dublin) signifying that the metal is of the standard required by law. The symbol, which is often based on the city coat of arms, is usually accompanied by a year mark.

associated (1): Term used of a set of silverware in which one part is of the same design but not originally made for it – e.g. of a teapot and associated stand.

associated (2): Of weapons, any part which is not original.

Assyrian: Objects, especially relief sculptures, produced in the Near East in the heyday of the Assyrian empire, which flourished between the C12 and C7 BC.

astragal: Moulding into which are set the glass panes of a cabinet or bookcase.

astrolabe: Instrument for plotting altitude and for charting the relative moments of planets and constellations, consisting of a telescope sight, a movable brass measuring ring and a planisphere.

astronomical clock: One that shows the phases of the moon and other astronomical phenomena. Usually C18 and very fine.

Asuka: The period of Japanese history AD 552-645.

atlanta: A male figure used as a support or as a decorative motif during C17.

atlas cloth: Indian silk and cotton fabric imported to Europe from C17.

atmos clock: One which uses slight changes in barometric pressure to rewind the main spring, hence, in theory, it never needs manual winding.

Attic: Very fine pottery made in the Athens region of Ancient Greece from the C7 to C4 BC, often with detailed scenes from myth painted in black or red figure.

Attwell, Mabel Lucy (1879-1964): Illustrator of children's books, postcards and nursery equipment, as well as money boxes and biscuit tins, now collectable.

Aubusson: French town producing tapestries, and tapestry-weave carpets, since C17 although formal workshops were not established until c1743.

auger flame: American term for the flame-type finials found on some cabinet pieces. See also Flambeau.

aumbry: Medieval cupboard, sometimes raised on a stand, and used for storing weapons or food. Also called a hutch.

aurene: Iridescent coloured glassware made by Steuben, New York, early C20.

aureus: The highest value of coinage under the Roman Empire, always of gold.

auricular: Any shell-like ornamental motif, derived from the Latin word for ear.

automata: Any moving toy or decorative object, usually powered by a clockwork mechanism.

automaton clock: One with mechanical figures which perform the strike.

automobilia: Antiques associated with the early history of motoring and motor sports.

autoperipatetikos: Greek for "self-walking"; term used of C19 clockwork dolls.

aventurin: Powdered gold found on some japanned items.

aventurine: Brown or blue quartz with gold inclusions; hence anything that resembles the mineral, such as aventurine glass (blue with minute threads of gold) and lacquer work of gold strands on a red or black background.

awl-pike: Infantry spear of the C15/C16, with a long spike and a disc-shaped handguard. The English name for an Ahlspiess.

Axminster: Knotted pile carpets made at Axminster, England, late C18 and early C19 imitating oriental and French styles. Not to be confused with the same factory's more recent cut pile carpets.

Aztec: Late Mesoamerican culture, much of whose jewellery and pottery was destroyed by the Conquistadores in early C16, but their highly prized sculpture is occasionally found.

B

baby doll: One in the form of a baby, as opposed to an adult.

baby house: Alternative name for doll's house.

baby walker: Device to enable a child to learn to walk and become mobile. They usually comprise a circular frame on castors which encircles and supports the child at the waist.

Baccarat: Group of factories in France and Belgium producing tableware and decorative glass from late C18, famous for paperweights.

Bacchus: The Roman god of wine, equivalent to the Greek god Dionysus, frequently portrayed on drinking vessels and in statuary as a young man crowned with vine leaves, or offering a cup of wine.

Bacchus glass: Pressed glass, made by George Bacchus & Sons, Birmingham, UK, C19; noted for ornamental bowls.

Bachelder, Ezra: Denver clock-maker, active 1793-1840.

bachelor chest: Small chest of drawers with a hinged foldover top to provide a larger working surface. They were designed for a gentleman's dressing room.

backboard: The unpolished back of wall furniture.

backplate (1): Brass plate which protects a drawer front from being damaged by the bail or by the hand as the bail is grasped.

backplate (2): Also called back stop, or back piece; the metal plate extending from the pommel to the guard of a sword.

backplate (3): Rearmost of two plates supporting a clock mechanism, usually engraved with the maker's name.

back stool: Term precisely designated to a stool with a back and not merely a single chair.

backsword: Sword with only one cutting edge.

bade-bade: Malaysian single-edged sheath knife; the sheath usually has a pronounced wing at the opening.

badekind: C19 china doll used as a bath toy.

Baehr & Proeschild: German makers of bisque head dolls, late C19 to 1930.

baff: Persian name for the knot used in carpet making.

Bagneux shade: Glass dome used in C19 to protect ornaments from dust, originally made in Bagneux, France.

baguette: In jewellery, a small stone cut into a rectangular shape.

bail: Curved metal drawer pull which hangs from metal bolts.

bail handle: One which rises over the top of the vessel, like a bucket handle, instead of being fixed and parallel to the sides.

Baillie-Scott, MacKay Hugh (1865-1945): British architect and designer whose furnishings for the Darmstadt home of the Grand Duke of Hesse did much to create a taste for Arts and Crafts style in Germany.

Bain, Alexander: Scottish inventor of the electric clock, patent granted 1843.

Bakelite: Early form of plastic, invented by L. H. Baekeland in 1913, and used for a wide variety of industrial and domestic objects, including Art Deco sculpture and electrical fittings.

Baker bayonet: A sword cum bayonet, common in early C19, with a knuckle guard, made to fit the Baker rifle.

Bakewell glass: From Pittsburgh Flint Glass Works, established c1800; first American producer of fine lead glass, noted for luxury tableware and chandeliers as well as inexpensive pressed glass.

Bakhmetev glass: Made in Moscow from the late C18 to the Revolution.

Bakhtiari: Southern Iranian nomads producing red, brown and blue rugs of cotton and wool with floral motifs, often in squares.

balance: Device in clock mechanisms used to control and counteract the force of the mainspring.

balances: Scales made for weighing in very small and very precise quantities; used by scientists, jewellers, etc.

balance spring: Spring acting on the balance wheel in a watch mechanism to control the oscillations of the mainspring. Equivalent in watches to the clock pendulum, developed c1675.

baleen: Whalebone, used C18 and C19 for buttons, and also carved into ornaments by sailors.

Ball, William: Liverpool porcelain maker, c1755-69, producing delftware and elaborate rococo sauceboats.

ball and claw foot: Type of furniture foot representing a

ball held by a claw. Introduced c1720. Said to be an adaptation from the Chinese of a dragon's claw clutching a pearl.

ball back: Descriptive of a country-made chair which has small wooden balls held between rails in the back. They were made in East Anglia and are sometimes known as Suffolk chairs.

ball clock: Clock in which the oscillations of the mainspring are controlled by the backward and forward movement of a steel ball in a see-saw. Also used of rare clocks driven by heavy metal balls.

ball foot: A round foot shaped as a ball which was in use at the end of the C17.

ball-jointed doll: One with ball-jointed limbs, able to swivel in all directions, as opposed to stiff-jointed.

ball knop: Ball-shaped formation on the stem of wine glasses, from early C18.

ballock dagger: Dagger with a cross piece (quillon) terminating in small spheres.

balloon back: Descriptive of a dining chair with a rounded back. They were made throughout the Victorian era.

balloon clock: Late C18 and early C19 mantel clocks with balloon shaped case, curving inwards below the dial.

ball stopper: On early glass bottles, a glass ball in a retaining cage which falls out to allow pouring when tilted and falls back to seal the neck when stood upright.

balsamarium: General term to describe any ancient glass or ceramic vessel, usually small, that might have been used to store perfume or unguent.

Baltimore glass: Glass from one of several factories in Baltimore, Maryland, such as Amelung glass, and Baltimore flint glass, esp. pressed glass patterned with a fig shape.

Baltimore silver: Early C19 silver carrying the assay mark of Baltimore.

Baluchi: Nomads of the Afghan/Iranian border region producing dark blue and rust red rugs with floral motifs.

baluster (1): A short pillar, often of turned wood or stone, used to support a stair handrail or parapet. A series of balusters is called a balustrade.

baluster (2): A shaped turning used as the centre column or legs of a table. Various designs were achieved, a familiar one being the vase shape used during C17.

baluster stem: Glass with a swelling stem, like an architectural baluster: "true" if the thicker swelling is beneath; "inverted" if above. From late C17.

baluster vase: Shaped like an architectural baluster, with a bulbous body and long neck.

balustroid: Lighter, slimmer version of the baluster stem glass; 2nd quarter C18.

bamboo: Giant tropical grass known as the Great Indian Reed. It has a hollow and jointed stem and is creamy yellow in colour. It was used to make furniture and was often imitated.

bamboo turning: Term used to describe the legs of furniture made in the Chinese taste during late C18 and Regency period which were turned to simulate bamboo.

banding: A contrasting strip of wood laid into another for decorative effect.

bandolier: Shoulder strap, first used in C16, for carrying powder charges or bullets.

band sword: Ornamental swords issued to drummers and military bandsmen from c1768, with a curving scimitar blade and cruciform hilt.

banister: Same as balustrade, but used specifically of the turned or square vertical supports for a staircase handrail or chair back.

banister back: Descriptive of a chair with vertical split banisters in the back.

banjo barometer: A wheel-type barometer, so called because of its shape; instead of a columnar scale, weights floating on the surface of the mercury and linked to pulleys, convert linear movements so as to turn a pointer around a circular dial.

banjo clock: Popular form of late C18 to mid C19 pendulum clock resembling an upturned banjo on a pedestal base.

banker: Old term for a bench.

banner screen: Portable cross-shaped screen comprising a piece of velvet or other rich cloth that hangs unframed from the horizontal bar and is weighted by tassels at the bottom. The horizontal bar can be raised or lowered on the vertical pole.

banquette: Long stool with high scrolling ends and a caned seat.

bantam work: Type of lacquerwork which has incised designs instead of the more usual raised designs. It originated in the Java province of Bantam in the C17 and is also known as cut work.

bar back: Descriptive of a chair which has the top rail formed as a bar.

barber's chair: Type of chair with a back which incorporates a head rest for the sitter to use while being shaved.

Barbizet-Palissy: Late C19 pottery made at Barbizet, near Paris, in imitation of C16 Palissy ware.

Barboteau: French designer of Art Nouveau bronze vases.

barbotine: Painting on pottery using coloured kaolin pastes, invented 1865 by Ernest Chaplet.

barbute: C15 Italian helmet modelled on those of ancient Greece, with curving cheek pieces but no visor.

bardiche: Long handled axe used by Scandinavian and Eastern European infantry, C16 and C17.

bargueño: Spanish cabinet with a fall front enclosing drawers. Also known as a varguéño.

Barker ware: From the Yorkshire factory of Samuel Barker, mid C19.

barley twist: Form of turning, popular in late C17 which resembles a spiral of rope.

17

Barlow sisters: Artists employed by the Doulton pottery in the 1870s, famous for their animal designs on the company's decorated tablewares.

Barnsleys: The Barnsley brothers, Sidney (1865-1962) and Ernest (1864-1962) founded the Cotswold Arts and Crafts movement with Ernest Gimson, based at Sapperton. Their furniture designs were inspired by rural and timeless wood-working techniques.

barograph: A form of barometer which measures air pressure by means of a vacuum chamber linked to a rib which draws a graph on a revolving drum, from late C18.

Baroque: A heavy, highly ornamental style which superseded classicism in the late C17, principally in Italy. A term which came to mean over-ornamented, florid or even grotesque.

Barr, G.: Bolton maker of Yorkshire style clocks, late C18.

Barraud & Lund: London company, active from mid C19, specializing in electric clocks.

barrel: The part of a clock mechanism that contains the mainspring and round which the string driving the train is wound.

Bartholomew babies: Now rare, carved wooden dolls made for sale at fairs in England, originally (1721) at the St. Bartholomew Fair at Smithfield.

basaltes: Black porcelain invented by Josiah Wedgwood with a polished, stone-like finish; modern reproductions are called basalt wares.

bascinet: Also known as basinet, basnet, basenet or basanette. The commonest type of helmet worn by men-at-arms in C14 Europe. Essentially a bowl-shaped helmet with chinstrap and chain mail neck protector and snout-shaped visor.

baselard: Dagger with an I-shaped hilt, late C13 to late C15, probably originating from Basel in Switzerland.

basin stand: Another name for a washing stand.

basket hilt: Perforated hilt, covering the whole of the hand, at the end of a sword.

basket top clock: Clock with a dome-shaped case, usually of metal.

bas relief: Term used to describe a carved or sculpted design which is slightly raised from the surface. Also known as low relief.

Bassano ware: Pottery produced near Venice from the C15, later specializing in porcelain imitations of Chinese wares.

bassenet: A basketwork cradle.

basset table: Small table for playing bassette, a card game.

Bassett-Lowke: Manufacturers of clockwork locomotives and scale models from c1910.

Bast: Sometimes also Ubasti; a feline goddess of ancient Egypt represented as a cat, and sometimes as a cat-headed woman.

bastard: C15 and C16 sword with an extended grip, but too short for double handed use unless the hands overlap.

bath chair: A type of mobile invalid's chair with a handle designed to be pushed from behind.

bath metal: Alloy of 32 parts of copper to 39 of zinc, made from the late C17 as substitute for gold.

batik: Dyed cloth in which wax is used to resist colour and produce the design.

baton: In jewellery, a large stone cut into a rectangular shape.

bat printed: Transfer printed, from the "bat" or sheet of thin paper that was used to transfer the decoration from the printing block to the ceramic vessel.

bat's wing fluting: Term to describe graduated gadrooning which radiates from a fixed point, somewhat resembling the outline of a bat's wing.

batten: Thin strip of wood.

Battersea enamel: Enamelled porcelain trinkets (snuff boxes, ornaments, decorative plates) from the London factory established mid C18.

battery metal: Earliest form of English brass, made in C16, named after a noted manufacturer, the Mineral & Battery Works of London.

Bauhaus: Influential German artistic style which was inspired by new industrial materials, such as stainless steel, with the emphasis on cubic, unadorned shapes. The term was coined by the architect Gropius who became director of the Weimar school of Arts and Crafts in 1919, and renamed it the Bauhaus.

Bayley & Upjohn: Late C18/ early C19 London makers of regulator clocks.

bayonet: Short blade made to attach to the muzzle of a firearm.

baywood: Another name for Honduras mahogany.

beading: Term used to describe two types of moulding. Either a small plain half or quarter round wooden moulding, or a moulding in the form of a string of beads.

bead-pattern hilt: Sword hilt decorated with five balls or beads on the knuckle guard, a late C18/early C19 military type.

beadwork: Decoration on material using glass beads of different colours.

bear-baby: Rare toy by Louis S. Schiffer, New York, in 1914, one half a bisque head doll, the other side a teddy bear.

bearer: See Loper (1) and (2).

bear jug: English stoneware jugs of C18 in the shape of a bear, first made in Derby and Staffordshire but widely copied.

Beauvais ware: Religious figures and tableware produced at Beauvais, France, from the late C14.

beaver: Also bevor; the front part of a helmet, hinged at the top so that the face guard could be raised or lowered.

bébé: French dolls made by Bru and others in the latter half C19, modelled on actual children of 8-12 years of age.

bed: The part of a drop leaf table top which does not hinge.

bedside cupboard: See night table.

bedstead: Framework of a bed, supporting the bedding.

bed steps: Two or three solidly constructed steps designed as an aid when climbing into a high bed. Some have a chamber pot fitted within them.

beech: A light brown wood with a distinctive flecked grain. It is very strong but is also prone to woodworm and rot. Often used for chair seat rails as it can be close-nailed without splitting.

beehive clock: Mid C19 New England mantel clock with a case shaped like a pointed Gothic arch, so called for its resemblance to contemporary beehives.

Behrens, Peter (1868-1940): German illustrator, architect and craftsman, designer of everything from glass to stationery to factory complexes. Founded the Vereinigte Werkstätten in Munich but later rejected Art Nouveau to create a new, simplified classical style.

Beilby glass: Made by the Beilby family in Newcastle, UK, up to c1778; celebrated practitioners of painting and enamelling on glass, especially armorials and Rococo ornamentation.

beinglas: Glass of milky appearance from the inclusion of bone ash; made in Bohemia, late C18.

bekerschroef: Dutch stand for a wine glass, usually of silver, from the C17.

bellarmine bottle: Bottle with a spout in the form of a grotesque human face; named after Cardinal Bellarmio (1542-1621) who sought to outlaw alcoholic beverages. Usually of salt-glazed stoneware from early C17 but still being produced mid C19 in many forms.

belleek: Very thin and iridescent parian ware, originally made at Belleek, in Ireland, late C19.

belle vue: C19 tableware made in Hull.

bellevue: Late C18 faience from the French factory at Meurthe on the Moselle.

bellflower: Hanging flower bud of three or five petals either carved or inlaid one below the other in strings, usually down a table or chair leg. See also Garya husk.

bell flyer: Horse brass consisting of one or more bells mounted in a frame so that they can swing with the movement of the horse.

bell metal: Copper and bronze alloy, so called because it was used in bell casting, but also for other ornaments.

bell pull/push: Bell pulls, attached to a cord and pulley system, became fashionable in C18 and were superseded by the electric bell push in late C19. Highly ornamented examples of both are found in metal, porcelain, glass and wood.

bell sundial: C18 French sundial with a lens designed to focus the sunlight at noon onto a thread which, on burning through, released a hammer which struck a bell or gong.

bell ware: Red stoneware made by Samuel Bell, Newcastle-under-Lyme, mid C18; or the products of the Glasgow factory of J & M P Bell, latter half C19.

Belper ware: C19 stoneware made by Bourne & Co., whose first factory was at Belper, Derbyshire.

belt pistol: Short pistols used by travellers in the C18, often in pairs, worn suspended from the belt; hence they have a belt-lock on the stock.

Beluchistan: Small rugs made for export since C19, originally used as prayer rugs, horse blankets, etc, of goat and camel hair, dark-red to brown with geometric motifs.

belvedere: Small look out tower on the roof of a house made for enjoying the view.

bench: A long seat, with or without a back. Also known as a banker. See also form.

bench book: The name given to a design or work book used by a cabinet maker or apprentice.

Benedict stove: Ornate cast-iron stoves made by Philip Benedict in Pennsylvania in early C19.

Beneman, Jean: German born cabinet maker who worked in Paris during late C18. He made a large amount of furniture for Queen Marie Antoinette and the French Court.

Benin: Ancient Nigerian kingdom whose artists produced bronze sculpture of great refinement, up to C16.

Bennington: Celebrated American pottery established early C19, producing red earthenware and stoneware vessels, parian wares and dark-brown mottled "Rockingham" type wares.

bent-limb doll: One made only to sit, with limbs permanently fixed in the seated position.

bérain: Rococo style ornamentation on French faience wares; originally blue and white, later polychrome, with a narrative scene surrounded by an ornate frame.

berber: Rugs from Morocco, now mass produced.

Bergama: Weaving centre in Turkey noted for prayer rugs in bright colours with geometric patterns.

bergère: Widely used French term for an armchair with cane woven sides and back, often with an excessively deep and low seat.

Bergner, Carl: German doll maker, active at Sonneberg, 1890-1909, specializing in two- and three-faced dolls.

Berlin faience: Products of several C18 factories in the Berlin region, delftware and vases of unusual shape and bold blue decoration.

Berlin porcelain: Tableware and figure groups, similar to Meissen and often made by former Meissen employees, from c1750.

Berlin tinware: Tin plate household wares, often japanned, made in Berlin, Connecticut, mid C18.

berretino: Greyish-blue glaze typical of Italian maiolica of the Renaissance period.

besagew: In medieval armour, a circular plate to protect the armpit.

beshir: Large dark red and blue carpets with densely packed designs.

Bessarabian: Carpets from the Romanian/Russian border region, characterized by naturalistic designs.

bevel: Slope cut at the edge of a flat surface. Usually associated with plate glass used in mirrors.

bezel: Metal rim to the glass covering a clock or watch face.

Bianchi: Noted maker of banjo-type barometers, often incorporating clocks and thermometers, working in Ipswich in early C19.

bianco sopra bianco: White glaze patterns painted over a greyish-white background, typical of C16 maiolica or C18 Delft.

bibliothèque-basse: Low French cupboard fitted with shelves for books.

bichwa: Also bich'hwa, Indian for scorpion; a dagger with a double curved, and occasionally double-pronged, blade.

biddery: Cheap metal wares imported from India in C19 made of a copper, lead and tin alloy.

Bideford: The most prolific of several Devon potteries producing wares for export to the American colonies; typically white glazed with sgraffito ornament revealing a red body.

bidet: Cleansing receptacle housed within a wooden support on legs and covered by a lid.

Biedermeier: An unpretentious and informal style of C19 German furniture.

bifurcated drop: Type of late C17 drop handle which divides into two branches at the end.

biggin: Small cylindrical silver coffee pot, with a cotton sleeve to hold the coffee grains, said to resemble the shape of a biggin or nightcap, hence its name. Sometimes with a stand and spirit lamp.

bijouterie table: Small table with the top formed as a glazed display case.

bilbohitt: Spanish broadsword, named after the port of Bilbao, with two large plate guards curving towards the pommel.

Bilderboge: German cut-out paper toys.

bill: C15 weapon consisting of a long cutting blade and back spike fitted to a long pole.

billiards table: Large table with a baize covering used for playing billiards, a game which originated in C15.

Billingsley: Porcelain painted by the flower artist, William Billingsley (1758-1828) who worked for Derby and other potteries, later founding his own at Nantgarw.

Bilston enamel: Door knobs, finger plates, boxes and trinkets of painted enamel on copper, made in Bilston, Staffordshire, latter half C18.

bim-bam: Name imitating the two-toned strike of popular early C20 German-made mantel clock.

bimbeloterie: French term for antique toys or, literally, "playthings".

bimetallic balance: One made of brass and steel whose different rates of expansion and contraction cancel each other out, so that the oscillations in a clock mechanism remain constant despite changes in air temperature.

Bing Artist's Dolls: Company based in Nuremberg making fine character dolls in the 1920s and 1930s.

Bing, Samuel: Native of Hamburg who opened a shop in Paris in 1885 specializing in Japanese art. He reopened it in 1895 to promote the new decorative arts of Europe, and called it "La Maison de l'Art Nouveau", from which the term Art Nouveau derived.

binnacle clock: One made for a ship with a dial marked with the nautical watches and striking one to eight.

birch: A close grained wood which is whitish yellow in colour.

birdcage: Small construction found under the top of some tables which enables them to revolve as well as tip up.

birdcage clock: C18 novelty, often ornate, in the shape of a birdcage with a hidden clock mechanism and a singing bird in place of a strike.

bird's eye: Marking of small spots associated with maple wood.

Birmingham Dribbler: Early toy locomotive powered by steam, heated by methylated spirits, so called because of its propensity to leak; mass produced in Birmingham from c1870.

Birmingham silver: Made in Birmingham, UK; before 1773 stamped with wheatsheaf and dagger assay mark of Chester, or the leopard's head of London; after 1773, acquired its own assay office and mark in the form of an anchor.

biscuit ware: Any unglazed pottery, but specifically unglazed figure groups first made in France, mid C18, and much copied elsewhere.

bismuth: Naturally occurring metal used as a strengthening agent in pewter and other alloys.

bisque: French term for biscuit ware, or unglazed porcelain.

bisque doll: One with a biscuit fired and unglazed ceramic head.

Bizarre: Name of a highly-colourful range of Art Deco tableware designed by Clarice Cliff and manufactured by the Staffordshire potter, A. J. Wilkinson Ltd, in the 1930s.

blackamoor: A negro figure. Often depicted as a page boy, perhaps as a support for a table top.

black figure: Pottery decoration technique invented in Ancient Greece around 700 BC in which figures from myth and legend are painted in black silhouette on a red-brown background. Much imitated in the C19. See also Red figure.

Black Forest clock: Simple but charming clocks of the C18 and C19 with a wooden movement; cases are often mildly Gothic in form and dials are sometimes painted with rustic scenes. Made by country craftsmen as a cottage industry.

black glaze: Dense, glossy glaze used on C18 English earthenwares; often dark brown rather than true black.

blackjack: Leather tankard or flask, usually with a silver rim and applied ornament, C17.

black mammy: Rare form of fabric doll designed by Martha Jenks Chase of Panstucket, Rhode Island, 1921-25 in the form of a negress.

black walnut: Variety of walnut which is also known as red walnut or Virginian walnut because it comes from that part of the United States. It was also grown in England and was used mainly during the William and Mary and Queen Anne periods. It is a dark red-brown colour and never displays any burr figuring. It is thus easily mistaken for mahogany.

bladed knop: Knop with a concave outward curve, culminating in a sharp edge.

blade sight: Thin, vertical leaf-shaped sight situated at the front of a gun barrel.

blanc-de-chine: French for Chinese white. Fine Chinese porcelain from Fukien with a pure white glaze, notably figures in swirling drapery, exported to Europe C17 and widely imitated C18.

blanc fixe: White decoration on a greyish, bluish or yellow background, typical of tin-glazed earthenwares.

bleeding knife: Medical instrument used for blood letting; best examples are those with a letting cup for catching the blood.

bleu persan: French for Persian blue, tin-glazed wares with blue decoration painted on a greyish-white or yellow ground in imitation of Middle-Eastern medieval pottery.

blind fret: Fretwork either glued to, or carved upon, a solid surface and therefore unable to be seen through.

blind front: Another term for a block front.

blinking eye clock: One with a dial in the shape of a human face and eyes linked to the movement which blink alternately in time with the tick. Originally German C16 but widely made in Europe and America C18 and C19.

blister: Marking which is thought to resemble a blister, usually associated with maple wood but also found in cedar, poplar, pine and mahogany.

block foot: Descriptive of a foot formed as a solid block.

block front: Term used to describe the solid unglazed doors of a cabinet piece. Also known as a blind front.

blond bisque: Bisque head dolls tinted pink to resemble flesh tones.

blown moulded: Method of mass-producing glass to standard shapes (e.g. wine bottles), where molten glass is blown into a mould, rather than shaped manually by spinning.

bludgeon: Mid C19 American short-barrelled pistol shaped like a small metal club.

blue and white ware: Porcelain ornamented with cobalt-blue on a white background in imitation of Chinese wares, such as willow-pattern.

blue dash: Broad blue dabs of glaze used to decorate the rims of earthenware tin-glazed vessels; common on C17 and C18 delftwares.

blue glass: Colour obtained by the inclusion of cobalt, popular in Renaissance Venice, revived Bristol C18.

blue-printed: The products of numerous Staffordshire potteries, decorated with a transfer-printed pattern in blue, produced in quantity late C18/early C19.

bluing: Heat treatment of steel or iron armour as a protection against rust and for decorative effect. Metal so treated is called blued steel, though the colour can range from blue to black.

blunderbuss: Heavy, short handgun with a flaring barrel designed to scatter a large quantity of shot at short range.

Blunt instruments: Various scientific instruments, including compasses and barometers, made by the American company of Edward and George Blunt.

boarded furniture: Simple early furniture constructed entirely of shaped boards held together by nails or pegs.

boat bed: American bed in the Empire style, shaped similar to a gondola.

boat-shell hilt: A heart-shaped sword guard, split on the upturned side to accommodate the forward quillon.

bob: Weight at the end of a clock pendulum.

bobbin turning: Style of turning in the form of bobbins, one on top of another. Popular during C17.

bocage: French for a small wood; figure groups, popular in the C18, set against a background of trees, foliage and flowers.

boccaro: Unglazed red and brown stonewares, made late C17/early C18 in imitation of similar Chinese imports.

body: The fabric of a pottery vessel, excluding the glaze.

bog oak: Type of oak taken from those parts of a tree which have been submerged in a peat bog. It is blackish in colour.

Bohemian glass: Used to describe ruby glass first produced in the late C17 in Bohemia, and high quality engraved glass produced in the region over four centuries.

bois durci: Wood-based substance made from fine sawdust and blood. It can be easily moulded and was used for ornamental decoration.

bokhara: Rugs of wool and jute, usually deep red and ornamented with repeated octagonal "flowers", made by tribes of the Iranian/Soviet border region.

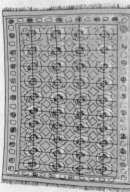

bokhara work: C18 and C19 quilts and coverlets embroidered with colourful floral patterns from the Bokhara region, now in the southern USSR.

bolection: Descriptive of a shape of ogee section used as a drawer front or as a projecting door surround.

Bologna: Centre of pottery production from C15, noted for large basins and jugs with applied decoration, produced up to C18.

bombard: Primitive and cumbersome cannon with a large mortar made of hooped iron staves used to propel stone-shot.

bombé: Term to describe a piece of furniture with a bulging rounded lower front.

bonbonnière: Small box, usually of porcelain and decorated with a whimsical scene, but also in silver, made to contain small sweet-meats or breath-fresheners.

bone china: Very strong, white porcelain invented by Josiah Spode at Stoke-on-Trent, c1790, made from china clay and bone ash.

bone glass: Milky glass made with added bone ash.

Bonheur du jour: Small French writing table of delicate proportions with a raised back comprising a cabinet or shelves.

bonnet dolls: American dolls with bonnets or hats fixed and integral to the head.

Bonnin & Morris: Very rare porcelain made in Philadelphia c1770-3, in imitation of Bow figurines.

book rest: Support for large books comprising a square or rectangular framework supported by a strut and adjustable on a grooved base. Sometimes incorporated into the top of a table.

book shelves: Series of shelves for books, made either hanging or free standing and with or without doors.

bookstand: Stand for books comprised mainly of open shelves and first made in late C18. Sometimes the base is a drawer or a cupboard and the top shelf is often edged with a brass gallery.

bootlegger or bootleg pistol: American percussion pistol with the striking hammer underneath the barrel, so called because the type was commonly used by New England smugglers.

Borchardt, Hugo: Leading Berlin gunsmith, late C19.

Bordeaux: Centre of faience and porcelain manufacture from C18; characterized by polychrome designs in the Spanish style.

Bordshali-Kazak: Caucasian carpets essentially of red and blue but with patterns, medallions, flowers and figures in many other colours.

bore: Internal diameter of the barrel of a firearm.

borlou: Turkish carpets with stylized patterns on a red or blue ground; floppy and not densely woven.

Borrell, Henry: London clock-maker, active 1795-1840, specializing in clocks and watches for export, often with Turkish numerals.

bosom bottle: Small decorative bottle, in glass or silver, worn as a pendant and often used to contain perfume.

boss: Circular ornament, usually placed to hide the junction of the ribs in a vault, but also any cone-like projection e.g. from a shield, or plaster ceiling.

Boston glass: Used of the products of C19 glassworks in Boston and Cambridge, New England, including the Boston Porcelain and Glass Co. and American Flint Glass Works; notably good early pressed glass and silvered glass.

Boston rocker (1): An American rocking chair with a tall spindle back and a seat which curves up at the front and down at the back.

Boston rocker (2): Rocking horse consisting just of the horse's head and a seat mounted on curved rockers.

bosun's pipe: Ship's whistle, used for giving orders at sea. Often of silver and ornamented with naval motifs, from c1750 to 1920.

boteh: Decorative motif in carpets, similar to European Paisley pattern, essentially a leaf-form with a curled or hooked tip.

boteh-miri: A small boteh.

Böttger: The earliest products of the Meissen factory, named after the supervisor, J. F. Böttger c1710-20; glazes somewhat bubbly and decoration in low relief.

bottle glass: Cheap glass made of impure materials, typically brown or green.

bottle tag: Silver label on a chain engraved with the name of a spirit (Brandy, Rum, etc) hung

around the neck of a decanter or bottle from early C18.

Boucheron, Frédéric (1830-1902): Founder of the French jewellery firm and leading Art Nouveau designer, especially for American clients.

Boucheron, Louis: Son of Frédéric, and head of the Boucheron firm of jewellers after his father's death in 1902; responsible for making Boucheron famous for its Art Deco designs after the First World War.

boudoir dolls: Dolls made as mascots or "adult toys" in the early C20, usually of very cheap materials and construction.

boulle: Type of inlaid decoration using fine strips of brass with tortoiseshell. Sometimes referred to as Buhl.

Boulle, André (1642-1732): A French artist, architect, engraver and bronze worker after whom the process of boulle marquetry is named. He did not invent it himself but perfected a particular type which satisfied the requirements of the time.

Boulton, Matthew (1728-1809): Ormolu mounts of the finest quality were made at his factory at Soho, near Birmingham.

Bourg-la-Reine: French porcelain and faience produced 1774-1806.

Bourne & Son: C19 factory based at Derby, producing large, inexpensive household vessels in stoneware.

Bow: Important London porcelain factory producing blue and white wares 1749-76, and polychrome wares 1754 onwards; early work shows Chinese influence (paeony and chrysanthemum flower decorations); later work in Meissen style.

bow front: An outwardly curving front.

Bowie knife: Heavy sheath knife with long curved blade, double edged near the point, named after the Texas pioneer Colonel James Bowie (1799-1836) and carried as a weapon.

box: Very close grained wood which is whitish yellow in colour. Often used for stringing and other inlay work.

boxlock: Type of flintlock in which the entire mechanism is contained within the gun breech.

box seat: Term to describe a seat that rises to provide storage space within.

box stool: Stool with a rising seat that reveals a storage space within.

box table: Table with a rising top that reveals a storage space within.

boys and crowns: Old term for a type of carved ornament found particularly on the cresting rails of some C17 chairs, depicting a crown supported by two flying, naked boys.

bracket (1): Small length of wood used to strengthen the joint between the leg and supporting rails of a chair.

bracket (2): See fly bracket.

bracket (3): Projection designed to support a shelf or mantelpiece, often carved with acanthus leaf.

bracket clock: Originally a C17 clock which had to be set high up on a bracket because of the length of the weights; now generally applied to any small mantel or table clock.

bracket foot: A type of foot for case pieces which appears somewhat shaped as a right-angled bracket below the front edge.

bracket lamp: Oil lamp of brass or iron with an integral bracket, designed to be fixed to a wall or partition.

Bradburys: Alternative name for Treasury Notes, UK paper money issued during the First World War, bearing the signature of John Bradbury, Secretary to the Treasury.

Bradford pewter: Pewter wares copying English forms made by Cornelius Bradford in Philadelphia, latter half C18.

Bradley, Langley: London clockmaker late C17/early C18, noted for very fine clocks.

Bradwell Wood: Late C17 Staffordshire pottery producing red stoneware teapots and cups in imitation of contemporary Chinese imports.

braganza foot: Furniture term to describe a type of foot, on an otherwise straight leg, which bends outwards a little at the bottom, similar to a hockey stick.

Bramah lock: Type of lock invented by Joseph Bramah in 1784 which was the first to be operated by a small and easily carried key.

Brameld: Family that acquired the Rockingham factory, Yorkshire, early C19; producers of fine bone china noted for its rich enamelling and gilt decoration.

Brampton: Pottery-making centre near Chesterfield, Derbyshire, noted for utilitarian brown stoneware vessels, some with internal green glazing.

branch notes: UK paper money issued by one of the thirteen provincial banks authorized by the Bank of England; scarcer and more valuable than "London notes".

Brander, W.: Leading London gunsmith, early/mid C18.

Brander, W. B.,: Leading London gunsmith, late C18/early C19.

Brander & Potts: Leading London gunsmiths, early C19.

brandesijkom: Silver bowl with handles, used to prepare a dish of hot brandy and raisins, Dutch C17.

brandistock: Pole weapon with retractable spikes concealed in the haft which swing out when the safety catch is released and the weapon is wielded.

brandy bowl: Shallow but wide silver bowl with handles used for warming and serving brandy from the C17, usually accompanied by a shallow ladle.

brandy saucepan: Bulbous or baluster-shaped small silver saucepan with a long handle at right angles to the spout, made for warming and pouring brandy.

brandy tumbler: Wide squat glass beaker with straight sides from C17, later often etched or engraved.

Brandt, Paul-Emile: Swiss Art Nouveau jewellery designer.

Brangwyn, Frank (1867-1943): English artist who served an apprenticeship with Morris & Co. and specialized in Art Nouveau furniture, textile and carpet design.

bras de cheminée: Wall mounted candle holders with several branches made in gilded wood, or metal from C17.

brass: Yellow alloy of copper and zinc, sometimes other metals in small quantities, made since antiquity for household objects and ornaments, furniture legs, knobs and handles, etc. Often used as an inlay.

bratina: Richly decorated, often enamelled and jewelled, drinking or loving cup of silver or gold, originally from Imperial Russia.

brattishing: An ornamental crest on top of a cornice; usually in the form of miniature battlements or a series of palmettes.

break: In firearms, the point at which the barrel block hinges open so that bullets or cartridges can be loaded into the breech; or the points at which the gun components can be dismantled for cleaning and casing.

breaker: Trade name for a piece of furniture that is worth more as raw materials.

breakfast table: Tilt-top table that can be used by a small number of people at mealtimes. Usually oval or circular and smaller than a dining table. Pembroke tables were also once known as breakfast tables.

break-front: Usually applied to bookcases or sideboards to describe a centre section which protrudes forwards from the line of the sides.

breath motivated: Toys that move or make a noise when blown.

breech: In firearms, the end of the barrel closest to the user (opposite to the muzzle).

breech-loading: Any firearm loaded through the breech of the barrel, as in a shotgun, as opposed to down the barrel.

Breguet: Important family of Paris clockmakers: Abraham, considered one of the greatest in his field, active 1770-1810, Louis from 1830-70 and Louise A. 1800-1833.

brewster chair: The name given to a type of C17 American armchair constructed of turned spindles and posts and a rush seat.

brianchon: A lustrous glaze, like mother-of-pearl, invented by J. J. H. Brianchon, and characteristic of late C19 Belleek wares, especially ornamented parian wares cast in the form of sea-shells.

briar pipe: Tobacco pipe of briar or rosewood introduced c1810, sometimes with a bowl carved in the form of a human head.

Bridges, Henry: English clockmaker, primarily an architect, active first half C18 and noted for astronomical clocks.

bridle joint: Joint used to set a table leg into the top frame.

Brigadier: Danish manufacturer of toy soldiers since 1946.

brigandine: Leather or canvas jacket lined with overlapping metal plates, invented C15 as a form of bullet-proof vest.

bright cut: Engraving on silver in which the edges of the lines that form the design are bevelled to reflect light and stand out more brilliantly.

brilliant: A precious stone cut so as to have 58 facets; 33 above the girdle, 25 below.

briolette: A jewel cut into pear shape and faceted all over, often pierced to hang as a pendant.

Brislington: A form of delftware made at Bristol mid C17 to mid C18.

Bristol: Important porcelain factory established c1749, producing delftware, and (c1770) enamelled and gilded wares decorated with flowers and swags. Also, C17 and C18 delftwares (bowls, figure groups, jugs) produced by several factories in the area.

Bristol glass: Coloured glass, especially blue, made in quantity in Bristol, C18, but also in other centres.

Bristol penny toys: Cheap wheeled wooden toys sold by street vendors, made from c1800 originally in Bristol, but also in London from 1850.

Britain, W.: Leading English manufacturer of toy soldiers and other figures, vehicles, etc. from 1893.

Britannia metal: A form of pewter used as a silver substitute in the first half C19; an alloy of tin, copper and antimony, harder and able to take a higher polish than most pewter, and lacking the dangerous lead content.

Britannia standard: Of higher quality than sterling silver, of 958.3 parts of silver per 1000; introduced 1697 to prevent silversmiths using melted-down coinage as a source of metal, and usually stamped with the figure of Britannia.

British plate: Nickel alloy made in the mid C19, objects often "hall-marked" in an attempt to pass them off as silver.

broadsword: From the C16 on, a sword with a flat double-edged blade, often used with a smallsword or rapier.

broken arch: See broken pediment.

broken corners: Term used to describe a rectangular shape or decoration, the corners of which do not extend to their natural point but are cut short and inwardly rounded.

broken pediment: A pediment on a piece of furniture, the centre part of which is missing i.e. broken. Also variously known as broken arch, goose neck, scroll top and swan neck.

broken set: A number of matching chairs but less than the original number in the set.

bronze: Bright golden alloy of copper and tin which develops a brown or dull green patina with time. Easily cast and used from antiquity especially for figurines and statues.

Bronze Age: The date when bronze was first discovered and used in preference to stone for tools and weapons differs from culture to culture. In Europe, Bronze Age means the period c2000-c700 BC.

bronzes d'ameublement: French term used to describe gilt or patinated mounts for furniture. See also Ormolu.

Brooklyn glass: Products of factories based in Brooklyn, New York, C18/C19, especially the Brooklyn Flint Glass Co., specializing in cut glass, which moved to Corning c1870.

Brownfield: Used to describe pottery from the Albion Works, at Cobridge, produced under the ownership of William Brownfield, mid C19; bone china figures, basketwork dishes and plates printed with the caricatures of Phiz (the illustrator of Dickens' works).

Brownhills: Staffordshire pottery, founded c1760,

producing transfer-printed salt-glazed wares.

brown oak: A sought-after variety of oak which is a deeper red brown colour caused by the pigment from a fungus that penetrates the whole tree.

Bru & Cie: Leading French doll maker 1866-99; noted for dolls in elaborate contemporary costumes.

Brunstrom pewter: Made by one of two pewterers of that name in late C18 Philadelphia.

Brunswick: C18 New Jersey pottery producing delftwares, and rococo figure groups.

brushing slide: Wooden slide found in some chests of drawers which pulls forward to provide a larger working surface.

Brussels carpets: Generic term for carpets of moquette-wool and linen brushed to resemble silk – made from the C16, not necessarily in Brussels.

bucchero: Black, highly polished ancient ceramic, burnished to resemble metal.

buckler: Small round shield used to ward off the blows of an adversary.

Buddha knop: Spoons with a knop or finial in the form of an eastern deity, perhaps Buddha, made C17 and especially associated with Raleigh Clapham, Devon silversmith, who marked his work with the initials RC.

Buen Retiro: Factory established 1760 near Madrid, producing pottery (including a famous set of porcelain furniture) for the Spanish court; noted for rococo style figure groups sculpted by Giuseppe Gricci.

buffalo willow pattern: American willow-pattern style plates depicting a child on a buffalo.

buffet: Name loosely applied to various structures of more than one tier, with or without enclosed sections. For the more correct names see court cupboard, livery cupboard and press cupboard.

Bugatti, Carlo (1855-1940): Italian designer of bizarre Art Nouveau furniture made of parchment, and interior decorator.

buggin bowl: Rare late C17 lead glass bowls so-called because some surviving examples are engraved with the arms of Butler Buggin.

Buhl: An old English interpretation of Boulle.

bulb: The bulging swelling found on some C17 legs and supports, more correctly known as a Portuguese swell.

bulb bowl: Oriental pottery form, a small bowl, about 12in (30cm) across with three feet, used for growing bulbs.

bulla: Ancient Etruscan bubble-shaped pendant, often in gold, used for storing precious liquids such as perfume or ointment.

bullet: Projecting piece in a keyhole designed to accept a suitable groove cut into the key.

bullion: Silver or gold blocks or bars; the state before being made up into coinage, vessels, jewellery, etc.

Bullock, Edmund: Shropshire clockmaker, active mid C18, his work usually signed and numbered.

bull's eye: Clear glass with a large centre gather. Used occasionally in cabinets.

bun foot: Similar to the ball foot but with the rounded shape slightly flattened.

Bunyan, Robert: Lincoln clockmaker, active late C18.

bureau: Writing desk with either a fall, a cylinder or a tambour front.

bureau à cylindre: See cylinder top desk.

bureau bookcase: Bureau with a glazed-fronted bookcase fitted above it.

bureau cabinet: Bureau with a solid-doored or mirrored cabinet fitted above it, often containing further fitted cupboards and drawers.

bureau de dame: Writing desk of delicate appearance and designed for use by ladies. Usually raised above slender cabriole legs and with one or two external drawers.

bureau-plat: French writing table with a flat top and drawers in the frieze.

bureau-toilette: A piece of furniture which combines the functions of a dressing table and a writing table.

Burges, William (1827-81): English architect and designer whose furniture is distinguished by ornate, neo-Gothic surface decoration, often painted.

burgonet: Originally a Burgundian steel cap worn by pikemen, but in C17 a cavalry helmet with a crested crown, peak and hinged chin pieces.

burl: The marking in wood of a knot or protruding growth which displays beautifully patterned grainings when cut as a veneer.

burr: Another name for burl.

bursa: Northern Turkish prayer rugs with a short pile, of silk or cotton, predominantly blue, red and ivory.

busby: Late C19 tall military cap of fur, with a plume and a bag suspended from the top, hanging over the right side of the face.

busted bonds: Share or loan certificates issued by defunct governments or enterprises e.g. Tsarist bonds which became worthless at the Russian Revolution.

butler's tray: A portable tray which rests on a folding stand.

butt: The rear-end of the stock of a gun, placed against the shoulder whilst firing.

Butterfield, Michael: Noted maker of pocket sundials, died 1724, but the name continued to be used on similar instruments well into the C19.

butterfly gate: Type of table leaf support which comprises a shaped flap board which swings out from the main frame to support the leaf. See also butterfly table.

butterfly joint: Joint shaped like a butterfly and used to join two pieces of flat wood end to end.

butterfly table: Drop leaf table which is so called because the leaves are supported by butterfly gates.

butterfly wing: Term used to describe a table which has shaped leaves similar to the wings of a butterfly. Usually applied to Pembroke tables.

butternut: Another name for white walnut.

butt hinge: Type of commonly used cabinet hinge which shows only a thin strip of metal.

button back: Descriptive of upholstered seat furniture where the back has been buttoned. See also buttoning.

button hook: Metal hooks, sometimes highly ornate with silver or ivory handles, used for fastening the buttons of close-fitting high boots and spats from c1840 to c1920.

buttoning: Process in upholstery whereby a button is covered with the fabric and drawn tightly into the furniture for decorative effect.

bygones: Term used to describe objects superseded by technology, usually agricultural and domestic implements and utensils.

byknives: Ceremonial small knives sometimes worn with a sword or dirk.

Byrne, Michael: Leading English gunsmith, mid C18.

Byzantine: The style of art developed in the Eastern Roman Empire, whose capital was Byzantium (now Istanbul) from the beginning of the C5 AD; early pottery, tile and mosaic depicts Christian symbols; later work shows Islamic influence.

C

cabbage ware: Tableware, first made at Worcester, of green porcelain with cabbage-leaf decoration in low relief.

caberet: Name given to a complete tea set in porcelain, consisting of teapot, milk jug, sugar basin, cups, saucers and tray.

cabinet: Descriptive of various case pieces of furniture having either drawers, shelves or compartments.

cabinet furniture: Handles, escutcheons, etc. for furniture, usually made of brass.

cable moulding: A decorative moulding of twisted rope appearance used during the Regency period on some chair-backs and columns. Such chairs are known as rope back or Trafalgar chairs as this moulding was a tribute to Nelson's victories at sea.

cabochon (1): Design motif comprising a domed or ball shape surrounded by leaves.

cabochon (2): Jewel cut into a dome shape, especially popular in C19 jewellery.

cabriole leg: Tall curving leg subject to many designs and produced with club, pad, paw, claw and ball, and scroll feet.

cachemire: Pattern of closely-spaced and interlaced flowers in many colours, copied from Chinese models and typical of Delft vases.

caddy: Usually silver (but also of ceramic, wood or enamel) container for tea with a lead-lined compartment; often two compartments with a spoon and glass bowl for blending two types of leaf.

caddy spoon: Late C18 accompaniment to a caddy, made with a short handle so as to fit into a compartment in the caddy, usually with a bowl of ornate shape or decorated.

cage cup: Drinking vessel ornamented with bars by grinding away surplus glass; found on ancient Roman glass; revived C19 in Germany.

caillouté: Gold circles on a deep blue background typical of mid C18 French porcelain.

cake basket: Silver or gilt dish with the sides pierced in a variety of patterns and two handles, variously used for serving fruit, bread and sweetmeats from the latter half C16. Later examples, from the C18, are oval rather than circular.

calabash: Originally a gourd used for storing liquids; any pottery vessel of similar shape, often African in origin.

calamander: Reddish brown hardwood imported from India and Ceylon and used as a veneer.

calcedonio: Marble effect in glass in imitation of precious minerals.

calendar clock: Clock with separate openings in the dial showing the day and month and, more rarely, the year.

calendar sword: One with signs of the zodiac or saint's feast days etched on the blade.

calibre: Diameter of a bullet or projectile, but often used as an alternative name for the bore, or internal diameter, of a gun barrel.

caliver: Early musket, in use in C16, with a short barrel and matchlock mechanism, fired from the shoulder.

Callot: Grotesque figure group, usually in porcelain but also in metal and glass, after the etchings of the French caricaturist Jacques Callot (1592-1635).

calorifere: Portable stove, usually made for heating conservatories and greenhouses.

caltrop: Iron ball with four projecting prongs used to impede horses in battle.

calyx: Decorative motif of leaves enclosing a bud.

camaieu: Porcelain decoration using different tones of the one colour.

camail: Chain mail curtain attached to the rear of a bascinet to protect the neck from sword blows.

Cambrian: Pottery from the factory of that name in Swansea, Wales, noted for pottery painted by the flower artist, William Billingsley, produced in the early C19.

camel back: Term to describe a chair or sofa with a back that curves somewhat like the hump of a dromedary.

cameo (1): Design carved in relief, usually on a semi-precious stone, and often with a contrasting background.

cameo (2): In furniture, a term used to describe the oval-shaped back of a settee. Occasionally used to describe other oval decorations.

cameo glass: A sandwich of coloured glass which is then cut or etched away to create a multi-colour design in relief. An ancient technique rediscovered by Emile Gallé and popular with Art Nouveau and Art Deco glassmakers in the early C20.

cameo parian: Mid C19 porcelain imitating cameo, originally white paste decoration on a blue ground; later many other colours were used.

camera lucida: A prismatic device, from early C19, used by artists to project an image on a sheet of paper so that the outline could be traced.

camera obscura: Box-like instrument containing lenses which project an image onto a black surface, used from the late C17 as an artist's aid.

camisarde: Shirt worn over armour, originally used in night attacks so that the wearers could distinguish each other from the foe.

campaign buttons: First designed in 1896, badges produced during American presidential elections promoting a candidate or party slogan.

campaign chair: Chair designed to fold flat and therefore convenient for travelling use.

campaign chest: A chest of drawers with brass protective mounts and no protruding parts (except possibly small feet, which may themselves be detachable) designed for travelling use. They sometimes have an outer tin-bound travelling box.

campana: Silver vase of exaggerated shape with a very pronounced waist.

camp canteen: Set of boxed cutlery and accoutrements such as salt and pepper cellars designed for travellers; the box often has retractable or folding legs to serve as a table.

camphor: Light yellowish brown wood from the East Indies. It has a distinctive smell and is used mainly for making trunks and boxes.

camphor glass: White or semi-opaque American pressed glass.

canapé: The French word for a sofa.

canary: Bright canary-yellow background to early C19 resist-lustre pottery.

candelabrum: Usually of silver and made in matched pairs or sets, a candlestick with two or more branches, ornate after the C18.

candle box: Square or cylindrical box of metal or wood for storing candles. Also a lidded compartment within a chest for the same purpose.

candle slide: Small wooden slide designed to carry a candlestick.

candlestand: Portable stand for a candlestick, candelabrum or lamp. Also known as a gueridon or torch.

candlestick: Candleholder designed for a single candle, in pewter, brass or silver, often of columnar form, sometimes in matching pairs.

candy: Cord that holds the sides of a rug in place and prevents fraying.

caneware: The name of a stoneware, produced by Josiah Wedgwood, of a creamy colour; developed for use on the earliest oven-proof wares in the mid C19.

caning: Method of seating furniture using rattan. The cane is interwoven in a mesh to give a strong but light seat.

cannon stove: Large bulbous stoves originally popular in Holland as early as C15 and made in Colonial America especially for heating public rooms.

canopy: Hanging or over-hanging covering usually associated with beds and high dressers.

Cantagalli: Late C19 maiolica factory founded in Florence by Ulysse Cantagalli and specializing in reproductions of Renaissance wares.

cantaro: Mediterranean glass drinking vessel, C18, with a wide spout for filling and a smaller one for pouring.

canted: Descriptive of a corner which is bevelled, chamfered or sloping at an angle.

canteen: Set of cased silver tableware or cutlery; or an urn, also of silver, with a tap at the base for dispensing contents.

canterbury: Small portable music stand with open partitions designed to hold sheet music.

canton: The general term for blue and white porcelains imported to the west in the C18 when Canton was the chief port for east/west trade.

capacity marks: After 1826, required by law on pewter tankards used in taverns, hence an aid to dating and provenance.

capacity mug: Any vessel marked to hold a specific quantity of liquid; used from C17 to measure beer and other liquors.

cap dispenser: In firearms, a metal dispenser, usually circular, fitted with a release mechanism that allowed one percussion cap to be released at a time. Usually suspended from the belt.

Cape Cod glass: Pressed and cut glass made by the Cape Cod Glass Co., second half C19.

Capodimonte: Porcelain factory established mid C18 in Naples, later moved to Buen Retiro, Madrid; noted for the figure groups carved by Giuseppe Gricci.

Cappadocian: Early hand-made pottery painted with geometric motifs made in the Cappadocia region of Anatolia around 2000-1800 BC.

capstan: Used to describe the shape of a salt pot or the finials or feet of a silver object, resembling the shape of a ship's capstan or a domestic cotton reel.

capstan table: Another name for a drum table.

Capuchine: Stoneware vessel which, turned upside down, resembled the pointed hood of a Capuchine, or Franciscan, friar; first made Nottingham c1700.

caqueteuse: Type of chair with a tall back and widely splayed arms capable of accommodating the full dresses of ladies in the late C16. Also known as a gossip's chair.

carafe: Glass vessel with a bulbous body and tall narrow neck for water, wine or liquor; C18 examples are engraved and made for table-use, C19 examples designed for bedroom use, often plainer and with a beaker that sits on the neck doubling as a stopper.

carbine: Cavalry musket, similar in most respects to infantry firearms but lighter and lacking a bayonet.

carbine bore: Smaller than a classic musket bore, at about 0.65in/1½cm.

carbine-thimble: Leather socket on the offside of a

cavalryman's saddle used to hold a carbine.

carbuncle: A garnet cut into a dome shape.

carcase: The main framework or body of a piece of furniture onto which the veneer is applied.

carcase furniture: General term for furniture used for storage purposes as distinct from tables and chairs.

card case: Small receptacle for storing visiting cards, usually of silver, popular from c1820 to end C19.

Cardew, Michael (1901-83): English art potter, taught by Bernard Leach, and inspired by oriental porcelain. Worked at the Winchcombe Pottery 1926-39.

card table: Table with a foldover top, the inside of which is lined with baize for playing card games. See also gaming table.

Carlin, Martin (d.1785): French cabinet maker working in the third quarter of C18. He was commissioned by Royalty and worked mainly with lacquer and with plaques of Sévres porcelain which he incorporated into his furniture.

Carlton House desk: A distinct type of writing desk which has a raised back with drawers which extend forward at the sides to create an "enclosed" central writing area.

carousel figures: Horses and other animals from fairground carousels or roundabouts, usually classified as either "jumpers" or "standers".

carpet: Strictly woven fabric with a cotton or linen warp and wool weft and pile; originally used to describe decorative wall hangings and only since the C17 to describe a floor covering.

carrara: Very fine white marble quarried in Tuscany and used by Michelangelo amongst others; also Doulton stoneware and C19 English parian ware made to imitate the appearance of white marble and very popular for decorative objects.

carriage clock: Originally one fitted with a device to ensure that the jolts common in the days of coach travel would not interfere with the oscillations of the balance spring. Now, any small portable oblong clock of rectangular form, popular from the C19 to the present day.

carrier: The metal clip which sits over the waistband, with two attached chains, for carrying the scabbard of a small sword.

cartel clock: C18 French wall clock in the shape of a shield, often with a gilded bronze case and elaborately ornamented in rococo style.

Carlton House desk

Carlton ware: Brand name of Art Nouveau pottery made by Wiltshaw and Robinson, a Stoke-on-Trent pottery founded in 1897.

Carolean: Term used for furniture made during the reign of Charles I (1625-1649).

cartonnier: Piece of furniture made in various designs but which usually stood at one end of a writing table and was intended to hold papers. Also known as serre-papier.

carton pierre: Pulped paper and glue invented in C19 as a substitute for stucco for making lightweight ceiling mouldings.

cartophilists: Collectors of cigarette cards, but the term also includes those who are interested in postcards, greetings cards, etc.

cartouche: An ornate tablet or shield surrounded by scrollwork and foliage, often bearing a maker's name, inscription or coat of arms.

cartridge: Casing of parchment or metal which fits into the bore of a firearm, containing a measured quantity of powder and either a projectile (ball cartridge) or not (blank cartridge).

carver: A dining chair with arms.

caryatid: An upright carved female figure used as decoration or support. Although, strictly, it implies a female figure, the term is sometimes used for a male figure.

cased glass: One layer of glass, often coloured, sandwiched between two plain glass layers or vice versa, plain glass between two coloured layers; outer layer engraved to create decorative effects. Ancient technique revived C19.

casein: Early form of plastic patented 1900 and much used for imitation horn and tortoiseshell objects.

casement: In architecture, the hinged part of a window.

case of swords: Two swords which clip together and fit into a single scabbard, sometimes made as duelling rapiers.

cassapanca: Type of Italian settle with a chest under the seat. Usually with a very high back.

Cassel: Short-lived German porcelain factory, 1766-88, noted for blue-painted coffee and tea sets.

cassone: Italian chest used for general storage of linen and clothes.

Castelford: Pottery near Leeds, established c1790, noted for glossy, white porcellaneous stoneware.

castellato: Little castle, popular motif in European porcelain painting, latter half C18.

castelli: Maiolica from the Abruzzi region of Italy, noted for delicate landscapes painted by members of the Grue family.

caster or castor: Cylindrical

vessel for dispensing sugar or spices, such as pepper, with a detachable dome often ornately pierced, from the C18.

cast glass: Glass cast in a mould.

casting bottle: Small silver container with pierced sides, filled with a perfume-soaked sponge and suspended from a chain as an air freshener, mainly in C18.

cast iron: A smelted mixture of iron and carbon used for mould-casting, etc from the C18. Brittle but cheaper to make than wrought iron, much favoured for architectural railings, pillars, balconies, etc in C19.

castors: Small wheels of wood, china, brass or leather on furniture allowing it to be moved without lifting.

cast spoons: Cast, rather than hammered and drawn, spoons of highly ornate design – the bowl, stem and finial all decorated – from the mid C18.

catoptrick: Instrument using curved mirrors which converts an apparently meaningless doodle into a recognizable picture. Novelty instrument made from the C18.

Caucasian: From the Caucasus, the range of mountains between the Black and Caspian Seas, forming today's Soviet/Turkish border region. Important rug-making centre; products characterized by geometric patterns, with a notable absence of curves.

caudle cup: Silver cup with a cover designed to keep the contents warm – originally for caudle (spiced gruel laced with wine).

Caughley: Shropshire factory, established c1750, producing porcelain very like that of Worcester, including early willow-pattern, often embellished by gilding.

causeuse: Large chair or small sofa to seat two people.

cavetto: A quarter round concave moulding.

cedar: Reddish brown wood frequently used for chests and drawer linings because of its fragrant and long lasting aroma which repels moths and woodworm.

celadon: Chinese stonewares with an opaque grey-green glaze, first made in the Sung dynasty and still made today, principally in Korea.

cellaret: Lidded container on legs designed to hold wine. The interior is often divided into sections for individual bottles.

celluloid: Early form of plastic, used from the 1870s for a great range of household objects but flammable and superseded in 1926 by cellulose acetate or "nonflammable celluloid".

cemetery rugs: Small Turkish prayer rugs with a design of cypress trees and tomb-like buildings.

centrepiece: Silver ornament, usually decorative rather than functional, designed to occupy the centre of a dining table.

centre table: Table designed to stand in the centre, or other open part, of a room and thus should look attractive when viewed from any side.

Chad Valley Co.: Late C19 English manufacturer of rag dolls and other toys.

Chaffers, Richard & Partners: Liverpool pottery manufacturer, operating around 1754-65, producing earthenwares resembling china and modelled on Worcester forms.

chafing dish: Silver vessel designed to keep plates warm, with a charcoal brazier or spirit lamp in the base and racks or supports above, from mid C17.

chain: Term sometimes used for the threads that make the warp or weft of a carpet.

chain fusee: A development of c1800; prior to that the fusee was connected to the mainspring barrel in clock mechanisms by gut whose expansion or contraction

jeopardized the clock's accuracy.

chain mail: Armour made of interlocking metal rings, in use until C17.

chair: Until C18 the term "chair" invariably meant an armchair, and what might now be called a chair was probably a back stool.

chair-back settee: A distinct type of settee with a back that looks like two or more chairs joined together.

chair-table: See table-chair.

chaise longue: An elongated chair, the seat long enough to support the sitter's legs.

chalcedony: Translucent semi-precious stone with a waxy appearance much used in antiquity for seals, stamps etc.

chalet style clock: Black Forest cuckoo clocks in the form of a mountain chalet, a style which first appeared c1850.

chalkware: Painted ornaments and figure groups made of plaster of Paris in imitation of porcelain.

chamber: The space in the breech of a gun barrel in which the charge is placed and in which the ignition takes place; larger than the rest of the barrel and originally detachable.

chamber clock: Strictly, small iron clocks of C15 and C16, scaled down versions of turret clocks; sometimes used of any domestic clock.

Chamberlain porcelain: Either that decorated by Robert Chamberlain, employed at the Worcester porcelain works, 1751-83; or that made by the firm of Chamberlain & Son, which he founded in Worcester in 1786.

chamfer: A bevelled edge.

champagne glass: C18 bowl form in the shape of a cyma, or double ogee. Today's simple hemispherical bowl introduced mid C19.

Champion, Richard: Founder of a porcelain factory in Bristol, late C18, noted for its clear, colourful glazes.

champlevé: Enamelling on copper or bronze, similar to cloisonné, in which a glass paste is applied to the hollowed-out design, fired and ground smooth.

Chanak Kate: C18 and C19 Turkish earthenware vessels, usually jugs in the form of stylized animals.

chanfron: Armour used to protect a horse's head.

channel moulding: A uniform grooved decoration often found on early oak furniture.

Chantilly: French porcelain factory operating in the C18, notable for its imitations of Japanese forms.

chape: Originally the metal tip of a scabbard, then the buckle by which it was attached to a belt.

Chaplet, Ernest (1836-1909): French potter inspired by the artist Gauguin and by oriental ceramics. Noted for his barbotine wares and flambé glazes, some of which are unique to him, for he destroyed the formulae before his death.

chapter ring: The part of a clock face on which the hours are inscribed – usually separate from the dial plate.

character doll: One with a naturalistic face, especially laughing, crying, pouting, etc.

character jug: Earthenware jugs, and sometimes mugs, widely made in C18 and C19, depicting a popular character, such as a politician, general, jockey or actor.

charger: Large, flat plate or dish, used for serving the main meat dish, or as a buffet dish on the sideboard.

Charleston iron: Wrought iron made in Charleston, South Carolina, and used for the ornate architectural iron-work characteristic of the region.

Charleville musket: Early American gun, used in the American Revolution, copied from French prototypes.

Charmes, Simon de: Huguenot refugee, noted for very fine clocks, in London 1700-10.

charpay: A rug approximately 4ft (1.2m) long.

Charpentier, Alexandre (1856-1909): French Arts and Crafts artist, sculptor and designer of furniture, ceramics, metalwork and leatherware.

chased silver: Decorated by producing an embossed design using hammer and punches, as distinct from carving or engraving.

chasing: The portion of a gun barrel between the breech and the beginning of the swell of the muzzle; or in modern firearms, where there is no swell, up to the muzzle itself. Also, decorative metal inlay, often found on the wheel-locks.

chatironné: Floral decoration, the outlines drawn in black, imitating oriental motifs, on porcelain.

Chelsea: Important London porcelain factory, founded c1745 and one of the first to exploit the discovery of the secret of porcelain manufacture made in 1742. Early forms imitate those of silver; from 1749-56, influenced by Meissen and noted for very fine figure groups, and fine botanical painting; from 1757-69, florid, rich blue and gold decoration and elaborate bocage groups.

chenet: French andiron, common C17, often ornate.

Chenghua (Ch'eng Hua): Chinese Ming dynasty emperor, 1488-1505.

chequer inlay: Dark and light wood squares inlaid alternately as on a chess board but forming a strip of inlay.

cherry: Hard close grained wood which is initially a pinkish brown colour but matures to a more reddish colour.

chest: A large box with a lid. Used for general storage and sometimes for travelling. See also coffer.

chesterfield: Type of large over-stuffed sofa introduced in late C19.

chesterfield ware: Mid C19 stone caneware, often decorated with hunting scenes.

chestnut: Two main varieties. Horse chestnut is a very light whitish wood used mainly for drawer linings. Sweet chestnut is a reddish brown colour when matured.

chest of drawers: Frame containing a set of drawers which developed from the plain chest as the tendency to increase the drawer space at the expense of the box became fashionable.

chest on chest: Another name for a tallboy.

cheval mirror: Large toilet mirror in a frame with four legs, the mirror being pivoted and adjustable within the frame. Also known as a horse dressing glass and a psyche. Made c1750 onwards.

cheval screen: A type of fire screen comprising two uprights each on two legs and enclosing a decorative panel.

cheveret: A small writing table of delicate proportions, often with a raised back containing small drawers and a shelf.

chi: Chinese symbol of immortality portrayed on carpet and ceramic designs as a cloud or sponge-like shape.

Chicago window: A window with a fixed central panel and two narrow sash windows at either side.

Ch'ien lung: Chinese C18 porcelain imitating various non-ceramic materials, e.g. horn, lacquer, wood, jade.

chien ware: Chinese stoneware with deep red to brown hare's fur glaze, used for tea-ceremony vessels from the Sung dynasty and produced in Fukien province.

chiffonier: Generally a twin door cupboard with one or two drawers above and surmounted by shelves.

chih: Chinese wine-tasting vessels.

child's chest: Name sometimes given to an exceptionally small chest.

child's furniture: Mainly small-scale furniture for children to use, as distinct from toy furniture.

ch'ilin: Mythical Chinese animal, symbol of goodness, with dragon's head, body of a deer and lion's tail. Motif frequently found on Chinese and oriental carpets.

chime: Of clocks, where the hours and quarters are sounded on more than one bell, as distinct from a strike.

chimera: Carved animal decoration found during the Regency period.

chimney crane: Hinged bracket of iron or brass fixed to the wall of a fireplace and used to suspend a pot or kettle over an open fire.

chimney piece: The frame around a fireplace opening.

chimney pot: Tall pot of terra cotta used to heighten the chimney, made from C15 onwards in a variety of fanciful shapes and now collected as garden planters.

china cabinet: Cabinet made especially for the display of china and porcelain.

china doll: Doll with a head and body made of glazed porcelain; from C18.

Chin dynasty: Period in Chinese history AD 1115-1260.

Chinese carpets: Mass produced since c1900 and characterized by designs in relief, formed by cutting the pile to different lengths. Often depict whole landscapes, and other scenes derived from Chinese water colour painting.

Chinese export porcelain: C16 to C18 wares made in China specifically for export and often to European designs.

Chinese Imari: Chinese imitations of Japanese blue, red and gold painted Imari wares, made from the early C18.

Chinese lacquerware: Objects of wood coated with layers of sap from the lacquer tree; considered inferior to Japanese lacquerware because of the inclusion of glues derived from animal bones and for the repetitiveness of the formalized designs.

Ch'ing dynasty: From 1644 to 1912, the period during which much decorated Chinese porcelain was exported to Europe.

Chinkin-bori: Japanese lacquerware in which the design is engraved in hairlines and filled with gold or coloured lacquer.

chinoiserie: The fashion, prevailing in the late C18, for Chinese-style ornamentation on porcelain, wallpapers and fabrics, furniture and garden architecture.

chintamani: Oriental carpet motif consisting of three balls arranged in a triangular form, symbol of the Buddha.

Chiparus, Demêtre: Rumanian-born sculptor working in Paris in the 1920s, noted for painted bronze and ivory figures, portrayed in exotic dance poses.

chip carving: Type of simple carved decoration associated mainly with oak, where the surface has been lightly cut or chipped away.

Chippendale, Thomas (1718-1779): A well known but little documented English cabinet maker, carver and furniture designer, particularly in the Chinese, rococo and Gothic styles.

Chippendale barometer: One with a case made by the celebrated cabinet maker, or in the Chippendale style.

chiton: Tunic worn by ancient Greeks, often depicted in classical statuary.

chlamys: Originally an ancient Greek cloak, but also ornamentation that imitates the hanging folds of a cloak.

chocolate pot: Similar in shape to a coffee pot but with a lip rather than a spout.

Chongzhen (Ch'ing Cheng): Chinese Ming dynasty emperor, 1628-44.

chosroes: Famous, much-copied C6 Persian rug.

Christian, Philip: Acquired Richard Chaffers' Liverpool factory in 1765 and continued producing china based on Worcester prototypes to 1776.

chrome dye: The dye now used in modern carpet production; more colour-fast, less likely to run, than aniline dye.

chromolithograph: Coloured prints taken from etched and polished stone, enabling a finer range of tints and shades than

was possible from metal plates; invented 1796.

chronometer: A timepiece of great accuracy, often marked with seconds or fractions of seconds, made for special purposes such as scientific research or navigation.

chryselephantine: Originally, made of gold and ivory, but now used of Art Deco statues made of ivory and another metal, typically bronze and very desirable.

church warden: Clay tobacco pipe with a long stem – up to 24in (60cm) – fashionable from c1750.

cider glass: Late C18 drinking glass, similar to an ale glass, but decorated with apple motifs.

cinerarium: Or cinerary urn; the name given to any ancient vessel used to preserve the cremated ashes of the dead; usually glass or ceramic with a lid.

cinquedea: C15 and C16 dagger or shortsword, so called because the blade measures five fingers (cinque diti) in length.

circular movement: A clock movement contained within circular, as opposed to rectangular, plates, a feature of French clocks after the early C19.

circumferentor: Surveying instrument consisting of several sights mounted over a compass and a brass circle marked with degrees of a circle, from the early C17, predecessor of the theodolite.

cire-perdue: French for "lost wax". Technique of metal casting in which the model is made in wax, coated with clay and then fired. The wax disappears leaving a cavity into which the molten metal is poured and cast.

cistern: Chamber containing the mercury at the base of a barometer column.

cistern cover: Piece of metal which shields a barometer cistern against accidental damage.

clair du lune: French for moonlight; Chinese porcelain with a pale blue glaze, or opalescent sapphire tinted glass.

claret jug: Silver jug or ewer made from C19 for serving claret, often indistinguishable from ewers generally.

Clarke, Arundell: Patron and retailer of Art Deco and Modernist furniture in London in the 1920s and 30s.

Classic: One of the principal divisions of Mesoamerican culture: the Pre-Classic era (*c*1500-200 BC) saw the development of cities; the Classic era (200 BC-AD 900) was an age of great artistic achievement; the Post-Classic era (900-1521) was a militaristic age, but much fine pottery, jewellery and metalwork survives.

Classical: Any style that relates to or copies ancient Greek or Roman art and architecture.

claw and ball foot: See ball and claw foot.

claw beaker: Late Roman and Saxon glass beaker with hook-shaped prunts projecting from the body, often in coloured glass; rare medieval German glass examples also known, and the style revived by the Köln Ehrenfield glassworks from 1879.

Clay, Henry: British furniture maker and originator of papier mâché furniture in C18.

claymore: Large double-edged broadsword used by Scottish Highlanders up to C18, with quillons angled towards the point.

clay pipe: The commonest and cheapest form of tobacco pipe, made of white Kaolin and produced from the late C16.

clay tablet: Ancient tablets of Near Eastern origin, dating to the 3rd and 2nd millennia BC, inscribed with cuneiform script and often containing economic or agricultural information.

clay ware: Objects made of sheet paper and glue, often gaily painted, made in late C18 by Henry Clay's factory in Birmingham, UK; especially trays, cups and boxes.

cleat: Strip of wood at the edge of a flat surface for neatness and extra strength.

Clements, William: Noted clockmaker, active late C17, specializing in anchor escapement mechanisms.

clepsydra: Any form of water clock; most, if not all, of those claimed to have been made in antiquity are more recent fakes or novelties.

Clermont-Ferrand: Briefly the centre of faience production in the mid C18; products now rare.

Clews, James and Ralph: Staffordshire potters making transfer-printed wares for export to America, early C19.

Clichy glass: From the factory founded in Paris but moved to Clichy-la-Garenne around 1840; specializing in cheap export glass but renowned for decorative paperweights, now much sought after.

Cliff, Clarice (1899-1972): Employed by A. J. Wilkinson Ltd, the pottery at Newport, Staffordshire, as artistic director in the 1930s. Designer of the colourful "Bizarre" and "Fantasque" ranges of mass-produced china.

clobber: Technique of applying coloured enamel glazes over blue and white underglaze colours.

clobbering: Re-decoration, or additional decoration, in polychrome glaze on old tin-glazed earthenware to enhance their value; practised as early as C17 in the Netherlands.

clock case: Container for a clock movement, often made by a different craftsman to the movement itself.

clock garniture: A matching group of clock and vases or candelabra made for the mantel shelf. Often highly ornate.

Clodion, Claude Michel (1738-1814): Designer who made figure groups in porcelain for Sèvres, in terracotta, pewter and bronze, noted especially for mildly erotic scenes.

cloisonné: Enamelling on metal with divisions in the design separated by lines of fine brass wire. A speciality of the Limoges region of France in the Middle Ages, and of Chinese craftsmen to the present day.

close band: Oriental carpet motif resembling strands of seaweed.

close-helmet: One made to cover the neck as well as the head, with a visor hinged at the temples.

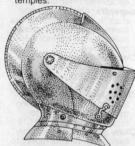

close plating: A fine layer of silver foil applied to knife blades to prevent them from rusting.

close stool/chair: Rectangular or drum-shaped boxed stool or chair designed to house a chamber pot and used for sanitary purposes. Also known as night stools or night chairs.

Clowes, James: Noted late C17 clockmaker.

club foot: Virtually the same as pad foot.

clustered column: Design whereby several pillars are clustered together, usually to form a leg.

Clutha glass: Art glass produced by the Glasgow firm of Couper Ltd from 1885, to the designs of Christopher Dresser; inspired by ancient glass, it is greenish, opaque and contains numerous bubbles and deliberate "flaws".

coaching clock: A large watch with a swivel handle for suspending in a coach or carriage, like a carriage clock.

coaching table: Small table which folds flat. So called because it could be carried on the side of coaches for use on picnic stops but its uses were really many and varied.

coade stone: Artificial stone invented by Mrs Eleanor Coade c1769. Frost proof and difficult to distinguish from real stone, it was widely used for casting garden statuary and architectural ornament in the late C18 and early C19.

coal box: Usually made in pairs to stand either side of the hearth, of brass bound hardwood with a drop-front and detachable lining. Some double as fireside seats; from the mid C19.

Coalport china: Porcelain manufactured at Coalbrookdale, Shropshire, from the 1790s, noted for the translucent felspathic wares produced from 1820 and the delicate colours of the figure groups.

coal vase: Tall and often ornate metal coal storage vessel, usually made in pairs to stand either side of the hearth.

coaster: Small silver tray with feet, sometimes wheels or castors, into which a bottle fits, so that it can be slid along the surface of a table.

cobalt: The mineral oxide used to give colour to blue glass; also used to describe glass of this colour.

cochineal: Brilliant red carpet dye derived from Central American insects; hence very precious and used only for the best rugs.

cock (1): In a watch mechanism, the bracket which, attached to the plate, supports one end of the balance spring.

cock (2): In early firearms, the metal jaw that clasped the flint or pyrites used to spark the powder. Later, the spring tensioned arm used to hold the firing agent. To cock means to set the tension ready for firing.

cockbeading: Small protruding moulding found on the edges of drawer fronts.

cockfighting chair: Chair with a curved T-shaped back and a saddle seat on which the sitter could sit back to front. They are said to have been popular to sit on while watching cockfighting.

cock metal: Copper and lead alloy, resembling pewter in appearance, used for cheap domestic wares in C19.

cock's head hinge: A twin plate hinge with finials shaped similar to a cock's head. It is usually found on furniture dating pre-1650.

codpiece: In armour, a protuberant box to protect the genitals and groin.

coffee pot: Silver vessel for mixing and serving coffee, often with a filter for the grounds, made in various shapes which offer a clue to dating from the late C17; early examples are flat-bottomed and of simple cone shape, later ones, from the late C18, more ornate, bulbous with a foot.

coffer: In strict definition a coffer is a travelling trunk which is banded with metalwork and covered with leather or other material. However, the word tends to be used quite freely to describe chests of various kinds.

coffin stool: The name given to some joined stools, especially those with a storage area under the seat, although strictly speaking this is incorrect for the domestic stool and applies only to those stools used as coffin biers in some churches.

coin glass: Goblet with a coin in the knop of the stem, a commemorative custom from late C17 onwards and often faked.

colichemarde: C18 leaf-shaped smallsword, wide at the hilt and rapier-like at the point; used for both cutting and thrusting.

Colinet, Claire Jeanne Roberte: Belgian-born artist who worked in France and produced many animated Art Deco figures based on mythology and dance.

collector's cabinet: See specimen chest.

collector's piece: Trade term, originally denoting a fine piece of interest to connoisseurs, now often used to describe pieces which appeal only to a minority taste.

Collier, sometimes Collyer, Benjamin: Noted London clockmaker active 1693-1730.

Collier revolver: Early C19 American revolver, the predecessor of the Colt, made by Elisha Collier.

Collinot: Decoration on porcelain resembling cloisonné; produced by the Collinot factory in Paris, late C19.

Colonial: Term used to describe American furniture made prior to c1680.

Colonna, Edward, known as Eugène (1862-1948): French artist who supplied Samuel Bing's Parisian shop, L'Art Nouveau, as well as clients in America, and who designed furniture, jewellery, pottery, textiles and art glass.

coloured glass: Glass coloured by the addition of a metal oxide.

colour twist: An air twist in a wine-glass stem in which the core of the twist or the outline is coloured.

Colt revolver: Mid C19 percussion pistol with an automatically revolving chamber, invented by Samuel Colt of Hartford, Connecticut, and manufactured in great quantity.

comb back: Descriptive of a country-made chair with a top rail and back shaped somewhat like a comb.

combed morion: Spanish C16 and C17 helmet with upturned peaks at front and rear, and crest shaped like a three-quarter moon.

combing: A pattern on earthenware of wavy parallel lines created by incising the surface, or drawing a pattern in slip, with a comb; common motif on C17 slipware.

cometarium: Instrument for plotting the path of a comet in relation to the sun.

comfit basket: Silver tray with pierced sides, smaller than a cake basket, for serving sweetmeats and crystallized fruits from the late C18.

commando knife: Short dagger-shaped knife with cross guard and razor-sharp edge, issued to commandos from the early 1940s.

Commedia dell'Arte: Figures from traditional Italian theatre (Harlequin, Columbine, Scaramouche, Pantaloon) often depicted in porcelain groups in C18.

commode: French word for a chest of drawers and borrowed from them to describe finely decorated chests of drawers for use in principal rooms. In C19 came to be used for a close-stool i.e. small cabinet containing a chamber pot for night use.

common furniture beetle: A wood-boring beetle which can infest furniture. The familiar tell-tale holes are the result of the adult beetle hatching inside the wood and boring out to escape from its nest. Commonly known as woodworm.

Communion tokens: Tokens of lead, pewter, leather or card, used widely in C18 and C19 in Protestant churches, to denote that the owner was entitled to receive Communion; sometimes with a religious text and the name of the church or parish.

Compagnie Dessin: Porcelain made to the orders of the Compagnie des Indes and exported from China in C18 and C19.

compass: Instrument for locating orientation by reference to magnetic north; ornate examples of the late C17 to early C19 are often of gold, silver, gilt or ivory.

compendiario: C16 maiolica, originally made at Faenza, with a high white glaze and restrained decoration, often in only one or two additional colours.

compendium table: Games table containing a variety of game boards and playing accessories.

compensated pendulum: One which compensates for variations in the pendulum length caused by temperature changes so as to keep the duration of each oscillation

constant; usually a gridiron of iron and steel is used, more rarely a mercury well.

compo: Short for composition. A form of plaster invented in the late C18 for making applied ceiling and furniture decorations.

composite: In classical architecture, the style that combines elements of the Corinthian and Ionic orders; capitals are carved with a volute and acanthus leaf.

composite set: Term given to a collection of chairs which are similar but not a true set. Also called a harlequin set.

compositiera: A small tray and matching sets of two or more silver vessels with lids and spoons, containing different types of spice, sauce or food to be mixed on the plate according to taste.

composition doll: One made of papier mâché or wood pulp and glue.

composition figures: Toy soldiers made out of a mixture of sawdust, kaolin and glue on a wire skeleton, plaster-like in appearance; from c1904.

compost: Fruit or dessert dish, often of silver, with a single foot.

compound twist: In a wine glass stem, any air-twist made of multiple spirals; e.g. lace twist, gauze and multi-ply.

concertina action: Descriptive of the way in which the frame of some card and gaming tables extends to support the foldover top. The back half of the frame is hinged in two sections and opens out for support.

condiment pot: Small silver pot, often with a glass or ceramic lining, for holding salt, pepper, mustard, etc.

confidante: Large sofa of French origin, the ends of which are formed as separate seats which face diagonally outwards.

console: A tall ornamented scroll-shaped bracket common in rococo architecture and fireplaces.

console table: Decorative side table with no back legs, being supported against the wall by brackets.

Constructivism: One of the styles of the 1920s developed in reaction to Art Nouveau, and associated principally with the Dutch de Stijl movement.

consular watch: The successor to the pair-case watch from the early C19, with a glazed bezel and a movement both hinged to the backcase.

conversation seat: Large circular upholstered seat divided into segments. Made during the C19 and perhaps more decorative than practical.

Cooper, J.: Leading English gunsmith, mid C19.

Cooper, J. M.: Leading Philadelphia gunsmith, mid C19.

coopered joint: A curved timber joint, as found on wine coolers.

Copeland: Wares produced by the Spode works after it was acquired by William Copeland, in the early C19.

Copenhagen: Porcelain works founded c1750, best known for the Flora Danica range, decorated with Danish flowers.

coperta: Literally a covering; a lead glaze applied over tin glaze in delftware or maiolica.

copper: Naturally occurring metal used on its own, or in an alloy, especially for kitchen pans etc., from the C17.

Coptic: The art of Egyptian Christians, renowned from the C5 onwards for colourful textiles decorated with pagan classical as well as Christian motifs, and for funerary portraits painted on wood.

cordial glass: Smaller version of a wine glass, with a thick stem, heavy foot and small bowl; evolved C17 for strong drink.

Corinthian: The most elaborate of the classical orders in which the capitals are decorated with acanthus leaf.

cork glass: Early hand-cut flint glass, late C18/early C19 from two short-lived factories in Cork, Ireland.

corn chest: Chest made for storing corn and, probably, other grains. Sometimes with small drawers and a shallow raised back.

corned powder: Powder ground to a specific grade to suit the firearm; coarse in the case of a cannon, fine for hand guns.

corner cabinet/cupboard: Cabinet designed to fit into a rightangled corner. The internal angle of the back is often greater than 90° to allow for cottage rooms which may not have perfectly symmetrical walls.

corner chair: Chair designed to fit neatly into a corner, being of squarish appearance with two side legs, one back leg and one central front leg. Also called a writing chair or roundabout.

cornice: Any moulded projection which crowns and completes the top of a wall, cabinet, window or door surround.

cornucopia: The horn of plenty, overflowing with fruits and vines, originally carried by Ceres, goddess of the harvest, but frequently used as a decorative motif, especially for wall-mounted brackets and candelabrum.

coromandel (1): Oriental carved lacquer work, used especially to create pictorial folding screens, so called because Coromandel, in Bengal, was the principal export port in the C17 and C18.

coromandel (2): Yellow and black striped wood from South America which is used mainly for cross banding.

correction chair: Tall, high-backed child's chair on which children were taught to sit correctly.

corridor carpet: Alternative name for runner; a long thin rug.

corridor stool: Long stool with raised ends, made throughout C19. They were never upholstered. Also known as a rout stool.

corseca: Also known as a corseque; a medieval weapon combining a hook, axe and spear.

corset back: Term describing a C19 American elbow chair with a waisted back.

corslet/corselet: Armour that covers the trunk but not the limbs.

costume doll: Dolls made from the C19, often intended for sale as souvenirs, dressed in national, regional or occupational costume.

cot: Child's bed, but by derivation one that is suspended between two uprights and swings, as distinct from the rocked cradle.

cottage clock: General term for small C19 New England mantel clocks with wooden cases.

cotton twist: A pattern of very fine white spirals in a wine glass stem.

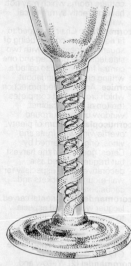

cotyledon: Decorative motif of stylized cup-shaped leaves sprouting from a bud.

couch: An old term for a day bed.

Coudyser, James: French Art Nouveau designer specializing in embroidery and lacework.

counter: A structure resembling a table but with a compartment underneath; so called because the top was used for reckoning accounts with counters, although it also had other purposes.

counter box: Often of silver but also of wood or ivory, used for storing gaming counters or tokens from the C17.

counterguard: Protection for the hand at the hilt of a sword.

countersink: The cutting of a bevelled hole to accommodate and conceal the head of a screw.

country furniture: General term for furniture made by provincial craftsmen; cottage furniture and especially that made of pine, oak, elm and the fruitwoods.

countwheel strike: Mechanism for controlling the number of strikes that mark the hours in a clock movement: consisting of a wheel with notches at increasing intervals around the rim; the lever, or detent, continues to strike until it catches in one of the notches.

Couper Ltd: The Glasgow firm of glassmakers that produced Clutha glass, from 1885.

coup perdu: Literally "lost beat": a clock whose pendulum beats half-seconds but whose second hand only moves every second.

couronne de feu: Iron candle-stick with two or more branches.

court cupboard: Two or three-tiered open structure used primarily for the display of plate and other finery.

couse: Medieval spear with a broad blade.

couter: In armour, the plate that protects the elbow.

Couty, Edmé (d.1917): French designer who worked for the Sèvres porcelain factory but also designed tapestries, book bindings and furniture in the Art Nouveau style.

cove moulding: Decorative plaster or wood frieze used to disguise the angle between a wall and the ceiling, usually concave in section.

cow creamer: Porcelain, or silver, cream boat or jug in the shape of a cow; its tail used as the handle, its mouth the spout.

crabstock: The handle, and sometimes the spout, of a C18 teapot formed in the shape of an apple-tree branch.

crackle: Hairline fractures in ceramic glaze, deliberately induced for decorative effect, found on Chinese porcelain and sometimes imitated by European manufacturers.

crackle glaze: Patterns of fine cracks in glazed ceramic, deliberately induced for decorative effect.

cradle: Box-shaped child's bed, but one specifically mounted on cross bearers as rockers. Many cradles were made with tall finials at the corners which enabled a mother to rock the baby from her bed.

cradle telephone: The earliest form of telephone produced in quantity, invented by Erickson of Sweden in 1892; early examples highly ornate, of gilded and japanned metal, ivory and horn.

Crailsheim: Faience from a C18 factory near Würtemburg, noted for its bright and colourful floral decoration.

cran: Iron tripod used as a kettle stand on the hearth.

crazing: A network of cracks in glaze, induced for decorative effect; alternative name for crackle.

cream boat: Long, low jug with a wide spout, smaller than a sauce boat, for pouring cream, often ornate and part of a tea set.

creamware: Earthenware with a thick buttery white or cream coloured glaze, made to imitate porcelain; developed by Wedgwood in the 1760s.

crèche figures: Dolls made principally in Italy and France as part of a tableau depicting the Nativity of Christ: not just the Biblical figures, but onlookers from all walks of life.

credence table: A side table became known in the C19 as a credence table when it was used ecclesiastically for the elements and cruets of Holy Communion.

credenza: Used today to describe a type of side cabinet which is highly decorated and shaped. Originally it was an Italian sideboard used as a serving table.

Creil: Late C18 and C19 faience from the French factory of that name, often imitating English forms and decoration.

crenellated: Originally battlemented; but also used to describe pottery vessels with a pie-crust or wavy rim. Also descriptive of a cornice which has battlements.

Crescent, Charles (1685-1768): French cabinet maker widely employed by Royalty during the first half of C18.

crest: In armour, the ridge of a helmet strengthened to protect the skull. Later a tuft of feathers or device worn on top of the helmet.

crested china: Pottery decorated with colourful heraldic crests, first made by Goss but, by 1880, being produced in quantity by manufacturers throughout the UK and in Germany.

cresting: Shaped ornament, usually on the top of a chair.

cresting rail: The top rail of a chair which joins the two uprights of the back.

crib: Child's bed of manger or feeding trough design and mounted on four legs. Quite distinct from the swung cot or the rocked cradle with which it is sometimes confused.

cricket stool: Term used in C17 to describe a small footstool. Both three-legged and four-legged stools were known as crickets.

cricket table: Country-made three-legged table with a round top.

crimping: Pattern of small parallel ridges created by pinching the clay, or earthenware.

crinoline stretcher: Semi-circular stretcher arrangement found on some Windsor chairs.

crockery: Pejorative term for cheap, mass-produced domestic china.

crocketted: Ornamented on the inclined side of a pinnacle etc.

croft: Small filing cabinet comprising many small drawers and a writing surface, designed especially for the library.

Cromwellian: Term used to describe furniture made during the Commonwealth (1649-1660).

Cromwellian chair: Term used to describe a type of C16 and C17 leather-upholstered chair. It is, however, something of a misnomer as such chairs were not particularly associated with Cromwell or the Commonwell period.

crooked dresser: An L-shaped dresser designed to fit into the corner of a room.

cross banding: A strip of wood cut across the grain and laid into another for decorative effect.

crossbill: Glass vessel with two interlaced necks.

crossbow: Trigger-operated weapon invented in antiquity and used by medieval foot soldiers. Designed to fire a bolt from a taut wire which had to be cranked-up to achieve tension.

cross hilt: Simplest and earliest form of hilt; the quillons consist of a simple bar, usually straight but sometimes curved towards the blade.

cross stretcher: Either a curved or a straight X-shaped stretcher.

crouch ware: Salt-glazed stonewares made at Burslem, Staffordshire, C17.

Crown Derby: Strictly, the products of the Derby Crown Porcelain Co., established c1877; sometimes used of C18 products of the Derby Porcelain Manufactory, which used a crown as its porcelain mark.

Crown Devon: The name of a range of pottery, influenced by Art Nouveau, introduced in 1913 by the Staffordshire firm of Fielding & Co.

crown glass: Early cabinet glass made by the process of blowing, and then flattened by spinning.

cruet: Small glass vessel for oil and vinegar at table, or wine and water in Christian ritual; later the collective term for a set of salt, pepper, oil and vinegar dispensers in a stand.

crusie lamp: Simple iron oil lamp consisting of a saucer in which a wick of moss or wool floated, common in Scotland and Ireland from the C18.

crutch: In a clock, the arm that connects the pendulum to the pallet.

crystal: Brilliant clear glass, resembling rock crystal, developed Venice mid C15 when it was named cristallo.

crystallized ware: The name given to the C19 technique of decorating tin-plate by coating with clear varnish and painting on top.

crystello-ceramic: Technique, developed in C18 France, of enclosing a ceramic ornament in glass, used for paperweights and commemorative glass.

C-scroll: A handle shape, resembling the letter C. Also a type of carved motif.

cuban mahogany: See mahogany.

cuckoo clock: First made c1730, a clock with an automaton in the form of a cuckoo whose call announces the hours.

cucumber slicer: Cylinder mounted horizontally with a circular blade at one end operated by turning a handle, from early C19.

cuenca: Decorative technique on early Spanish pottery achieved by stamping the vessel to leave a raised outline and glazing the area within, thus keeping glazes from running into each other.

cuerda seca: Medieval technique for preventing glazes from running into each other by painting an outline of grease and manganese onto the vessel, which burnt off during firing.

cuirass: In armour, sometimes used to describe the breast-plate alone, sometimes the breast-plate and back-plate combined. Alternatively, the latter may be called a pair of cuirasses.

cuisse: In armour, a plate protecting the front of the thigh.

cuivre d'argenté: The technique of applying silver foil to a copper vessel and burnishing, or applying gentle heat, to make it adhere.

cuivre d'oré: Rare gold-plated copper, the gold applied as a film and gently heated or burnished so that it adheres to the copper.

culet: In armour, the skirts or plate that protects the buttocks.

culverin: C16 cannon with a long narrow barrel, providing a relatively high degree of accuracy of aim; also a similarly shaped early hand gun.

cuneiform: The ancient script of Near Eastern peoples, consisting of wedge- or arrow-shaped characters, found on baked clay tablets of the 3rd and 2nd millennia BC.

cup and cover: Carved decoration found on the bulbous turned legs of some Elizabethan furniture.

cup hilt: One with a hemi-

46

spherical guard, typical of Spanish and Italian rapiers of the C17/C18.

Cupid: Roman god of love, son of Mercury and Venus, frequently portrayed in art as a young boy or infant with a bow and arrow. Equivalent to the ancient Greek god Eros.

Cupid's bow: Term describing the typical top rail of a Chippendale style chair which is shaped like a bow.

curl: Descriptive of a curly or feathery grain pattern in timber as a result of being cut from the junction of a side branch with the main trunk.

curling irons: Scissor-like implements common until *c*1900, used for producing ringlets and curls in hairstyling.

cushion drawer: Drawer with a convex front which is usually found disguised as a moulding near the top of a chest on stand, an escritoire or similar piece.

cushion stool: A joined stool with a fixed upholstered top. Made during C16 and C17.

cusp (1): The point at which two curves meet. Usually descriptive of the shaped corners of some table tops.

cusp (2): Faceted knop on a wine glass stem; the point formed by the intersection of two arcs in tracery ornament.

cut-card work: Silver ornamentation achieved by laying a sheet of silver, cut through with fretwork patterns, onto the body of the vessel, often as a border, typical of Huguenot work, from C17.

cut down: Trade term for a piece which has been made into a smaller and more saleable item.

cut glass: Glass carved with revolving wheels and abrasive to create sharp-edged facets that reflect and refract light so as to sparkle and achieve a prismatic (rainbow) effect. Revived Bohemia C17, and common until superseded by pressed glass for utilitarian objects.

cutlass: Short single-edged sword with a flat, wide, slightly curved blade. The standard British naval sword in the C18.

cutlass pistol: Rare type of firearm consisting of a heavy single-edged blade, fitted with a panel on the blunt edge, incorporating a percussion mechanism and trigger in the cross piece.

cutlery stand: Small stand with compartments for holding cutlery and plates. Also called a supper canterbury.

cuttoe: English C18 single-edge short sword, sometimes called a hunting-hanger because favoured by hunters.

cut work: See bantam work.

Cycladian: Pre-historic pottery and sculpture from the Greek islands called the Cyclades, highly regarded for the purity and simplicity of the forms.

cylinder-top desk: Desk or bureau with a rounded or cylindrical shutter to enclose the interior working area. See also tambour.

cyma: Double-curved moulding. Cyma recta is concave above and convex below; cyma reversa the other way round. Also known as ogee and reverse ogee moulding. Popular with late C18 cabinetmakers.

Cymric: The trade-name used by Liberty & Company for a mass-produced range of silverware, inspired by Celtic art, introduced in 1899, and often incorporating enamelled pictorial plaques.

cypher: An impressed or painted mark on porcelain which gives the year of manufacture; each factory had its own set of codes; used principally mid to late C19.

cypress: A pale to dark brown wood which is similar to cedar and noted for its resistance to decay.

cyst: The swelling at the base of a glass bowl.

D

dado: The lower part of a wall, between the skirting board and the chair rail. Also used of ornamental wood panelling made to fit that space.

daftun: Comb-like carpet-making tool used for compacting the weft threads.

dagger: Any short-edged and pointed weapon with a cross hilt used for thrusting and stabbing.

Daghestan: Rug-producing region on the western shores of the Caspian Sea, now in the USSR.

daguerreotype: Early form of photograph but of metal containing a high proportion of silver, coated with light-sensitive iodine and developed using mercury vapour. Invented 1839 by Louis Daguerre.

daimyo: Japanese nobleman; during the Edo period (1614-1867) they sponsored or retained master craftsmen with whose names their objects are sometimes associated.

daisho: A pair of Samurai swords, one long (dai) called the katana, the other short (sho) and called the wakisashi.

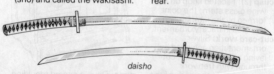

daisho

daisy pattern toys: Tin plate toys made from 1815 with cast iron wheels, so called because of the pattern made by the spokes.

damascene: Inlay of gold or silver onto another metal such as steel; named after Damascus from which fine examples derive.

damascening: Sword decoration of inlaid gold or silver; true damascening involves hammering metal into V-shaped grooves; counterfeit damascening is laid on to a cross-hatched surface and is shallower, easily worn away.

Damascus barrel: In firearms, a barrel ornamented with spiral bands of iron, originally from Damascus; also known as a twist barrel.

Damascus rugs: Brightly coloured angora wool rugs so called because they were exported through Damascus although made in Africa, Spain and Turkey.

Dancing Jack: Flat cardboard or wooden dolls with limbs joined by string, sometimes mounted on a frame.

danske chest: Softwood chest said to have been imported from the Baltic port of Danzig.

Daogung (Tao Kuang): Chinese Qing dynasty emperor, 1821-50.

date aperture: Opening in the face of a clock displaying the day of the month.

Daum: The Daum brothers (or Daum Frères), Auguste (1853-1909) and Antonin (1864-1930), were contemporaries of Emile Gallé who turned to art glass production in Nancy, France, in 1889. They specialized in Art Nouveau and Art Deco designs in cameo, etched and pâte de verre glass, and invented their own faceted martelé glass, resembling beaten metal.

davenport (1): Small writing desk with a sloping top and a series of real and false drawers below. Some have a writing surface which slides forward and rising compartments at the rear.

davenport (2): American term for a day bed or reclining sofa with headrest.

Davenport (3): Important factory at Longport, Staffordshire, founded 1793 by John Davenport; originally manufactured earthenware, but noted from 1820 for very fine botanical wares and Imari style decoration.

Davidson, Joseph: Leading English gunsmith, active early C19.

Davidson, Peter Wyler (d.1933): English jewellery designer in the Art Nouveau style.

day bed: Couch with one sloped end to support the head and back whilst reclined. Either upholstered or caned and sometimes with six or eight legs. Made from C16 until the mid-C18. Also known in the U.S. as a davenport.

deadbeat escapement: Invented c1715, it eliminates the recoil of a clock's escape wheel as the pallets catch in its teeth, thus improving accuracy.

deal: See Scots pine.

Dean's Rag Book Co.: English manufacturer of printed rag dolls and rag books from the late C19.

decanter: Originally (C17) a glass wine pourer, like a bottle but in clear glass; later a variety of shapes developed, often cut, enamelled or chased in silver, usually with an ornate stopper.

deception table: Small table similar to a Pembroke table but containing a secret compartment which is revealed, on close inspection, by a flap hanging downwards and outwards.

décor à la corne: Design on mid C18 French faience consisting of a cornucopia, birds, flowers and insects.

décor à la guirlande: Design on C18 French faience consisting of garlands of flowers; usually on plate rims and often enclosing a a scene from mythology.

Dedham: Art pottery from Dedham, Massachusetts made from c1900 by the Robertson family and others, notably fine designs using Chinese style glazes.

Dehua: Alternative spelling of Te Hua, the region in the southern Chinese province of Fukien, famous for its blanc-de-chine white-glazed porcelain.

Delander, Daniel: Noted London clockmaker, active late C17/early C18.

Delft: Dutch tin-glazed earthenwares named after the town of Delft, the principal production centre. C16 Delft shows Chinese influence but by C17 the designs are based on Dutch landscapes. Similar pottery made in England from the late C16 is usually termed "delftware".

Della Robbia: Florentine Renaissance sculptor who invented technique of applying vitreous glaze to terracotta; English art pottery made at Birkenhead, late C19, in imitation of his work.

demi lune: Half round; usually descriptive of a table top.

De Morgan, William Frend (1839-1917): Artist who manufactured stained glass and tiles in the 1860s, rediscovered the process of making colourful lustre glazes, established the Chelsea pottery works (1871), and later the pottery at Fulham (1888-1907). A medievalist whose style was much influenced by William Morris as well as Renaissance and Islamic pottery.

denarius: The standard silver coin under the Roman Empire.

Denby: Stoneware made by Bourne & Son, at Denby, C19; also known as Bourne pottery.

dentil frieze: A frieze moulding comprising a series of small rectangular blocks resembling teeth. Often used to ornament a cornice.

depthed: Term used of clock mechanisms mounted with the aid of a depthing tool, so that the wheels and pinions are correctly meshed and run true, hence more accurate and less susceptible to wear.

derbend: Rugs from Daghestan on the Caspian Sea.

Derby: Important porcelain factory founded 1756, producing very fine figure groups – often called English Meissen – as well as painted wares decorated with landscapes and botanical scenes.

Derbyshire chair: Another name for a Yorkshire chair.

derringer: Small, inexpensive pocket pistol invented by Henry Deringer (with one "r") of Philadelphia c1825 and produced in great quantity by many gunsmiths. Those made by Deringer's firm, stamped PHILADEL DERINGER on the lock plate, are eagerly sought after.

Design and Industries Association: The organization established in Britain in 1915 by Ambrose Heal and others to promote high quality in mass-produced furniture, and responsible for simple but elegant designs inspired by the Arts and Crafts work of Ernest Gimson and the Barnsley brothers.

design registration mark: Insignia used on English porcelain after 1842, which provides a date for the design, though not necessarily for the particular design since some designs continued in production for many years.

desk: A piece of writing furniture made in various designs. Generally comprising two pedestals of drawers with a writing and working area above. See also cylinder top desk, kneehole desk, pedestal desk and roll top desk.

dessert stand: Shallow silver dish on a short pedestal, from the C17.

de Stijl: Dutch artistic movement founded around 1917 in reaction to Art Nouveau, associated with the abstract painter Piet Mondrian. Furniture and furnishings are typically decorated with bold, rectangular blocks of vivid primary colour.

deuddarn: A Welsh variety of the press cupboard with two tiers. The full name is cwpwrdd deuddarn.

Deutsche Blomen (Blumen): Means "German flowers"; flower painting on German porcelain and faience, noted for its subtle shading and botanical accuracy.

dha: Burmese national sword, curved with a single-edged blade and guardless hilt.

dhurri: Indian flat rugs without a pile.

Diaghilev dancer: Popular motif in Art Deco statuary; figures based on the revolutionary ballets choreographed by Diaghilev in the 1920s and 1930s.

diagonal barometer: One with a tube set at a slant so that the mercury moves further than it would in a vertical column as pressure changes, enabling more accurate readings. C18 examples often ornate.

dial plate: The front plate of a clock mechanism to which the chapter ring is attached, or on which the numerals are painted.

diamond-cut: Glass cut into facets in imitation of diamonds, or lozenge shapes.

diamond-point: Glass engraved with a diamond-tipped tool.

diaper: Surface decoration composed of repeated diamonds or squares, often carved in low relief.

diepper model: Model ship made of ivory, usually encased in a glass dome, made by sailors in the late C18 early C19; also made of wood.

die-sinking: Method of making a metal object by hammering sheet metal into a mould to produce two identical halves which are then soldered together; the hollow often filled with lead or pewter.

die-stamping: Method of mass-producing a design on metal by machine which passes sheet metal between a steel die and a drop hammer. Used for forming toys as well as stamping cutlery etc.

dinanderie: Brass objects and vessels made at the French factory in Dinant, near Lièges, C15.

Ding yao: Northern Chinese pottery of the Sung and Yuan dynasties, characterized by carved or moulded floral decoration covered with rich ivory coloured glazes with pale green or brown patches.

dining chair: Chair designed for use at a dining table and supplied in sets.

dining table: Large table used for dining and made in various designs. Many are capable of extending when required to seat many people.

Dinky toys: Die cast model cars, aeroplanes etc. produced by Meccano Ltd from April 1934.

dinner wagon: A set of open rectangular shelves or trays on castors, used for transporting food into the dining room. Also known as a "running footman".

Dionysus: The Greek god of wine, portrayed in ancient art as a young man crowned with vine leaves; equivalent to the Roman god Bacchus.

diorama: Realistic scenes recreating famous battles using hand-painted toy soldiers on a fixed base.

diplomatic sword: A sword with no cutting edge, worn as a sign of rank.

Directoire/Directory: The style prevalent in France in the last decade of the C18; neo-classical motifs but combined with forms based on bold curves.

dirk: The pointed dagger of a Scottish Highlander (carried strapped to the calf) or of a naval midshipman.

Disbrowe, Nicholas (1612/13-1683): The earliest known American furniture maker. He was one of the first settlers in Connecticut but was born in Essex, the son of a joiner.

dish cover: Dome-shaped lid, often of silver or plate, with a handle, intended for covering a plate and keeping the food warm until served.

dished: Term used to describe the shallow depressions in gaming tables used for holding counters or money; also known as guinea pockets.

dish-hilt: Saucer-shaped sword guard introduced c1625 and the precursor of the cup hilt.

dish ring: Ring of silver, often with fretwork ornament, designed to suspend a dish over a spirit lamp to keep it warm.

Disneyana: Any objects associated with the characters and films of Walt Disney.

display cabinet: See china cabinet.

display pieces: Advertising figures made of stout card — more rarely in metal or plaster; tobacco store Indians, Highlanders and Blackamoors are among the earliest and most collectable examples.

display table: See bijouterie table.

dis-torba: Small carpet bag used for carrying salt or household utensils.

distressed: Term used to describe furniture in need of obvious repair.

distressing: The deliberate superficial damaging of furniture in order to make it appear aged, as might be carried out by a faker.

dobutsu: Japanese name for objects carved in the shape of real animals, as opposed to mythical ones (kaibutsu).

Doccia: Mid C18 porcelain factory in Florence producing white and painted figures and maiolica.

dockyard model: Perfect scaled-down model of a ship, produced as a prototype by dockyards from the late C17 to the late C19.

document drawer: Thin drawer in a desk for important papers.

dog-leg staircase: Staircase which rises to a half-landing and then turns back on itself.

dog lock: Type of safety-catch on a flintlock, so called because the head of the lever holding the flint resembled a dog's head.

dognose spoon: Derived from the trefid spoon but no longer cleft, so that the terminal is one continuous trefoil shape, with a pronounced central lobe, said to resemble the head and projecting snout of a hound. Early C18.

Dog of Fo: Mythical Chinese animal, resembling a lion-spaniel, guardian spirit of the temple of Buddha (Fo).

dogwood: Whitish yellow wood occasionally used for inlay and marquetry in the early C18.

dole cupboard: Term which strictly applies to hanging or other structures used in churches and institutions for the charitable dispensing of food.

don wares: Earthenware, and occasionally bone china, with painted decoration produced in Yorkshire, C19.

Donyatt: Somerset pottery producing yellow glazed slip wares, C17.

Doolittle, Isaac: New Haven, Connecticut, clockmaker, active 1742-90.

door furniture: Collective term for fittings, such as finger plates, knobs, locks, knockers, letter boxes and escutcheons which serve a decorative as well as functional purpose on doors.

door knocker: Used on external doors since the early C15, originally of wrought or cast iron, later of brass, and ranging in style from simple rings and scrolls to lion's heads, dolphins and human heads.

door stop: First made at the end of the C18, and used to hold open doors. Usually of lead, bronze or cast iron, sometimes with a carrying handle and often ornamented with foliage.

Doric: Earliest of the classical orders, in which the capitals consist simply of a cushion. Greek Doric columns have no base whereas Roman Doric columns do.

dormant: Another name for a trestle.

Dorotheenthal: German faience factory, founded early C18, producing brightly coloured wares decorated with leaf and strapwork.

Dorst, Julius: German maker of wooden dolls, active at Sonneburg, 1865 to early C20.

doruye: Reversible carpet with a different design on each face.

dos-à-dos: Meaning back-to-back and used of a ceramic group in which two identical figures face in opposite directions.

dosser: Old term for the headboard of a bed.

dot Meissen: Meissen porcelain of the late C18 marked with a dot between crossed swords; the late C18 is generally considered to be the period in which much of the finest Meissen was produced.

double action: Firearm that may either be cocked manually, or automatically (self-cocking), when the trigger is depressed.

double "D": A moulding in the form of a capital "D" above another capital "D".

double ogee bowl: Bowl of a glass drinking vessel, consisting of two S-curves, one large one above another; often found on pre-C19 champagne glasses.

doubler: Pewter bowl with a wide slanted rim, from the C17.

doucai: Chinese for "contrasting colour", enamel decoration introduced under the reign of the Ming Emperor Chenghua (1465-87).

douche: Early medical instrument resembling a very large syringe used for administering a jet of water to the body's internal organs.

Doulton: London pottery established 1815 to produce household vessels; from the 1860s, revived brown stoneware and salt-glaze art pottery; employed the Barlow sisters in the 1870s to create decorated fancy wares; began making enamelled "siliconware" china in the 1880s and figurines from 1913. Received royal warrant in 1902 and products now known as "Royal Doulton".

Doune pistols: Pistols made in the C18 in the town of the same name in Stirling, Scotland; highly decorative with no trigger guard and an all metal stock; standard issue to soldiers of the Black Watch infantry regiment.

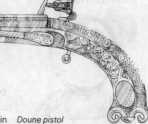

Doune pistol

douter: Scissor-like implement for snuffing out a candle flame.

dovetail: Type of joint usually seen in drawers. Two pieces of wood are joined at a right angle by wedge-shaped interlocking pieces. Such joints are either a Through dovetail or a Lap dovetail.

dowel: Wooden pin used to secure timber joints. Also known as a trennell (treenail).

dower chest: Chest used to store the trousseau of a bride-to-be. Also known as a marriage or hope chest.

dozar: A carpet of two zars in length; about 6ft (1.8m).

dragon carpets: Old Caucasian carpets decorated with heraldic dragons.

dragon-lung/dragon-loang: Male dragon symbol on Chinese carpets.

drake foot: Another name for duck foot.

dram cup: Small silver cup with two handles; smaller than, though similar to, a porringer.

dram glass: Short-stemmed glass for strong liquor, with small bowl on a heavy foot.

drawer: Lidless box within a framework from which it can be drawn. It was originally known as a till.

drawer stop: Small block of wood fixed within a carcase

which mates with another block on the underside of a drawer to prevent the drawer being pushed in too far.

draw leaf table: Another name for a withdrawing table.

dredger: Cylindrical silver vessel with a perforated top, like a caster, but usually with finer holes for sprinkling powdered sugar, etc.

Dresden: Faience production centre from the early C18 noted for large jars and pots.

Dressel, Cuno & Otto: Long-established German doll-making firm producing composition, waxed and bisque dolls.

dresser: A piece of furniture on which food was dressed. Some appear as a sideboard-type base and are known as low dressers while others have a rack, or superstructure of shelves above and are called high dressers.

Dresser, Christopher (1835-1904): Influential English pottery and glass designer who was inspired by Japanese art and worked for Tiffany as well as the pottery firms of Ault, Linthorpe and Pilkington.

dressing mirror: Small mirror mounted above a drawer or bank of drawers, designed to be stood on top of a table or tallboy, made since the early C18.

dressing table: One designed for the bedroom or a gentleman's dressing room and made to many designs, either as a squarish piece with drawers and a top comprising two opening flaps with an array of internal fittings, or as a single small table with one or more drawers now commonly called a lowboy. See also Duchess and Rudd's table.

dress sword: One with no cutting edge worn on ceremonial occasions.

DRGN: Emblem of the German Toy Federation; the mark found on early German mass-produced toy locomotives and other items from c1890.

drop: The short, blunt support that links the handle to the bowl of a spoon; a later development of the rat-tail.

drop handle: Hanging brass handle, either solid or hollow and attached to the drawer by snapes.

drop-in seat: Upholstered chair seat which is supported on the seat rails but which can be lifted out independently.

drop leaf: Descriptive of a table with one or two hinged leaves which can be lowered when not in use. Many types of drop leaf tables are known by other names e.g. Pembroke, sofa, gateleg.

druid's eggs: Term used to describe any ancient Egyptian or Roman decorated glass beads. Sometimes also known as Adder's eggs.

drum clock: Early portable clock in the shape of a drum or cannister with the dial and movement arranged horizontally, rather than vertically.

drum table: Large circular table with a deep frieze containing drawers. Also known as a capstan table.

dry edge: Unglazed areas of a ceramic vessel, such as the rim.

dry-plate camera: Invented by George Eastman, 1879 and produced even after the roll camera was invented in 1888. Usually constructed by cabinet makers, of mahogany and brass.

Dublin delftware: Mid C18 tin-glazed earthenware with blue or purplish decoration, made by the Irish Delft Ware Manufactory.

Duché: Pottery made by the Duché family in Philadelphia, Charleston and Savannah in the early C18; principally stoneware and redware, but also porcelain.

Duchesne clock: Early C18 musical clocks made in England by the French clock-maker Claude Duchesne.

Duchess: Term used to describe a type of large Victorian dressing table with a variety of drawers, a raised and mirrored back and a footboard.

Duchesse: Type of long seat formed out of two bergère chairs facing each other and joined by a stool in the middle.

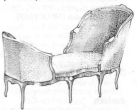

duck foot: American term for a three-toed club foot found mainly in furniture from the Delaware region. Also known as drake foot and web foot.

duck's egg: Porcelain produced briefly in the early C19 at Swansea, of a delicate translucent bluey-green colour.

Dudson: Earthenware decorated with inlaid mosaic made by James Dudson, Hanley, late C19.

duelling pistols: Pistols made in matched pairs of exactly the same weight and balance for settling disputes, known from the mid C17 onwards. Flintlock pistols were superseded by faster percussion pistols in the early C19. Boxed pairs with all their accoutrements are highly prized.

Duesbury: Porcelain decorated in the studio of William Duesbury (1725-86), especially the products of the Chelsea factory, and the Derby works which he co-founded.

duet stool: Piano stool for two people, as when playing a duet.

Dufrène, Maurice (1876-1925): French Art Nouveau designer of jewellery, furniture, textiles, wallpaper and book bindings. Towards the end of his career he became a leading exponent of Modernist design based on industrial materials.

dug out furniture: Furniture which is formed from a solid log of timber; usually chests but chairs are also known.

dumb stove: C19 American stove with several chambers grouped around or above the fire box, sometimes cast in the shape of human figures.

dumb waiter: A dining room stand with either two or three circular revolving trays. Some examples are more elaborate having special compartments for bottles, plates, etc.

dumps: Heavy glass object, such as a paperweight or door stopper, often dome-shaped and decorated with air bubbles.

Dunand, Jean (1877-1942): Swiss sculptor who produced beaten metal vases in Art Nouveau style, then in the more geometric shapes of the Art Deco genre.

Du Paquier: Porcelain from Vienna, especially chinoiserie wares produced early C18.

durlach: German late C18 faience, especially chinoiserie

wares decorated with celadon-green, orange and cobalt blue.

dussack: Medieval shortsword with a straight, single-edged blade.

dust board: A board found between drawers as part of the carcase in some chests of drawers.

dust chamfer: The chamfered bottom edge of a panel frame enabling dust to be more easily cleaned away.

dust mould (1): The moulding which is applied to cover the gap where two doors meet.

dust mould (2): A strip of quarter round moulding found along the inside lengths of a drawer. Introduced early C19.

Dutch doll: Early imported doll, probably made in Germany, rather than Holland.

Dutch drop: A type of drop handle shaped similar to the head of an axe.

Dutch stove: Stove which stands away from the wall or chimney recess, with a flue rising from the top and angled to join the chimney.

Dutch strike: Clock which gives advance warning by striking the next hour half an hour before on a smaller bell with a higher note; common on German as well as Dutch clocks.

Dutch tile: Tin-glazed tiles, decorated with chinoiserie or landscapes, made to decorate areas around a stove.

duty dodger: A hallmark removed from a small piece of assayed silver and applied to another, larger piece so as to avoid paying duty on the latter; a practice prevalent between 1720 and 1758 when duty was levied on silver by weight.

Dwerrihouse & Carter: Makers of clocks with Sheraton and Empire style cases, London, active early C19.

dwt: Abbreviation for "penny weight" – the smallest weight in the Troy system of weighing gold, silver and precious stones.

dynastic: Ancient Egyptian objects which cannot be dated to a precise Dynasty, but which belong to the mid-3rd, 2nd or 1st millennia BC, the period of the thirty Egyptian dynasties.

Dyottville: Early C19 glass-ware made in Philadelphia by the firm of Thomas W Dyott, decorated with masonic and patriotic emblems.

E

eagle head sword: Early American sword with an eagle-head motif on the pommel.

Eames, Charles (b.1907): Designer of the famous Eames chair of 1940, but also the talented creator of children's toys, and of prefabricated houses, based on the Japanese style.

ear: Small shaped piece of wood applied to either side of the top of a cabriole leg.

ear dagger: Renaissance dagger with ear-like flanges at the hilt.

earthenware: Pottery with a porous body, not watertight unless glazed; fired at lower temperatures than stoneware or porcelain so that not all of the silicates fuse.

East, Edward: Celebrated London clockmaker, court horologist to Charles II, active mid C17.

Eastern Han: Period in Chinese history from AD25-220, during which pottery and stoneware were produced. Many tomb figures of servants, buildings etc. were also made.

East Liverpool: Earthenware factory in Ohio, C19; one of the first to develop Rockingham wares in America.

Ébéniste: A cabinet maker, so-called since the C17, when French furniture-makers first used ebony as a veneer.

ebonised: Wood stained black to simulate ebony.

ebony: Finely grained hard wood which is black in colour. Used for stringing and other inlay work.

echinus: Moulding decorated with egg and dart motif.

Eckenförde: Short-lived faience factory in Schleswig-Holstein, founded mid C18, noted for lively decoration.

écuelle: C17 vessel, usually of silver, but also of ceramic, for serving soup. Has a shallow, circular bowl with two handles and a domed cover. It often comes complete with a stand.

Edo: Era in Japanese history 1615-1867, when Tokyo (Edo) became the new capital and in which the arts flourished: 1661-73 is known as the great age of porcelain and 1716-36 the period when lacquering and netsuke-making reached their zenith.

Edwardian: Term used to describe pieces made during the reign of Edward VII (1901-1910).

Edwardo glass: Manufactured by the father and son, both Benjamin Edwards, in Belfast late C18/early C19.

Edwards stoneware: Products of the Dale Hall pottery, founded at Burslem, mid C19.

egg and dart: Decorative pattern used in friezes and mouldings consisting of alternate egg shapes (ovolo) and arrow heads. Sometimes called egg and tongue.

eggebrecht: Faience produced by the Meissen factory, late C17, before the development of porcelain.

egg opener: Scissor-like device for removing the top of a boiled egg, in use from c1890.

eggshell porcelain: Very thin, tough porcelain with a mother-of-pearl lustre produced at Belleek, but also by various Staffordshire potteries, late C19.

eglomisé: Painting on glass, associated with clock faces: often the reverse side of the glass is covered in gold or silver leaf through which a pattern is engraved and then painted black.

Egyptian blackware: Alternative name for Basaltes, the black stoneware developed by Josiah Wedgwood.

eight-day movement: Clock movement which runs for eight days without rewinding.

Elastolin: German makers of composition toy soldiers and zoo figures, 1904-55.

elbow: Part of the arm of a chair.

elbow hinge: Brass hinge of two straight lengths joined at the centre similar to a compass. Also known as a rule hinge.

elder: Whitish wood occasionally used for inlay.

election pottery: Plates and mugs produced from the mid C18, especially in Bristol, promoting a parliamentary candidate or celebrating a political victory.

Electric Bright Eye: Teddy bear, made from c1909, whose eyes light up when a paw is shaken.

electroplate: The process of using electrical current to coat a base metal or alloy with silver, invented 1830s and gradually superseding Sheffield plate.

electrotype: Non-metallic object, such as a flower or leaf, coated with gold or silver using electrical and chemical methods.

electrum: Naturally occurring but brittle alloy containing silver and gold used in antiquity for coinage; an alloy of copper, zinc and nickel used for household wares since C19.

elephant clock: Novelty clock of the C18 and C19 with a case in the form of an elephant.

elephant's footprint: Alternative name for the gul, or octagonal stylized flower motif in oriental carpets.

Elers redware: Early stonewares, made by the Dutch Elers brothers in Staffordshire before 1700.

Elizabethan: The period in England 1558 to 1603, covering the reign of Elizabeth I.

Ellicott, John: Most celebrated of a noted London family of clockmakers, active mid C18.

Elliot repeater: American Civil War period six-barrelled pepperbox pistol made in New York.

Ellis doll: C19 American doll with painted wooden head, body and limbs made by Joel Ellis of Springfield, Vermont; had complex joints that enabled the doll to be manipulated into many positions.

elm: Two main varieties. English elm is a golden wood with blackish figuring used extensively in country furniture and as veneer. Hard-wearing but prone to warping. Wych elm has a particularly attractive grain and takes a polish well.

Elton ware: Art pottery, late C19/early C20, made by Sir Edmund Elton at Clevedon Court, Somerset.

email ombrant: Pottery design in relief overlaid by a transparent glaze to create a shadowy, chiaroscuro effect; developed France mid C19.

embossed silver: Of vessels with relief ornament applied by beating the metal into shape from the reverse side, often using a mould.

Empire: Style prevalent in France 1800-30, neoclassical but with much ornate applied and gilded decoration.

enamel (1): In ceramics, a second coloured but translucent glaze laid over the first glaze.

enamel (2): Coloured glass, applied to metal, ceramic or glass in paste form and then fired for decorative effect.

enamelled coins: Large, high value coins, usually of silver, in which the central motifs were highlighted in enamel; produced as commemorative souvenirs and as jewellery (especially as cufflinks) from c1880 to c1920.

enamelware: Metalwares given a coating of powdered glass and fired to create a hard smooth surface.

en arbelette: Used to describe a double curved shape like that of a crossbow.

encaustic: Engraved patterns on ceramic filled with a coloured slip; a technique used to produce wall and floor tiles in the Middle Ages, revived in the C19.

encoignure: French term for a corner cupboard with a marble top and ormolu mounts.

encrusted: Of glass, applied decoration, often of metal, mineral or stone.

encrusting: Engraved silver or gold ornament on a sword; stands proud of the surface in contrast to damascening which is inlaid.

end-of-day glass: Small glass ornaments, so called because they were said to have been made of scraps left at the end of a day's work, but also mass produced in quantity as novelties from the late C19. Still popular today.

end standards: The two uprights (when there are only two) that support a table top at the centre of either end.

endstone: A jewel, either real or artificial diamond, upon which the arbor pivots in a timepiece mechanism.

Enghalskrüge: German earthenware tin-glazed jug with pot-belly and tall neck, sometimes with a pewter foot-ring and lid; from the C16.

English dial: Type of C19 wall clock, often hung in public places such as railway stations, with a large painted sheet-iron dial, anchor escapement and pendulum.

English plate: American term for Sheffield plate, i.e. silver-plated copper.

engraved glass: Glass decorated using a diamond-tipped tool.

enjoyed: Toy-collectors' term for an object that has evidently been played with and has suffered an acceptable level of damage, as opposed to "playworn" or badly damaged.

ennecy: Carpets decorated with cruciform motifs and used as door hangings.

Ennion glass: Ancient Near Eastern glassware bearing the trade-mark "Ennion" in Greek characters.

en suite: Meaning "in the same way"; a set or part of a set, the components usually similarly decorated.

entablature: In classical architecture, all the mouldings above the capitals, consisting of architrave, frieze and cornice.

entrée dish: Silver dish and cover, oval in shape and sometimes with a stand and spirit lamp; from the mid C18.

Enty, John: Leading London gunsmith, early/mid C19.

envelope table: Card table with a top comprising four hinged segments which open out to reveal the baize playing surfaces. These tables are invariably Edwardian.

EPBM: Electroplated Britannia Metal; Britannia metal, originally developed as a silver substitute, used widely from c1840 as a base metal for electroplating and often stamped with these initials.

épergne: Centrepiece of silver consisting of a tray incorporating a number of small dishes around a central bowl.

EPNS: Electroplated nickel silver; i.e. nickel alloy covered with a layer of silver using the electroplate process.

equation clock: One with a special mechanism and dial which shows the difference between mean time and solar time. The dial has two hands: one points to the day of the month, the other indicates how far solar time is behind or ahead of mechanical time.

Erfurt: Factory in Thuringia, founded early C18, specializing in brightly coloured faience tankards with pewter lids.

Eros: Greek god of erotic love, better known by the Roman name of Cupid, frequently portrayed in art as a young boy, blindfolded and carrying a bow and arrow.

ersari: Carpet from western Turkestan, dark red and blue patterned with large guls.

escapement: The part of a clockwork mechanism that controls the driving force of the spring, checking and releasing it by means of pallets which engage and disengage in the teeth of the escape wheel.

escritoire: French word given to a piece of writing furniture. They are usually of walnut and comprise a large cabinet with a front that drops down for use as a writing surface and reveals an interior fitted with many small drawers and secret compartments.

escutcheon: Any applied metal plate but especially the ornamented plate around a keyhole, or a plate bearing a maker's name on a clock face.

espangolette: Decorative motif of a female head surrounded by a large stiff collar.

estate-made doll: One made by a craftsman employed on an aristocratic estate for the children of the house.

étagère: Small two- or three-tiered French work table often with a brass gallery. Also known as a table à ouvrage.

etched glass: Technique of cutting layers of glass away, using acid, much favoured by Art Nouveau and Deco glassmakers. Such sculpture in high relief is known as deep-etched, and layers of multi-coloured glass were often treated in this way to make cameo glass.

Etruscan: Art of the pre-Roman peoples who flourished in the region of modern Tuscany between the 8th and 4th centuries BC, strongly influenced by ancient Greek models, but with its own distinctive forms of pottery, metalwork and jewellery.

Etruscan maiolica: English and American lead-glazed earthenwares of the C19, so called for their resemblance to Tuscan products.

Etruscan style: Style of decoration based on ancient Greek and Roman ornamentation. Associated with the work of Robert Adam.

étuis: Small box or flat case of silver or other materials for storing oddments such as pins, pencils, etc.

everted: Ceramic or glass rim form, in which the edge is turned over to create a double thickness.

ewer: Jug with a narrow neck, bulbous body and wide spout, often in silver but also in glass and porcelain, sometimes with a matching bowl, for pouring water.

excise marks: Required after 1824 on British pewter vessels in which liquor was sold to a specific measure: usually combining a crown, a local emblem, and letters or numbers indicating the date and person carrying out the test.

Exeter carpets: Hand-knotted carpets made mid-C18 in Exeter by Claude Passavant.

exotic woods: Woods such as zebrawood, partridge wood and snakewood are sometimes called exotic woods.

express rifle: One with a light, high-velocity bullet, invented in the mid C19 for big-game hunting.

F

Fabergé: The great Russian jeweller, Peter Fabergé (1846-1920) is best known for jewel-encrusted Fabergé eggs but also produced many other ornaments in gold, silver and precious stones in the Art Nouveau style.

facet-cut: Glass cut into sharp-edged planes in a criss-cross pattern to reflect light. Popular 1760-1810.

Façon de Venise: Late C16/early C17 glass imitating Venetian forms, often made in the Netherlands by Venetian emigrés.

factory fresh: In mint condition, as made, with packaging.

faience: Also spelled fayence; tin glazed earthenwares, named after the town of Faenza in Italy, but actually used to describe products made anywhere but Italy, where the same wares are called "maiolica".

faience-fine: Sometimes used to denote faience of the best quality, but correctly the cream-coloured earthenwares produced by several C19 factories in imitation of English creamware.

The courtship of Victoria life

fairings: Mould-made figure groups in cheap porcelain, produced in great quantity in the C19 and C20, especially in Germany; often humorous or sentimental. So called because they were sold, or given as prizes, at fairs.

fake: Item made to simulate a genuine piece with deceptive intent.

falchion: Curved broad sword with the cutting edge on the convex side.

fall front: The opening flap of a bureau.

falling ball clock: Clock of spherical form suspended from a chain linked to the mechanism so that the weight of the clock provides the driving force; the hours are marked on a moving band around the circumference.

false edge: Used to describe the back-edge of a sword which, normally blunt, has been sharpened for some of its length.

false teeth: Early examples were made of silver or ivory.

Falstaff jug: Toby jug made in the form of Shakespeare's comic drunkard.

famille jaune: "Yellow family"; Chinese porcelain vessels in which yellow is the predominant ground colour.

famille noire: "Black family"; Chinese porcelain in which black is the predominant ground colour.

famille rose: "Pink family"; Chinese porcelain vessels with an enamel (overglaze) of pink to purple tones.

famille verte: "Green family"; Chinese porcelains with a green enamel (overglaze), laid over yellows, blues, purples and iron red.

fancy back: Spoons decorated on the back of the bowl.

fanlight: Semi-circular window over a door, with radiating glazing bars like the ribs of a fan. Made in cast iron in many shapes from the mid C18.

fan pattern: Term describing the back of a chair with ribs spread to resemble a half-opened fan.

fantasie vögel: Colourful, often imaginary, birds painted on Meissen porcelain and widely copied elsewhere.

Fantasque: Name of a colourful range of household china designed by Clarice Cliff and manufactured in the 1930s by the Staffordshire pottery, A. J. Wilkinson Ltd.

Faris, William: Philadelphia clockmaker, active 1755-90.

farmer's watch: C19 mass produced watches so called because the dials were painted with rural scenes.

farthingale chair: Misnomer for a joined and upholstered chair. So called because of the belief that the design was influenced by the wide farthingale dress which it could accommodate.

fatamid pottery: Islamic and Christian pottery produced in Egypt under the Fatamid dynasty, AD 969-1171, often in the form of birds, animals and human figures.

fauld: In armour, the skirtlike plate that protects the stomach and groin.

fausse-montre: Literally "false-watch"; a C18 dummy worn at one end of a watch chain to balance the weight of the real watch at the other end.

fauteuil: French open-armed drawing room armchair.

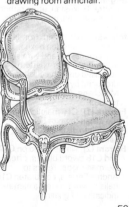

Favrile/finger joint

Favrile: Trade name used by Tiffany Studios for the company's metallic, iridescent art glass.

feather banding: Inlaid banding found in walnut veneered furniture. Two strips of veneer are laid at rightangles to each other to give a herringbone effect. Also called herringbone.

feather-edge: Bright-cut patterns of small lines around the finials of silver cutlery from the late C18.

Federal style: Term used to describe American furniture made between 1785 and 1830.

feldspar: Form of porcelain patented by the second Josiah Spode (1754-1827) containing the crushed mineral feldspar; popular from 1800, especially for export to countries which taxed imported true porcelains.

feldspathic glaze: Very high temperature glazes, and therefore very hard and glassy, based on using the mineral feldspar.

fender: Low guard around a fireplace designed to catch falling ash. Made since the late C17, originally of iron, then of brass.

fender stool: A more ornate form of fender with a low upholstered bench supported by a balustrade running around the hearth. Sometimes called a club fender.

feng-huang: Female halfdragon, half-phoenix motif on Chinese carpets.

feraghan: Carpets from central Iran with a strong cotton warp visible on the underside, dense short pile and herati motifs on a red or blue ground.

fergana carpets: From Kirghiz, central Turkestan, often rather loosely woven, predominantly red.

fernware: Actual fern fronds applied to wooden boxes, firescreens, etc and varnished; more rarely, a fern pattern stencilled onto the surface. Produced by William Smith of Mauchline, Ayrshire from 1900 to 1939.

Ferrara (1): C16 maiolica from the Italian town of Ferrara, difficult to distinguish from Faenza maiolica.

Ferrara (2): Name found on C17 and C18 sword blades, often German-made; refers to Andrea Ferrara, celebrated C16 Italian swordmaker; a name indicative of quality.

ferrule: Wire band or metal cap used to secure the binding of a sword grip, found at each end of the grip.

Ferrybridge: C19 Yorkshire pottery, founded by William Tomlinson and Ralph Wedgwood, specializing in earthenwares and stonewares.

festoon: Decorative motif characteristic of the Baroque style, consisting of a garland of flowers or ribbons suspended at either end so that it dips in the middle, like a hammock.

fibula: Roman bow-shaped brooch, clasp or buckle made of bronze.

fiddleback: Descriptive of a particular grain of mahogany veneer which resembles the back of a violin.

fiddle spoon: One with a handle terminating in a shape similar to that of a violin.

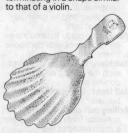

field: The whole of the central area of a carpet within the frame or borders.

fielded panel: Panel with bevelled or chamferred edges.

Fielding & Co.: Staffordshire pottery that manufactured Crown Devon wares, with Art Nouveau designs, from 1913.

figuring: General term for the patterns in a piece of cut timber.

filigrana: From filigree, a lacy pattern in glass, developed C16 in Venice.

filigree: Lacy openwork of silver or gold thread, produced in large quantities since late C19.

fillet: Thin strip of wood.

fin de siècle: One of the decorative styles prevalent at the end of the C19 in Europe; used of highly ornate objects combining baroque, rococo and art nouveau motifs, with the implication that the art was decadent or gross.

fine-line: On engraved glass, a matt background or infill of close-set incised lines.

finger joint: Wooden hinge

mechanism of the supporting leg or bracket of a foldover or drop leaf table. Also known as a knuckle joint.

finial (1): Spire-like ornament used to finish off any vertical projection, carved in many forms from human and animal figures to columns or obelisks. In furniture a small decorative turned projection.

finial (2): In silver spoons, the ornamented piece at the opposite end of the shaft to the bowl.

Fiora: Notable maker of banjo barometers with Sheraton style inlaid cases, working in Nottingham early C19.

firangi: Indian sword with an imported European blade. A corruption of the word "foreigner".

fireback: Cast iron plate for the back of the fireplace often ornately decorated and sometimes made to commemorate specific historic events. Beware the many modern reproductions.

fire board: Board used to cover a fireplace cavity when not in use. Many C19 examples are embroidered, painted or lacquered.

fire box: That part of a stove which contains the fire as distinct from the cooking compartments.

fire cats: Same as andirons or firedogs, but with many legs; so called because if dropped they will always land on their feet.

fireclay ware: Large urns and vases produced C19 by Bell of Glasgow as a cheaper alternative to Wedgwood's Basaltes; featuring classical scenes and overglazed with black enamel.

fire crack: A crack in a porcelain body which appears during firing.

firedogs: Alternative name for andirons; sometimes used to describe smaller, unadorned examples.

fire gilding: Early technique of gilding copper or other metals by painting with an amalgam of gold and mercury and heating until the mercury vaporizes.

fire insurance mark: Plaque bearing the emblem of an insurance company and a serial number, for affixing to the exterior of a building from 1722 to 1865, the period when insurance companies

organized their own fire brigades which dealt only with the premises of their clients.

fire irons: Collective name for a matching set of tools for stoking and cleaning a fireplace, consisting of tongs, shovel, brush, poker and sometimes a fork. C18 and C19 examples of brass are often highly decorative and made to match the fender.

fire polishing: Technique used to make pressed-glass resemble cut glass, by reheating to polish the surface and remove the mould seam.

fire screen: A panel, often embroidered, mounted on a stand designed to protect the face from the heat of an open fire. Also known as an Ecran.

firing glass: Drinking glass with a solid heavy base and stem, made from C17 for banging on the table in approval or applause, or at the conclusion of a toast.

fish-head: Porcelain ornaments of this form, often naturalistic, produced by various English factories in the late C18/C19.

fish slice: Broad-bladed silver knife, shaped like a trowel, with pierced or engraved ornament, from the mid C17.

fish tail: Decorative carving resembling the tail of a fish. It is typically found on the cresting rail of a banister back chair.

Fitzhugh: Pattern of flowers, insects and fruits in underglaze blue on Nanking Porcelain, possibly named after a merchant/importer.

Fitzroy barometer: Mass produced barometer introduced c1870 and named after Admiral Fitzroy, the first weather-forecaster whose predictions were published in *The Times* from 1860. The broad oblong case has printed charts and guidance notes pasted to it; some have a "storm glass" intended to measure static electricity.

Five Dynasties: Period in Chinese history AD 907-960.

fixed eyes: In dolls and toys eyes, other than painted eyes, that do not move.

flagon: Larger version of a tankard; flat bottomed with slightly tapering sides, a handle and thumbpiece, and often a hinged pewter lid; usually in salt or tinglazed stoneware.

flag seat: Term sometimes used to describe a seat woven with rush.

flail: Weapon consisting of spiked ball head attached by a chain to a staff.

flambé: Deep red pottery glaze much favoured by Art Nouveau and Art Deco potters, in imitation of the "sang-de-boeuf" (bull's blood) colour of Chinese porcelain.

flambeau: A finial which is carved to resemble flames. See also auger flame.

flamboyant blade: One with a wavy or undulating edge.

Flanders Baby: Alternative name for C19 imported dolls from Eastern Europe.

Flanders furniture: General name given to panelled furniture imported from, or via, Flanders in the early C16.

flash: In cased glass, the outer layer, designed to be cut or incised to reveal the layer below.

flask: Small vessel used for storing liquid. Examples from antiquity are usually of very fine moulded or blown glass with a bulbous body and narrow neck.

flatback: Popular mantelpiece ornament, made by numerous Staffordshire factories, in the form of a brightly coloured figure group, with an unglazed flat back.

flat carpets: Those without a pile: dhurries and kilims.

flat chasing: Hammered ornament in low-relief on silver.

flats: Two-dimensional toy soldiers cast in lead or tin alloy and made by Nuremberg toy-makers from the C16 and widely exported C18 and C19.

flatware: Collective name for flat pottery, such as plates, trenchers and trays, as opposed to cups, vases and bowls.

Fleischmann, Adolf: German maker of papier mâché dolls from the mid C19 to 1930.

Flemish scroll: Descriptive of a curving, double scrolled X-shaped stretcher found on furniture of the William and Mary period.

fleurs chatironées: Flower painting on porcelain characterized by bold black outlines.

Fleurs des Indes: Flowers of India; decoration on porcelain imitating oriental flower painting especially lotus and paeony blossoms.

fleurs fines: Flower painting on porcelain characterized by subtle shading and botanical accuracy.

Flight & Barr: Worcester porcelain of the years 1792-1804 when bone china was first introduced and the glazes were slightly less translucent, with a yellow tinge, than the preceding period.

flight of stairs: A staircase without any intermediate landings.

flint glass: Strictly, glass made from powdered flint, but used generally of any strong brilliant glass.

flintlock: The standard firing mechanism used for firearms from the C17 until superseded by the swifter and more reliable percussion mechanism in the early C19; a flint held in the cock strikes a steel to create a spark which primes the powder in the pan.

flip glass: Glass beaker, usually straight-sided, for making or serving flip: fortified and heated wine mixed with sugar and beaten egg.

flirting eyes: American name for dolls whose eyes move from side to side.

floral carpets: Term normally used to describe carpets made in industrial centres, rather than by nomads; decorative rather than functional, and with floral motifs instead of geometric.

Florence maiolica: Very early (C15) tin glazed earthenwares from Tuscany, predominantly green in colour.

Flörsheim: Late C18 German faience from Flörsheim, noted for brightly coloured floral decorations.

flowered: C18 glass ornamented with floral engravings.

fluke: Sharp triangular point on a halberd head, used for piercing armour.

flute glass: Glass with an exaggerated tall narrow bowl; evolved Netherlands C17.

fluting: Close-set concave grooves running vertically up a column or decorative panel.

fly bracket: Small hinged support for the flap of a table.

flying stretcher: Descriptive of a type of stretcher typically found on early oak dining tables spanning the single supporting leg at either end.

fly leg: A leg without stretchers which swings out to support a table leaf.

Fo: Lion with a flowing mane, a motif found on Chinese Buddhist carpets.

foible: The weakest part of the sword, most likely to break in battle, from the mid-point of the blade to the tip. See also forte.

foil: Light sword with a button on the point used in the sport of fencing.

folded foot: Of wine glasses, the edge of the foot folded under to give extra strength and thickness; common before the mid C18.

folding spoon or fork: One hinged above the bowl or the tines with a lock device so that it can be folded in half.

foldover: Descriptive of card, gaming and certain tea tables which have a top that folds over onto itself when not in use.

Foley: Name of a Staffordshire pottery founded by H. Wileman in 1860 and acquired by E. Brain in 1880, famous for its "Intarsio" polychromatic wares. Renamed Shelley Potteries Ltd in 1925.

folio stand: Adjustable stand with open slatted leaf supports designed for holding large sheets of paper etc.

foliot: A simple form of balance found in early clocks consisting of a bar and suspended weights, designed to counteract the thrust of the crown wheel against the pallets.

food hutch: Another name for an aumbry.

fore-end: In firearms, the part of the stock that runs beneath the barrel.

forgery: See fake.

form: Long bench seat with no back.

form watch: Any watch of an unusual decorative form, shaped like a skull, animal, musical instrument or crucifix, for example: popular C16 and C17 novelties.

forte: The thickest and strongest part of a sword blade, from the mid-point to the hilt.

Fortin's barometer: One with a device, such as a moving scale or a cistern that can be raised and lowered, which overcomes errors due to the fluctuating volume of mercury in the tube.

four-coloured watch: One whose case is decorated with gold inlay tinted with alloys to provide four colours; pure gold, blue, white and green. Common late C18 in France.

four-poster bed: Bedstead with four tall posts supporting a tester.

fourquette: Long, forked staff carried by C17 infantrymen to support their gun muzzles.

fox-head: Small C18 vessels in the form of a fox head, often in ceramic (e.g. sauce or cream jugs) but also in glass and silver (e.g. stirrup cups).

Frankenthal: Bavarian porcelain factory of the latter half C18, noted for symbolical and mythological figure groups.

Frankfurt: The leading German centre for the production of faience from the latter half of the C17.

Franklin clock: Early American weight-driven clock said to be based on Benjamin Franklin's design; also the name of a clock with a wooden movement manufactured early C19 by Silas Hoadley of Plymouth, Connecticut.

Franklin stove: Early American heating stove with bulbous body and short legs. Originally invented by Benjamin Franklin in 1742, but produced in numerous decorative forms until the beginning of C20.

free-blown: Glass vessels blown and shaped by spinning without the aid of a mould.

freedom box: Small commemorative silver boxes given to prominent citizens when they were presented with the Freedom of a city in the C18 and C19.

Freeman, John: Leading London gunsmith, mid C18.

Fremington: Inexpensive earthenwares made at Fremington, Devon, latter half C19.

French fashions: Elaborately dressed dolls made in the 1860s, wearing the latest of fahionable clothes.

French lock: The commonest type of flintlock firing mechanism, developed in France in the early C17. It has a notched tumbler which acts as the sear catch.

French plate: Copper plated with silver applied as a thin sheet of foil and either heated or burnished.

French polishing: Process of applying a solution of shellac onto a timber surface leaving a high gloss finish.

French stool: Another name for a window seat.

fresh: Used of swords in very fine condition.

fretwork: Wood cut into an intricate pattern for decoration. See also blind fret and open fret.

Friend Petz: Early name for German-made teddy bears.

Friesland clock: C18 Dutch bracket-clock with an ornate brass or gilt openwork case.

frieze (1): An ornamented band of painted or sculptured decoration.

frieze (2): The surface just below the top of a table or chest of drawers etc.

frigger: Novelty object made of glass in the shape of a walking stick, cane or rolling pin.

fringe: Decorative border to a carpet or rug, formed by knotting the warp threads.

frit porcelain: Soft paste porcelain containing ground glass; one of the ceramic types developed in the search for true porcelain.

frizzen: Striking plate of a flintlock; situated just above the pan, and designed to create a spark when struck with the flint. Also known as the frizzle, or steel.

froe: See riving iron.

Fromanteel clock: Early English pendulum clocks of very fine quality made by a Dutch family working in London in the C17 and early C18.

frontal: Piece of armour used to protect the forehead of a man or a horse.

frosted glass: Glass with a surface pattern made to resemble frost patterns or snow-crystals; common on pressed glass vessels for serving cold confections.

frosted silver: Matt surface decoration achieved by etching the surface with mild sulphuric acid; or engraving multiple small lines; or hatching.

Frozen Charlie: Male version of a Frozen Charlotte.

Frozen Charlotte: C19 china doll, so called because the head and limbs are not moveable.

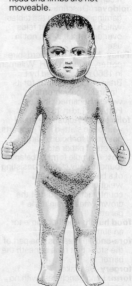

fruit basket: Silver container with fretwork sides and a handle for serving fruits.

fruit knife: A folding knife, first made c1780, used for peeling fruit and for picnics, often with a silver blade and an ornate handle of ivory, horn, mother-of-pearl or tortoiseshell.

fruitwood: Apple wood, pear wood, cherry wood, etc.

Fu: Chinese bat motif, symbol of good fortune, found on carpets and porcelain.

fuddling cup: Earthenware vessel of several cups linked in such as way that anyone challenged to empty one of the cups was in fact, forced to drain them all.

Fukugawa: Japanese porcelain company based in Arita, founded 1689 but only C19 products are common.

Fulda: Factory at Hessen that produced some of Germany's best faience in the mid C18; in the late C18 turned to producing Meissen-style porcelain.

Fulham: London pottery of the early C18 noted for fine salt-glazed figures modelled by John Dwight as well as early stonewares.

Fulham carpets: Hand-woven carpets from a short-lived mid C18 factory run by Peter Parisot in London.

full cock: A firearm ready to fire when the trigger is pulled, as opposed to halfcock when the hammer is raised and under tension but held in place by the sear which prevents the trigger from moving accidentally.

fuller: Groove running down the centre of a sword or dagger blade.

full stocked: Any firearm in which the fore-end of the stock extends the full length of the barrel.

fulminate: Mercury-based explosive material used in percussion caps and cartridge detonators, designed to explode when struck by the firing pin.

fumé: Glass with a smoky appearance.

fundame: Japanese term for matt gold decoration as opposed to bright gold, or kinji.

funnel: From the mid C18, a silver funnel with a cloth filter for straining wine into a decanter.

Furnival ironstone: Painted and relief decorated tablewares produced in great quantity by T. Furnival & Sons of Cobridge, from the mid C19.

Fürstenberg: German porcelain factory, founded mid C18, noted for plaques and ceramic pictures for hanging on walls.

fusee: C18 clockwork invention; a cone shaped drum, linked to the spring barrel by a length of gut or chain. The shape compensates for the declining strength of the mainspring thus ensuring constant timekeeping.

fusil: The steel used for striking a spark in a tinderbox; also the name of a light C17 flintlock musket.

fustic: Exotic wood from the West Indies used occasionally as a veneer or for inlay. It is a yellow colour when first cut, turning to a darkish brown.

Fu ts'ang lung: Chinese dragon symbol found on carpets and porcelain.

fyfot: Reversed swastika, or cross with L-shaped arms, found as a motif on Indian carpets, in ancient mosaic borders and on friezes.

G

Gabbeh: A much sought-after domestic rug type from south Persia, coarsely woven, with thick chunky wool, bright colours and bold designs.

gadrooned: Ornamented with convex vertical lines; the opposite of fluted.

gadrooning (1): Pattern found on the rims and handles of C18 silver, consisting of a series of raised convex curves.

gadrooning (2): In furniture a repetitive ornamental carved edging of curving alternate convex and concave sections.

gaichi: Scissors used for trimming the yarn in carpetmaking.

Gaillard, Lucien (1862-1933): French silversmith and jeweller, member of the Paris school of craftsmen.

Gainsborough chair: Open armchair of rectangular appearance made in England in the C18. Also known as a Hogarth chair.

galena: Powdered lead sulphide used by medieval potters as a glaze; ranging from almost colourless to rich yellow.

gall: The source of black or dark brown dye used in oriental carpets.

Gallé, Emile (1846-1904): Father of the French Art Nouveau movement and founder of a talented circle of designers based around Nancy. Simultaneously, in the 1880s, he designed delicate furniture embellished with marquetry and began experimenting with new glass techniques. In 1889, he developed cameo glass; in 1897 "marquetry in glass", or "marquetrie de verre". After his death, factories continued to produce his wares, signed Gallé but marked with a star, until the 1930s.

gallery: A brass or wood open decorative raised edging to a flat surface.

gallipot/gillypot: Small earthenware pot, traditionally used for storing lard, oil or ointment.

galtuk: Carpets from the Arak region of northern Iran.

gamboge: Bright yellow colour in carpets and textiles, named after the resin from which it is derived.

gaming table: A card table, but usually associated with those that have guinea pockets.

garde du vin: Type of cellaret designed en suite with a sideboard under which it would stand.

Garde Meuble de la Couronne: Department which dealt with furnishing of the royal palaces in France and whose records survive nearly intact as a useful source of reference.

garden carpets: Ornamented with a garden scene, chiefly from western Iran.

Garden, Francis: English founder in the mid C18 of a porcelain factory near Moscow.

garden furniture: Benches, seats and tables for use out of doors. Cast and wrought iron and timber are the commonest materials and the decoration is often rustic in theme.

Garnier: Paris family of clockmakers, including Paul Jean, active from 1825.

garnish: Collective name for a set of tableware usually of silver, but also of pewter or porcelain.

garniture: Collective term for a group of porcelain figures or ornaments, often including a clock.

garya husk: A stylized flower like a wheat husk or bluebell

used as carved or inlaid decoration. Usually associated with furniture in the styles of Hepplewhite and Adam.

gate leg table: Type of drop leaf table with leaves that are supported by legs with stretchers (called gates) which swing out from the main frame of the table.

gatling gun: Early machine gun named after its mid C19 inventor.

Gaudi, Antoni (1852-1926): Spanish Art Nouveau designer and architect who combined Moorish elements into his work and later created freeform, asymmetrical elements to produce a unique and bizarre style of his own; the work of imitators is often called Gaudiesque.

Gaudreau, Antoine (d.1751): French cabinet maker who was much patronized by the Royal family during the early C18.

gaudy: Used to describe cheap and colourful ceramic ornaments e.g. gaudy Dutch, Staffordshire wares painted with oriental designs and exported to America in quantity in the early C19.

Gaultier dolls: Late C19/early C20 bisque head dolls produced at the Gaultier porcelain factory in Paris.

gauntlet: Armour plate glove used to protect the hand and wrist.

gendje: Brightly coloured Caucasian rugs with linear decoration.

Georgian: Specifically the period 1760 to 1800; but sometimes the term is used to cover the whole period from 1714 to 1830, and subdivided into Hanoverian (1714-1760), Late Georgian (1760-1800) and Regency (1800-1830).

gera: Porcelain from Thuringia, late C18, imitating Meissen.

German metal: Nickel or tin-based alloy intended to imitate silver.

German silver: White metal alloy, composed of nickel, copper and zinc, used in the C19 for silver plating in preference to copper which showed through where the silver coating became worn through constant use.

gesso: Composition of plaster of Paris and size which was used as a base for applying gilding and usually moulded in bas relief.

ghashoghdoun: Small carpet bag used by nomadic peoples for transporting clothes and household utensils.

Ghiordes knot: One of the two principal knots used in carpet making (see also Sehna), characteristic of the Caucasus and Turkey. The knot is formed by passing the yarn over two threads, turning them under and bringing the ends up through the space between. Also known as a Turkish or symmetric knot.

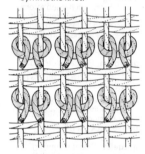

Ghiordes rugs: From the Turkish town of the same name; small, very high quality rugs in wool or silk with a dense, highly ornate pattern.

ghoum: Carpets from the Teheran (Qum) region of Iran, decorated with rows of multi-coloured motifs.

gien: French C19 faience imitating earlier styles, and sometimes transfer printed.

Gilbody, Samuel: Liverpool potter c1753-61, whose factory produced blue and iron-red wares with a silky glaze.

gilding: Process of applying thin gold foil to a surface. There are two methods. Oil gilding involves the use of linseed oil and is applied directly onto the woodwork. Water gilding requires the wood to be painted with gesso.

Gilliland: Glass made by John L. Gilliland and Co., C18, before it became the Brooklyn Flint Glass Co.

Gillow, Robert: Prominent English joiner and cabinet maker whose workshop in Lancaster began business in the mid C18. One of his apprentices was Hepplewhite.

giltwood: Wood which has been gilded but has not been further embellished by the application of gesso.

gimbal: Mounting for a ship's compass, clock or navigational aid which keeps the instrument horizontal no matter which way the boat tilts.

Gimson, Ernest (1864-1920): Founder, with the Barnsley brothers, of the Cotswold Arts and Crafts workshops, based in Sapperton, Gloucestershire. Designer of simple but elegant rustic furniture.

gin bottle: Stoneware jar or flask often modelled in the C19 with the caricature of a political figure.

ginger jars: Tall richly engraved silver vessels with lids from the C17, so called because of their shape, similar to oriental vessels used for storing crystallized ginger.

ginori: Early maiolica made by the Ginori family in Doccia, Italy; also C19 reproductions of older forms.

girandole: Mirror for suspending on a wall, the earliest type and made from the mid C17, usually with a highly ornate frame.

girandole clock: Early C19 banjo clock of especially ornate appearance, with applied gilt scrolls, eagles, etc.

Giustiniani: Family of C18 maiolica makers based in Naples.

glaive: Used of various types of long-handled weapons that can be used both for cutting and thrusting; thus combining the functions of the lance and the sword.

Glasgow delftware: Mid C18 tin-glazed wares made by Lambeth potters who founded a factory in Glasgow.

Glasgow School: Originally the name of the Glasgow School of Art at which Charles Rennie Mackintosh studied in the 1880s, and whose new buildings he designed in the 1890s. Now used to describe the style developed by Mackintosh and his followers, a simplified linear form of Art Nouveau highly influential on Continental work of the period.

glass case: Small decorative case of shelves used for the storage and display of drinking glasses and other delicate items.

glass paste: Coloured glass, used in jewellery as a cheap substitute for precious and semi-precious stones.

Glastonbury chair: Name given to a type of X-frame chair with elbowed arms which link the chair seat to the top of the back.

Glatigny: French porcelain workshop, established in the 1890s and noted for its Art Nouveau designs.

glazing bars: See astragal.

global clock: One of spherical shape with a moving band marked with the hours around the circumference, rather than hands and a dial.

globe: Model of the earth showing the seas and continents mounted so that it revolves around the axis.

Go: Pseudonym of a Japanese master craftsman; his adopted name.

goblet: Drinking vessel, in ceramic or glass, with a stem, foot and lid.

goffered/gauffered: Pattern usually achieved by passing material through a pair of rollers; raised on one side, incised on the other.

goffering iron: Domestic implement used, when heated, to crimp lace and other materials.

gofum dolls: C19 Japanese dolls with cloth bodies, faces made from a paste of crushed shell (gofum), usually with a squeak.

Goggingen: Faience factory in Bavaria, founded mid C18, noted for richly coloured flower designs and chinoiserie.

gold lustre: Metallic gold oxide used by C19/C20 art potters to give a red-to-coppery gold sheen to their wares.

Goldscheider: Porcelain factory established in Vienna in 1886 and famous for Art Nouveau vases and Art Deco figures.

Goldsmiths and Silversmiths Co., Ltd: British company, established in the 1890s, noted for its Art Nouveau designs for tableware, photograph frames, clockcases, etc.

goldstone: Glass with a golden lustre by the inclusion of copper oxide; often used in paste jewellery.

golliwog: Black faced soft toy with fuzzy hair named after a character in a children's story illustrated by Florence Upton in 1895, traditionally dressed in blue top coat, bow tie and red or striped trousers.

gombron: Persian blue and white pottery imported in quantity to Britain in the C17/C18.

googly eyes: Disproportionately large round dolls' eyes looking to one side.

goose neck: See broken pediment.

gorgelet: Oriental drinking vessel with spouts or jets, made for export from the C17.

gorget: In armour, the plate that protects the throat.

Goss: Various wares made C19 by W. H. Goss in Stoke-on-Trent; principally known for crested china souvenirs, but also producing parian wares and jewel-inlaid porcelain.

Goss doll: Rare bisque dolls produced in England by the firm of William Henry Goss during World War I when German imports were stopped.

gossip's chair: Another name for a caqueteuse.

Gostelowe, Jonathan (1744-1806): Exceptionally skilful American cabinet maker who produced Chippendale style furniture of outstanding quality.

gotha: Porcelain produced in Thuringia, Germany, from the mid C18.

gothic: Furniture style which is derived from Gothic architecture and is characterized by curved pointed arches.

gothic clock: C15 and C16 iron clocks, made chiefly in Germany, in the shape of a tower with four pillars, an arched canopy and pinnacles. Sometimes also used of C19 clocks with Gothic ornament or surmounted by a steeple.

Gotzkowsky: Repeated pattern of flowers set in panels, named after the originating artist at the Meissen porcelain factory.

Gould, Christopher: Celebrated London maker of longcase clocks, active late C17.

Gouthière, Pierre (1732-1813): Leading French cabinet maker who was widely employed by Royalty and nobility but who died in poverty after being declared bankrupt.

gnomon: Shadow-casting element of a sundial, often a rod and a triangular pointer, sometimes made in the form of a bird, or decoratively pierced.

Graham, George: Eminent London clockmaker, active 1695-1720.

Grainger Worcester: Bone china from Thomas Grainger's factory, established in Worcester, early C19; noted for parian ware leaf-form jugs.

gramophone: Patented 1887 by Emile Berliner; differs from Edison's phonograph in that the gramophone plays a disc, not a cylinder.

grande sonnerie: Clocks which strike the quarter followed by a repetition of the hour, usually on different bells. Dating from the late C17.

grandfather clock: Popular name for large longcase/tallcase clocks.

grand feu: French for great fire; high-temperature colours used in faience and maiolica decoration; principally cobalt blue, manganese purple, iron red, copper green and antimony yellow.

grandguard: In armour, a boss fitted to the breastplate to protect the heart.

grandmother clock: Popular name for smaller longcase/tallcase clocks, generally under 6ft (180cm) in height.

granite marbled: Purplish lead glaze sprayed onto earthenware to imitate marble; invented C18 by Wedgwood and widely copied.

graniteware: Earthenware covered with cream coloured glazes which contain numerous blue to black flecks and spots, so resembling granite.

granulation: Small specks of metal soldered to silver or gold metalwork for decorative effect, often polished so as to sparkle.

graveyard rugs: Turkish prayer rugs with a design of cypress trees and small tomb-like buildings.

gravity clock: Any type of clock which, suspended from a chain or ratchet, is powered by its own weight.

gravy pot: Double-walled vessel, often in silver or silver plate, with a central well for the sauce or gravy and an outer compartment for hot water to keep the gravy warm.

greaves: In armour, the plates that protect the legs below the knee.

Grecian key: A geometrical carved decoration of straight and right-angled lines somewhat resembling a maze.

green glass: Alternative name for bottle glass; the natural colour of glass made from unpurified silica which contains iron oxide.

green-glazed wares: Pottery covered in the translucent green glaze invented by Wedgwood mid C18 and typical of cabbage and cauliflower wares.

greenwares: Products of the Don pottery in Yorkshire in the early C19 when it was owned by John Green.

Greenwich armour: Armour made at the Royal Armoury, Greenwich, in the C16 and C17.

Gregory, Mary: See Mary Gregory.

Greiner, Ludwig: C19 American manufacturer of papier mâché dolls' heads.

Grenobles wood: High quality French walnut.

grés de Flandres: Grey saltglazed wares produced in the Flanders region from C14.

Gretton, Charles: Noted clockmaker, active late C17/early C18.

gridiron pendulum: One made of several rods of steel or iron linked to rods of brass; the differences in the rates of expansion and contraction between the two metals cancel each other out, keeping the length constant, and therefore also the duration of the swing.

grille: Brass latticework used as a filling for the doors of some cabinet pieces.

grisaille: Type of monochrome used to decorate furniture during the C18.

Griswold, A. B. & Co.: Leading New Orleans gunsmith, C19.

Grödnertal: Wooden dolls with carved combs in their hair, named after the place of origin, early C19.

Groszbreitenbach: Porcelain factory, founded late C18 in Thuringia, Germany, producing imitations of Meissen.

grotesque: Originally the ornamental style associated with grottoes. Any fanciful ornament composed of distorted faces, mythical animals (satyrs, sphinxes), and fantastical fruit and flower forms.

Gruber, Jacques (b.1870): Important French designer of Art Nouveau furniture and jewellery, working in Paris and Nancy.

Grueby: American pottery, established 1894 by William H. Grueby, specializing in architectural tiles and vases ornamented with floral or geometric designs.

Gruel, Léon: French bookbinder whose Art Nouveau designs are based on stylized plant shapes.

gryphon: Mythical beast with the head of an eagle and the body of a lion.

Guangxu (Kuang Hsu): Chinese Qing dynasty emperor, 1875-1908.

Guan yao: Chinese for "imperial ware"; Sung dynasty porcelain with blue or grey crackle glaze, much copied in the C18.

Guanyin: Alternative spelling of Kuan Yin, the Buddhist deity of compassion, often portrayed in blanc-de-chine porcelain.

guard (1): Part of the border motif in oriental carpets, a narrow outer band running parallel to the main one.

guard (2): Any part of a firearm fitted as a safety feature, hence the trigger guard designed to prevent the trigger being struck accidentally.

Gubbio: In Umbria, Italy, centre of maiolica production in the Renaissance period, noted for the gold and ruby lustre decoration of Giorgio Andreoli.

guéridon: Small two or three-tiered table designed to carry some form of lighting. See also candlestand.

Guernsey: Pewter vessel with a lid, originally from the Channel Islands, for measuring a precise quantity of a liquid.

guild silver: Silver ceremonial vessels marked with the insignia of a trade guild.

guilloche: Pattern of interlaced or plaited bands, or ribbons used to ornament a moulding. Also found as a motif on the borders of mosaic floors and carpets.

Guimard, Hector (1867-1942): French Art Nouveau designer, best known for his ornate cast-iron entrances to Métro stations in Paris. As an architect he designed all the interior fittings as well as the building, everything from the lock plates to the kitchen crockery.

guinea pockets: Shallow dishes set into the baize of a gaming table to hold money or gaming counters.

guisarme: Medieval weapon consisting of a short curved blade at the end of a long handle.

gul: Literally a "flower"; a common motif in oriental carpets, based on a rose but stylized out of recognition; geometric in form. Each nomadic tribe had its own identifying version.

gulestan: Rose garden; oriental carpet design.

gul-henna: Henna flowers; motif on carpets from Persia, often used as an allover pattern.

gun metal: Strong alloy of copper and tin used for making gun stocks, but also for casting candlesticks, furniture ornaments, etc in the C19.

gunpowder: Explosive mixture of saltpetre, sulphur and charcoal used to propel the shot in firearms until superseded by cordite c1880.

guri: Scroll patterns carved into alternative layers of red and black lacquer.

gusset: Chain mail used to protect the vulnerable points at the junction between any two pieces of plate armour.

gutta foot: Square section foot which is slightly broader at the base and incised on each side.

gutta percha: Synthetic rubber-like substance used for making dolls, latter half C19.

gyobu: Irregular gold flakes imbedded in Japanese lacquerwork.

gyroscope: Various forms of a spinning wheel which, mounted within a ring, remains stable through centrifugal forces; made as toys, as scientific instruments demonstrating the

characteristics of motion, and as a means of stabilizing ships' instruments.

H

Habaner faience: Made by strict Moravian protestants from the late C16. Though influenced by contemporary European designs, animal representations were taboo.

hacienda silver: Silver jewellery and objects from Mexico or Peru.

hadklu: Small rugs from central Asia with the field divided into four quadrants by a cross.

Hadley chest: American dower chest made in New England at the turn of the C17. It has distinctive carving of vines and leaves which cover the front.

Hadley ware: From late C19 pottery established by James Hadley, noted for Art Nouveau vases, later taken over by the Royal Worcester Co.

haematite: Oxide of iron used to give glass a ruby red colour.

Hafner ware: Lead-glazed pottery and tiles, sometimes with relief moulded designs, produced in Southern Germany and Central Europe from C13.

Hague porcelain: Made briefly at The Hague in Holland in the late C18, sometimes with gilded decoration on a blue ground.

Hagueneau: Faience factory near Strasbourg noted for floral painting in the latter C18.

Hahuko: Period of Japanese history AD 672-685.

hair trigger: Trigger designed to fire at the slightest pressure.

halberd: C16 weapon consisting of a spike, hook and axehead combined at the end of a long pole.

half-armour: Armour plate covering the trunk and arms but not the legs.

half-cock: In a firing mechanism, when the hammer is raised and ready for firing but held in place by the sear, thus preventing the trigger from moving until the hammer is raised again to full cock; a safety feature that did not always work, hence the expression "to go off at half cock".

half-hunter: Watch with a protective hinged front cover which has a central glass covered aperture so that part of the dial is visible even when the cover is closed.

half-stocked: Any firearm in which the fore-end of the stock extends only part way down the length of the barrel.

half tester: A canopy that covers only the bedhead half of a bed.

Haigh, Thomas (fl.1771-1779): British cabinet maker who was a partner of Thomas Chippendale.

Hall, John: Leading London gunsmith, mid C18.

hall chair: Strongly constructed chair which lacks intricate ornament and upholstery, being designed to stand in a hall to accommodate messengers and other callers in outdoor clothing. At the same time it had to be attractive enough to impress more important callers and was often carved with a crest or coat of arms for this purpose.

Hallifax barometer: Early C18 barometer designed by John Hallifax of Barnsley, the first barometer with a dial, predecessor of the wheel barometer, similar in appearance to a longcase clock.

hallmark: Collective term for all the marks found on silver or gold consisting of an assay office, quality, date and maker's marks; sometimes the term is used only of the assay office mark.

hall porter's chair: An armchair with the back and sides extended upwards to form a sheltering canopy. Designed for the draughty hallways and corridors of large houses and mansions. Also known as a watchman's chair.

Hall rifle: Breech-loading flintlock gun used by the American army and invented in the early C19 by John Hancock Hall of Maine.

Hamadon: Capital of the western Iranian region of the same name, centre of the local carpet industry; products often of cotton or wool with a central medallion.

Hamburg ware: C17 faience jugs often decorated with the Hamburg coat-of-arms though the precise location of the factory is not known.

Hamilton silver: Made by a British firm of silversmiths in Calcutta in the C19, usually for civil-service or military use.

hammer: In percussion firearms, the arm which strikes the firing pin. Sometimes used erroneously for the cock. In the snaphance firing mechanism the hammer is the striking plate.

hammering: Method of beating out silver, gold or pewter to form a vessel without using heat. Usually leaves a regular pattern of closely spaced decorative hollows in the surface of the metal.

hammer price: Actual price achieved by an antique at auction as opposed to an estimate, reserve price or bought-in price.

Hammonton: New Jersey glassworks, established early C19, noted for high quality flasks.

Han: In Chinese history, the period 206 BC to AD 220, usually divided into two periods: Western Han 206 BC to AD 24, and Eastern Han AD 25 to 220.

hanap: Large silver goblet with a lid but no handles; sometimes also found in stoneware with silver mountings.

Hanau: Faience factory founded by Dutch settlers in Hanau, Germany, in the mid C17. Noted for narrow-necked jugs decorated with Baroque flower and bird patterns.

hand-and-a-half sword: One with a grip long enough to be grasped by both hands, overlapped, in order to strike a forceful blow.

hand bayonet: Common early C19 bayonet made to be detached from the rifle and used as a shortsword.

hand cooler: Glass egg, often decorated like a paperweight, traditionally said to be used for keeping the hands cool at balls and assemblies, especially by ladies who were not supposed to perspire!

hand gun/hand cannon: Early primitive form of pistol consisting of a barrel mounted on a wooden stock, fired by placing a smouldering brand at the touch-hole.

handkerchief table: Table with a triangular top and a single triangular leaf. This arrangement enables it to fit into a corner when closed and form a square when opened.

Handwerck, Heinrich: German makers of bisque dolls, late C19/early C20.

hanger: Late C17 to C18 single-edged shortsword hung from the belt.

hangfire: In firearms, the term used to describe the delay between pressing the trigger and the ejection of the projectile. The whole development of firing mechanisms was dictated by the desire to reduce the duration of the hangfire.

Haniwa: Japanese bronzes and distinctive red pottery of the C1 to C4 AD.

Hankar, Paul (1859-1901): Leading Belgian architect and furniture designer, whose rectilinear style ran counter to the prevailing Art Nouveau genre and was inspired by Japanese art and the Cotswold Arts and Crafts movement.

Hanley: Important Staffordshire pottery town producing diverse wares, late C18 and C19, often closely copying Wedgwood developments.

Hanoverian: The period 1714 to 1760, i.e. covering the reigns of George I (1714-27) and George II (1727-60), the first two monarchs of the House of Hanover.

Hanoverian spoons: The style, popular under George I, of relatively simple forms with a long bowl and a central spine running up the face of the handle. The predecessor of most modern cutlery forms.

Hans and Gretchen: Boy and girl character dolls manufactured by Kammer & Reinhardt from 1910 to the early 1920s, also known as model 114.

Hansen-Jacobsen, Niels (b.1861): Danish Art Nouveau sculptor and ceramist.

hard metal: Highest quality of pewter, made with a high proportion of tin with bismuth as a hardening agent. Made from c1700.

hard paste: True porcelain made of china stone (petuntse) and kaolin; the formula was long known to, and kept secret by, Chinese potters but only discovered in the 1750s in England, from where it spread to the rest of Europe and the Americas.

hardware: General term for objects made of metal.

hardwood: One of two basic categories in which all timbers are classified. The hardwoods are the broad-leaved deciduous trees which replace their leaves every year. See also softwood.

hare's fur: Oriental glaze in which the mineral inclusions form extremely fine lines, usually in black on red/brown.

harewood: Sycamore which has been stained a greenish colour is known as harewood. It is used mainly as an inlay wood and was known as silverwood in the C18.

Harlaam: Dutch town which began tin-glazed earthenware production before Delft and was the first to produce the blue and white Chinese-style decoration characteristic of early delftwares.

Harlequin: Character in Italian commedia dell'arte, distinguished by his colourful diamond-pattern tunic; hence any similar lozenge pattern. Often portrayed in porcelain partnered by Columbine.

harlequin set: See composite set.

harlequin table: Combined card and tea table created by having a series of folding tops. Also known as a triple top table.

Haroun: Village in Iran, now a by-word for coarse or poor quality carpets.

harshang: Oriental carpet motif, a flower whose outline resembles the shape of a crab.

Harvey, Agnes: British designer of Art Nouveau metal and enamel jewellery, associated with the Glasgow school.

hatchli: Literally "marked with a cross"; carpet design based on a cross, especially one that divides the field into quadrants.

Hatschlou: Alternative name for central Asian Hadklu rugs, characterized by a four part field divided by a cross shape.

Hauberk: Chain mail tunic, reaching to the knees.

Haufenbecher: Set of cups, usually of pewter or silver, designed to fit one inside the other. German, from late C16.

haunch pot: Baluster-shaped pewter, more rarely silver, tankards of the C16 and C17.

Hausmalerie: German for homepainting; ceramics decorated by out-workers rather than in the factory.

Haviland: Porcelain factory established by David Haviland in France in 1842 and acquired by its director, Ernest Chaplet in 1885. In 1892, Theodore Haviland, David's son, established a new factory of the same name specializing in Art Deco tableware.

Haviland-Limoges: Art pottery made at Charles Haviland's factory in Limoges, France; late C19.

hayburner: Early American prairie stove of cast iron or brick, designed to burn hay where coal and wood was scarce.

Heal, Ambrose (1872-1959): English cabinet maker who joined the family business of furniture retailers, based in London, in 1893 and extended its business to include the whole range of interior furnishings. Important patron of young Arts and Crafts designers and co-founder of the Design and Industries Association (1915).

Heathcote wares: Earthenware and bone china decorated with blue transfer printed scenes from early C19 Fenton pottery in Staffordshire.

Hedwig glass: Early medieval cut glass beakers from the Near East with thick walls, decorated with animals and foliage in high relief.

Heian: The period of Japanese history AD 794-1185.

Heinrichsen: Nuremberg manufacturer of flat and solid toy soldiers 1870-1920.

Heinrichsen scale: Alternative name for Nuremberg scale, the standard size of German-made toy soldiers: 30mm for infantry, 40mm for cavalry.

heliograph: Early form of photographic print; a metal plate coated with light-sensitive chemicals which can be used to make a portrait or engraving; contemporary with Daguerreotypes but less efficient.

Hellenistic: Art produced between the C8 and C4 BC under Greek colonial rule and showing the influence of ancient Greek art alongside native styles.

helm: In armour, a helmet that completely enclosed the head and which could be bolted to the back and breast plate.

helmet: Any piece of armour that protects the head.

helmet badge: Brass or cloth military badges, attached to the front of helmets.

hemispherium: Sundial with a bowl-shaped dial.

Henderson wares: Products of David Henderson's factory in Jersey City, established C19 and noted for stoneware and Toby jugs.

Henri Deux: Henry II; rare C16 French earthenware decorated with coloured clay inlays, and C19 reproductions of the same.

Hepplewhite, George (d.1786): British cabinet maker and furniture designer. Well known for his chairs with shield and oval backs but a wide range of furniture and smaller items appear based on his designs.

Herat: Town in Afghanistan, major market for the tribal rugs of the region; also C16 to C18 carpets from the region whose design gave its name to the Herati motif.

Herati motif: Rosette contained within a diamond; motif common on oriental carpets, often used in allover patterns.

Hereke: Turkish town noted for very fine silk rugs with a close-clipped pile, with designs on an ivory ground.

Herez: North-western Iranian carpet-making centre, noted for large carpets with angular patterns on a red field.

herm: Rectangular pillar terminating in the helmeted head of Hermes, the messenger of the gods in Greek mythology. See also term.

Herree: Short-lived C19 faience factory in Norway, producing bowls and trays decorated with blue paint and manganese colours.

herringbone: Another name for feather banding.

Heubach: German doll manufacturer active 1820-63 (under Gebrüder Heubach) and 1887 to the 1920s (under Ernest Heubach), specializing in bisque head and character dolls with fabric or composition bodies.

hexafoil: Six-cusped figure which resembles a symmetrical six-lobed leaf or flower. Some early drop handles have brass hexafoil backplates.

Heyde: Dresden manufacturer of flat and solid toy soldiers, 1870-1944.

Heylin: Leading London gunsmith, late C18.

hickory: An American wood which is similar to ash but a little darker in colour. It turns well and is strong without being heavy.

Hida Takayama: Region of modern Japan in which craftsmen still make netsuke, inro, etc in the style of the Meiji and Tokugawa (Edo) periods.

hieroglyphs: Ancient Egyptian writing, in which words are represented by pictures.

Higgs & Evans: Late C18 makers of ornate musical clocks.

highboy: Tall American chest of drawers mounted on a stand with further drawers and raised on cabriole legs. The top is usually heightened by finials, etc. which help to create a uniquely American piece.

high chair: Tall chair used to sit a child at a table.

high dresser: See dresser.

high standard silver: Used of silver which contains a higher proportion of pure metal than sterling silver i.e. better than 925 parts per 1000 pure silver.

Hill, Matthew: Late C18 English maker of mural and Act of Parliament clocks.

Hilpert, Andreas: Late C18 German toymaker credited with the invention of toy soldiers standing on a base plate, cast in tin or pewter.

hilt: Handle of a dagger or sword.

himation: Originally an ancient Greek cloak thrown over one shoulder and fastened under the other. Used of any cloak draped over a nearly-nude statue.

himotoshi: The drilled hole in netsuka and inro through which the cord passes, often artfully disguised as part of the carving.

hipped: Term used to describe a cabriole leg which continues at the top above the seat rail. Usually found on better quality pieces.

hippocamp: Sea-horse with two fore-feet and the tail of a fish, portrayed in antique art.

Hirado: Japanese porcelain with figure and landscape painting in blue on a white body, often depicting boys at play, made exclusively for the Lords of Hirado, near Arita, mid C18 to mid C19.

hira-makie: Flat decoration in Japanese lacquerware, as opposed to carving or relief.

hirame: Irregular gold or silver inclusions in Japanese lacquerwork.

Hird's foot: Silver spoons of the late C17/early C18 with a cleft finial.

ho: Chinese bronze vessel for heating wine.

hochschnitt: German for "high cut". Decoration in high relief on German glass of the late C17.

Höchst ware: C18 German faience figures and covered dishes noted for fine floral painting.

hock glass: Glass specifically for drinking white wines from the Hoch Rein district of Germany, with a pale green or golden bowl on a long clear glass stem.

hock leg: Variation of the cabriole leg but with a broken line to the inner curve of the knee.

Hoffmann, Josef (1870-1956): Pupil of Otto Wagner in Vienna and a founder of the Weiner Werkstätte (1903). As a designer, he bridged the transition from Art Nouveau to Art Deco, reviving an appreciation of square and rectangular forms in furniture.

Hogarth chair: Another name for a Gainsborough chair.

Hogen: Honorary title bestowed on a Japanese painter or craftsman.

Ho Ho bird: The phoenix bird which is occasionally used as a furniture decoration. It is more commonly found on mirrors.

Holbein: Turkish Renaissance carpets imitating contemporary European paintings, notably those of Holbein.

holitsch: Mid C18 faience and creamwares from Hungary.

Holland and Green: Factory in Longton, Staffordshire, noted for brilliantly coloured glazes and fine stoneware, established latter C19.

Hollands porcelain: Dutch late C18 imitations of Ming dynasty porcelain.

hollow cast figures: Toy soldiers with a hollow core, made by a process invented by W. Britain Ltd, c1893.

hollow column clock: Early C19 type in which the weights are concealed in hollow columns that appear to be a part of the case.

hollow cut: Pattern of concave forms, especially on glass.

hollow stem: C18 wine glass with a hollow in the upper stem for collecting wine sediment.

hollow ware: Term used of bowls and cups, especially of pewter, as distinct from flatware plates, etc.

holly: A hard wood with a close grain. It is white and is used for inlay and marquetry work.

holster pistols: C18 short-barrelled pistols made in pairs for horse-back travellers and cavalry soldiers, seated in leather holsters at the front of the saddle.

holy-water sprinkler: In weaponry, ironic name for an iron spiked ball on the end of a flail.

home-service helmet: Military helmet of the C19 worn by officers for ceremonial, often with a spiked crest.

Honan: Sung dynasty Chinese stoneware with a purple-black glaze, originally made in Honan province.

Honduras mahogany: See mahogany.

Hongwu (Hung Wu): Chinese Ming dynasty emperor, AD 1368-98.

Hongzian (Hung Hsien): Last Chinese emperor, installed as ruler of Manchu, for one year only, 1916.

hood (1): Term used to describe the taller, enclosing part of a cradle.

hood (2): The superstructure of a longcase/tallcase clock containing the movement and dial. In old clocks this lifts off the clock so that adjustments can be made; hinged front doors were a C19 innovation.

hoof foot: A foot resembling an animal's hoof which was used on early cabriole legs.

Hooke barometer: Rare late C17 wheel barometer made by Robert Hooke, the predecessor of the banjo-type common from the late C18.

hooked rugs: European and American rugs made by hooking strips of yarn through a liner or canvas backcloth.

hoop back: Descriptive of the back of a Windsor-type chair which has a top rail bent round like half a hoop.

hooped tankard: Pewter tankard or mug with a swelling, barrel-shaped body, said to be based on wooden models, especially in Scandinavia.

Hope, Thomas (1770-1831): British furniture designer, architect and scholar whose designs were both formal and classical.

hope chest: Another name for a dower chest. This term is more commonly used in America.

hop glass: Drinking glass, especially an ale glass, ornamented with hop vines.

hornbeam: A pale wood which is similar to ash but harder. It is good for turning but was little used in furniture.

Hornby: Manufacturers of clockwork and electric locomotives from c1910, best known today for the "Dublo" range, introduced mid 1940s.

horse brass: Decorative brasses made to be fixed to the horse harness. Of hand-hammered brass from the C16 to the mid C19, cast 1830-70, and mass-produced by die-stamping 1870 to the present day.

horse dressing glass: See cheval mirror.

horsehair: Mane and tail hair of a horse which was mixed with wool flock and used for stuffing upholstery.

horse screen: See cheval screen.

Hotchkiss: Early type of machine gun, named after its inventor.

hotel silver: Marked, as the name suggests, with the name or trade mark of an hotel; often of high quality silver plate rather than pure silver, from C19.

hot milk jug: Made as a partner to, and smaller version of, a coffee pot but with a shorter spout.

hourglass: Waisted glass cylinder in a wooden or metal frame filled with powder or sand to give a precise measurement of the time taken for the sand to flow from one globe to the other.

hourglass clock: American early C19 mantel clock with a case of hourglass shape.

hourglass gauntlet: Armoured glove, tapering from the knuckles to the wrist and out again in an hourglass shape.

Houston, Mary Galway (b.1871): British author and artist, best known for her books on historical costume and ornamental styles.

Howard clocks: Banjo clocks manufactured mid C19 by Edward Howard, later the American Waltham Watch Co.

Hubertusberg: Factory founded by Frederick II of Saxony producing fine earthenwares, late C18/C19.

Hughes ironstone: C19 pottery produced in quantity for export to America by Thomas Hughes at Brownhills, Staffordshire.

Huguenot: Antiques especially clocks and silver made by French Protestant refugees who settled in England, the Netherlands and America after the Revocation of the Edict of Nantes in 1685, an Edict which had previously given them a degree of civil and religious freedom.

Hull: Centre of earthenware production in Yorkshire, C19.

Humpen: German or Swiss glass beaker usually with a silver lid, often made in exaggerated sizes, enamelled or engraved with armorials or Biblical scenes.

hunter: Watch with a solid hinged cover protecting the glass over the dial. This cover has to be opened in order to read the time.

hunting carpets: Rare and highly prized Persian carpets decorated with hunting scenes against a background of flowers.

hunting cup: Small silver cup without handles used for drinking before going hunting. Often in the shape of a foxhead and also known as a stirrup cup. Some are inscribed round the neck. Latter half of C18 onwards.

Huntley and Palmer: Reading, Berkshire, biscuit manufacturer whose early C20 tin boxes, some designed to function as money boxes when empty, are now sought after and collected.

Hurdals verk: Glass from the Norwegian factory of that name, operating late C18/early C19.

Hurd silver: Made by a Boston family of silversmiths of that name in the C18.

husk: See bellflower and garya husk.

husk finial: Decorative finial at the end of a silver spoon resembling the shape of an ear, or husk, of wheat; popular mid C18 motif.

Husson, Henri (1852-1914): French Art Nouveau goldsmith and jewellery designer.

hutch: Another name for an aumbry.

Hüttenglas: German term for free blown, or hand-made glassware.

Hyalith: Black glass, inspired by Wedgwood's basaltes wares, ornamented in gold, made at Nove Hrady, Bohemia, early C19.

hydria: Large ancient Greek vessel in earthenware or bronze, used for storing water. Often with three handles: two horizontal ones for lifting and a vertical one for pouring.

hygrometer: Device for measuring humidity, often incorporated in barometers from the late C18.

Hylton: Factory near Sunderland, one of the first to produce transferprinted earthenware, lustreware and Wear Bridge jugs, late C18/early C19.

hyperboloid platform: A triangular platform base with concave sides.

hypsometer: Instrument for measuring altitude; a metal vessel with integral spirit lamp and thermometer used to measure the boiling point of water which falls progressively as the altitude increases.

I

ice glass: Glass with appearance of cracked ice, achieved by a sudden drop in temperature in the furnace or, more reliably, by sprinkling broken glass onto the surface of the hot vessel; technique developed in Venice and Liège C16.

ice pail: Silver or plated metal bucket on feet, with two handles, a central cavity for a wine bottle, and an outer cavity for ice.

iga ware: Japanese stoneware vases of the C17, with a matt surface.

Ilmenau: German porcelain factory established late C18.

imari: Japanese porcelain made from early C18 for export through the port of Imari. Commonly decorated with a flower-basket pattern in blue, red and gold.

imari pattern: Flower-basket pattern in red, blue and gold copied from Japanese wares and popular on European porcelain of the C18.

impasto: Paint applied to maiolica or faience so thickly that it creates a pattern in low relief.

imperial yellow: Distinctive yellow enamel, developed by Chinese imperial potters in C15 and reserved for the imperial household.

important: Antique dealers' term for a fine piece by a leading maker, especially one that has been shown at exhibitions or featured in text books.

improved: Term used to describe objects, such as silverware, given additional decoration some time after its original manufacture.

Ince, William (fl.1760): British furniture designer, and partner of Thomas Mayhew. Their business enjoyed a good reputation and their furniture often incorporated Gothic or Chinese designs.

incense clock: Oriental time-measuring device consisting of a metal pan with a continuous groove in the base into which a trail of slowburning incense was laid.

incised laquer: See bantam work.

inclusion: Particles within the body of a glass vessel either deliberately introduced for decorative effect or by accident, when it is a flaw.

indestructibles: Dolls made of plastics or resin from mid C19, so called because they were less liable to damage than dolls with ceramic heads.

India pattern bayonet: Standard type of bayonet originally made for the British army in India and then used during the Napoleonic wars.

Indian carpets: Generally those made in India from late C16 to early C19, handknotted and based on Persian forms but more naturalistic.

indianische blumen: Indian flowers; painting on porcelain in the oriental style, especially on mid C18 Meissen and Höchst.

indigo: Dark blue of oriental carpets, named after the plant from which the dye was obtained.

ingle bench: Bench designed to fit into the inglenook i.e. the recesses either side of a large open fireplace.

inlay (1): In furniture a decoration of contrasting wood, bone, ivory, shell or brass, etc. inset into the solid wood.

inlay (2): In firearms, precious materials such as gold, platinum and ivory used to decorate the stock.

inner stripe: Part of a carpet border design; a narrow band between the field and the main border.

inro: Small Japanese compartmented medicine box worn on the belt (obi) and attached by the netsuke, or toggle.

intaglio: Incised gem-stone, often set in a ring, used in antiquity and during the Renaissance as a seal. Any incised decoration; the opposite of carving in relief.

intaglio eyes: Eyes of a doll incised into the bisque head.

intarsia: Inlaid pieces of different coloured woods to form a pictorial decoration.

inventory numbers: Numbers to be found either painted or branded on French furniture made for the Royal households. Sometimes accompanied by a palace letter.

Ionic: One of the orders of classical architecture. Ionic capitals have a scrolled volute.

ipek: Turkish word for silk, used of carpets.

iridized: Glass decorated with metallic oxides to give a lustrous surface; favourite technique of Art Nouveau/Art Deco art glassmakers.

Iron Age: In Europe, the period from c700 BC to the beginning of Roman colonization.

iron clock: Earliest form of domestic clocks, made in Germany from C15 often in the form of a church tower, with four pillars enclosing the movement.

iron stand: Stand of brass or iron used to hold a hot smoothing iron when not in use; typically pierced with ornate patterns, and made from c1700 to c1940.

ironstone: Stoneware, patented 1813 by Charles James Mason, containing ground glassy slag, a by-product of iron smelting, for extra strength.

Isfahan: Ancient capital of Persia, and site of the royal carpet manufactory, late C16 and C17, noted for rich silk rugs often incorporating gold and silver thread. Since 1900, producing very fine rugs with floral designs and a central medallion.

Isleworth: Variously used of bone china from a Liverpool factory of that name producing c1800; and of colourful flatwares produced at Isleworth, Middlesex, C19.

islim: Floral design on Persian carpets, characterized by elaborate serpentine foliage trails.

Isnik ware: Ottoman-Turkish pottery, C13 to C19, from the workshops of Isnik, Western Anatolia. Typically painted with blue floral and geometric designs on a white ground.

Isparta (1): Turkish centre of rug making, the ancient Greek city of Sparta.

Isparta (2): Alternative name for Sparta carpets, actually made in Smyrna but so-called to distinguish higher quality products from inferior Smyrna products.

istoriato: Narrative scenes, often painted on maiolica.

isu: Japanese for wood of the *prunus* species, principally cherrywood.

Italic: Name given to ancient pottery produced in Italy prior to C4 BC and the beginning of Roman domination of the peninsula.

Ives, Joseph: Brooklyn clockmaker active 1820-30.

ivoride: Early and rare form of plastic made from 1868, simulating ivory.

ivory: White, fine-grained dentine derived from the tusks of elephants and narwhales. Used in Europe, in the Middle Ages, for carving religious groups, by sailors to make scrimshaws and for numerous mass-produced ornamental objects in the Orient. Old ivory has a mellow patina which can, however, be faked.

ivory porcelain: Development of C19, similar to parian but ivory coloured in biscuit form.

ivory-tinted: Earthenware with an ivory coloured glaze developed by William Copeland at the Spode works, C19.

J

Jackfield: Black glazed, sometimes moulded and gilded, tableware and figures first developed by the Jackfield factory in Shropshire, mid C18, and widely copied.

Jacob, Georges (1739-1814): Prominent French furniture maker whose speciality was chairs, although he did make other items such as beds.

Jacobean: Period 1603-25, spanning the reign of James I; sometimes used more loosely to cover the period 1603 to the Restoration of 1666, since characteristically Jacobean styles continued long after the death of James I.

Jacobite: Wine glasses engraved with symbols of the Jacobites (supporters of Prince Charles Edward Stuart's claim to the English throne). Genuine examples date to between 1746 and 1788. Countless later copies and forgeries exist.

Jacobite blades: Basket-hilt swords etched with inscriptions or symbols in support of the Jacobite cause, mostly made in Germany for export to Scotland in early C18.

Jamaica wood: Old name for mahogany.

jamb: Armour plates protecting the legs.

jambiyah: Arab dagger with a sharply curved blade, bending almost at right angles from the hilt.

Jameson, George: Early C19 maker of ornate clocks and chronometers.

janina: Motif found in the borders of Turkish carpets; stylized pattern with a central leaf and two circular fruits either side.

japanning (1): European and American version of Oriental lacquering.

japanning (2): Of swords, a black varnish coating on the hilt, sometimes over-painted or decorated with gold, for decorative effect and to prevent rust.

japonaiserie: Designs based on Japanese forms and decorative motifs.

jardinière: Stand or other piece with a lead or zinc lining for containing plants indoors.

jasperware: Perhaps the best known product of the Wedgwood factory; very fine hard coloured stoneware, originally decorated with slip, but later with high relief decoration, medallions and pictorial scenes; from late C18.

jelly glass: Cone-shaped dessert vessel with a short stem, often with two handles and matching saucer, first made C18.

jelly mould: Ceramic from mid C18 to c1830, thereafter of metal as well and glass after 1935; made in many shapes and sizes. Complete matching sets and unusual forms especially collectable.

Jenkins, Henry: Maker of fine astronomical clocks latter half C18.

Jennens and Bettridge ware: Early C19 papier-mâché objects, especially furniture. Sometimes inlaid with mother-of-pearl, and made by the Birmingham firm of the same name.

Jensen, Georg (1886-1935): Danish designer of silverware and jewellery, whose workshop was established in 1904 in Copenhagen. Famous for his prize winning rose-lidded teapot.

jeroboam: Named after the Biblical "mighty man". A large goblet or drinking vessel of glass, or an outsize bottle.

Jersey glass: Early American pressed glass from the Jersey Glass Co., founded early C19, and other factories in the same locality.

Jesuit china: C17 and early C18 porcelain made in China to the order of Jesuit missionaries and decorated with New Testament scenes.

jeton: Coins used in gaming and as counters from the C12, usually of base metal and often in imitation of the genuine coinage of the day, but without a legend, or with a central hole.

jetware: Popular black-glazed earthenwares produced C19 by numerous Staffordshire potteries.

jever: Now rare faience produced late C18 in north Germany by a former Meissen employee.

jewel: In furniture, a raised decorative ornament.

jewelled porcelain: Inlaid with foil-backed glass imitation gem stones; first developed at Sèvres, late C18, copied by Copeland and others in England mid C19.

Jiajian (Chia Ching): Chinese Ming dynasty emperor, 1522-66.

Jian yao: Chinese Sung dynasty pottery from the Jian (Chien) region of Fukien province, noted for its hare's fur glaze.

Jiaqing (Chia Ch'ing): Chinese Qing dynasty emperor, 1796-1820.

jingling johnny: Toy consisting of a frame and numerous small bells which jingle when shaken.

Joel, Betty: London-based manufacturers of Art Deco furniture in laminated wood.

joey: Small glass or tumbler made to contain a tiny quantity of strong liquor.

Johnson, Mason & Taylor: American C19 makers of rag dolls.

Johnson, Thomas (fl.1756-1758): British designer and carver best known for his mirrors and console tables in the rococo and Chinese styles.

joined: Term used to describe furniture made by a joiner.

joined stool: Stool made by joinery. Such stools are also referred to as joint stools but this is merely a corruption of the correct name.

joint: Where two pieces of wood are attached to each other in construction.

jolly boat: Coaster for circulating wine or liquor, in the form of a boat on wheels.

jomon: Earliest known Japanese pottery, from the period *c*7000 to 300 BC.

jona: Staffordshire earthenware flatback figure of a dog.

jordan: Large decorated pot or bowl, especially a chamber pot.

joshagan: Central Iranian carpets with stylized flowers, each framed by a diamond, on a rich red or blue ground.

ju: Early Chinese stoneware, made briefly in C12, with a blue-grey glaze.

Judaica: Objects, especially silver, relating to the Jewish faith.

jufti: Double knot in carpet making; the yarn wraps around four threads of the warp instead of two, resulting in a less dense pile.

Jugendstil: German Art Nouveau style, named after the magazine *Jugend*, published from 1896 in Munich. Characteristically the style transforms plant shapes into sensual, but limpid, abstractions.

jug head: Cork or stopper surmounted by a china head.

julep: American straight-sided beaker, sometimes tapering to the base, late C18 and early C19, usually in silver and originally awarded as a prize or trophy.

Jumeau, Pierre François: Important French doll maker, noted for "Parisiennes", active 1842-99.

jumping jack: Acrobatic wooden figure, mounted between parallel bars, which can be made to somersault when a string is pulled.

Jungfrauenbecher: C16 and C17 large silver cup made for wedding feasts in the form of a young girl with two cups: one held above her head, the other formed by her skirts when she is inverted.

Jun yao: Chinese Sung, Yuan and Ming dynasty pottery from Jun (Chun) in Honan province with an opalescent blue to purple glaze, typically thickest at the foot, thinner towards the rim.

Jupiter: The heavenly father, or supreme deity, of the ancient Romans, equivalent to the Greek god Zeus.

K

kaba: Term used by carpet sellers to denote rugs made of coarse fibres.

kabistan: Caucasian carpets decorated with birds and animals, notably peacocks.

kabuto: Japanese samurai warrior's helmet.

Kaga: Japanese province which is famous for its Kutani ware.

kagamibuta: A netsuke that incorporates metalwork.

kagi: Japanese term for keys and other small items worn on a cord suspended from the waist sash (obi).

kaiba: Caucasian rugs of a particular size: 48-56in (1.2-1.4m) × 112-128in (2.8-3.2m).

kaibutsu: Japanese name for objects carved in the shape of mythical or imaginary animals.

kakemono: Japanese water colour painted on silk and mounted between two wooden rollers.

Kakiemon: Family of C17 Japanese potters who produced wares decorated with flowers and figures on a white ground in distinctive colours: azure, yellow, turquoise and soft red. Widely imitated in Europe.

kakihan: Mark of the craftsman or sponsor handcarved or painted, as opposed to one applied by stamping or impressing with a stone seal.

kamakura: Period of Japanese history 1185-1333.

Kammer & Reinhardt: German doll maker, active 1886 to early C20, noted for character dolls introduced 1909. Dolls combined unusually fine quality with high level of innovation. Merged 1919 with Simon & Halbig.

Kangxi (K'ang Hsi): Chinese Qing dynasty emperor, 1662-1722.

Kaolin (china clay): A fine white granite clay used in hard-paste porcelain.

karabagh: Carpets from the southern Caucasus, often Persian, rather than Caucasian, in style and some influenced by French design; i.e. floral rather than geometric.

karabele: Originally Turkish, but mostly Polish C17 and C18 sabres characterized by a stylized bird's head grip.

karaj: Northern Iranian carpets, typically decorated with three medallions, the central one larger than the other two.

karamani: Turkish term for flat woven rugs (kelims).

karatsu: C16 and C17 pottery made by Korean craftsmen working in Kyushu, Japan. Of pale-coloured glazes.

kard (1): Near Eastern dagger, often with a hilt of stone or ivory and a watered-steel blade.

kard (2): Cross-hilted sword from the Sahara region, often fitted with an imported European blade.

kar-haneh: Workshop or factory; used of rugs made in a workshop rather than by nomads.

kas: Large wardrobe with a heavy cornice and arched

panels separated by twisted columns. Usually on ball feet.

Kashan: Rug-making centre south of Teheran, Iran, noted for high quality products, often with a central medallion.

kashgai: Rugs woven by Iranian nomadic tribes, notable for the springy lustrous texture, and finely detailed rectilinear designs.

Kashmir: Civilization of northern India which produced extremely fine sandstone sculptures, principally of Hindu deities, between C9 and C18. Also the northern Indian centre of silk and wool carpet making.

Kastrupz: Copenhagen faience factory operating latter C18.

kast-stel: Set of five delftware vases; three baluster-shaped, two straight sided, used to decorate cupboard cornices in late C17/C18.

katabori: Fully three-dimensional netsuke, in which all of the available surface is carved.

katana: Long sword in a pair of Samurai daisho.

katar: Indian dagger with a sharply pointed blade and bar pommel.

Kayser, Engelbert (1840-1911): Chief German exponent of the Art Nouveau style in pewter; range sometimes described as Kayserzinn pewter.

Kayseri: Turkish town noted for silk rugs with designs based on well-known oil paintings.

kazak: Rugs from the central Caucasus; decorated with stripes, zig-zags, diamonds and stars.

Keene glass: Glassware from one of two factories operating in Keene, New Hampshire, C19.

Keley/Kelly: Particular size of carpet: 78in (2.6m) × 60in (1.5m).

kelim: Flat woven rugs lacking a pile; also the flat woven fringe used to finish off the ends of a pile carpet.

Kellinghausen: Late C17 to C19 earthenware and faience, with bright floral designs, made in Schleswig-Holstein.

Kelsterbach: C18 porcelain figures made by former Meissen potters and imitating that factory's style.

kenareh: Runner or side carpet; one made to flank the main central carpet.

Kennedy: Late C19 factory in Burslem, Staffordshire, noted for porcelain decorated with impressed scenes.

Kent, William (1684-1748): British architect and designer who instigated a classical revival based on an overall concept of design for both a house and its furnishings.

Kentucky rifle: Early rifle developed in Colonial America from European prototypes, with a long barrel, often ornately decorated.

kepi: French military cap with a flat top sloping down to the front and a horizontal peak.

kerki: Carpets from the Bokhara region, now in Soviet Asia, usually decorated with gul motifs.

Kermanshah: Western Iranian centre of carpet production; carpets usually multi-coloured.

Kestner, J. D.: Important late C19/early C20 German maker of high quality bisque head dolls.

kettle hat: Helmet worn by men-at-arms in the C14 and C15, shaped like a basin and protecting the crown of the head.

kettle stand: Small galleried table used while taking tea.

kewglas: Late C19 art glass produced at Somerville, Massachusetts, made of milk glass, overlaid by etched coloured glass and finished with a layer of clear glass.

kewpie: Baby dolls with a topknot based on Rose O'Neill's cartoon character of 1910; said to be a corruption of "cupid". Some early examples have wings.

khalichen: Term used to describe carpets that measure 5ft (1.5m) × 8ft (2.5m).

khamseh: Term used to denote carpets of above average quality from the Hamadan region of western Iran.

khandar: Indian longsword with double-edged blade and long pommel for two-handed use.

khanfar: Persian dagger with a curved pommel.

khanjar: Indian dagger with a curved blade and handle often of precious material such as ivory or jade.

khilin: Oriental carpet motif, a stylized deer.

Khirbet Kerak ware: Pottery of C3 BC found in Palestine, Syria and Egypt, remarkable for its highly polished fabric and applied ornament.

khorassan: North east Iranian carpets decorated with herati motif, sometimes characterized by tripling of the weft thread every few rows.

khotan: Chinese-influenced carpets from Soviet Central Asia, around Siankiang.

kian: Sung dynasty Chinese ceramics from Kiangsi decorated with resist designs.

kibitkas: Nomadic wood-framed tents hung with carpets; also used of carpets made for this purpose.

Kidderminster: Carpet weaving centre in the English Midlands since the early C17; motifs based on Flemish tapestries and early products highly prized.

Kiel: Faience produced in Schleswig-Holstein, latter half C18, noted for lively floral decoration on an almost pure white ground.

kimono: Japanese silk robe, essentially T-shaped with wide sleeves and often ornately embroidered with pictorial scenes. Tied at the waist with a sash (obi).

kinchaku: Japanese money purse suspended from the waist sash (obi).

kindjal/kindjhal: Caucasian double-edged shortsword or dagger with broad blade and no quillons.

kinetoscope: Both an early form of moving picture projector and a scientific instrument for demonstrating curvilinear motion.

King, Jessie M.: Scottish book illustrator and binder associated with the Glasgow School.

King's Lynn glass: C18 wine glasses and tumblers decorated with a series of horizontal grooves around the bowl, thought to have been made in King's Lynn.

kingwood: Coarse-grained yellowish brown wood with darker stripes which varies considerably in hardness and comes from Central and South America. It was known in the C17 as princes wood and is also known as violet wood.

kinji: Japanese term for bright gold finish as opposed to matt gold finish (fundame).

kinrande: Japanese porcelain with gilt decoration applied over deep colour glazes.

kirigane: Japanese for "cut metal"; small geometric shapes cut out of gold foil inlaid in lacquer.

kirman: Fine, densely woven carpets of cotton and wool from south-east Iran, decorated with floral designs around a central medallion.

kirman laver: Term used to distinguish modern kirman rugs from old or antique ones; similar in style but the floral designs often more intricate.

kirshehir: Small prayer rugs from central Turkey, relatively primitive.

kist: Name sometimes used for a chest or coffer, particularly in the north of England.

Kit-Kat glass: Balustroid glasses with a trumpet bowl, so called because they are depicted in early C18 portraits of members of the aristocratic Kit-Kat Club.

Kley & Hahn: German maker of bisque head dolls, early C20.

Kling, C. F.: German maker of glazed porcelain dolls from mid C19.

klismos: Type of chair made during the Regency period with concave tapering legs and a curved back.

Kloster-Veilsdorf: Factory in Thuringia, founded latter half C18, producing imitation Meissen porcelain before developing its own style.

knee: Curved top of a cabriole leg. It is often carved.

kneehole desk: Writing desk with a space between the drawer pedestals for the user's legs.

Knibb: Family of clockmakers based in Oxford and London, late C17 onwards: John, active c1680, made very fine longcase clocks.

knob handles: Term usually applied to the wooden handles found on much late Victorian furniture.

knole settee: Upholstered settee which can be reclined by means of ratchets. First made in early C17.

knop (1): Knob, protuberance or swelling in the stem of a wineglass, of various forms which can be used as an aid to dating and provenance.

knop (2): In furniture, a swelling on an upright member.

knoped spoons: Those made with a decorative knop or finial (Apostle, Virgin, seal-top, etc.) at the opposite end of the stem to the bowl.

Knopf im Ohr: Means "button in ear"; soft toys manufactured by the Steiff company, so called because the trademark was a button in the left ear.

knot: Threads that form the weft of a carpet and loop through the warp to form the pile. The more densely packed the knots the finer the carpet; the quality is sometimes designated by the number of knots per square inch: 150 is average, 500 or more very fine.

knotted pine: Second quality pine which was originally used only when painted. Today the paint is often removed, the knotty appearance having come into favour.

Knowles ware: C19 factory in East Liverpool, Ohio, noted for its thin translucent lotus ware.

Knox, Archibald (1864-1931): English designer of the Cymric range of silverware and Tudric pewter for Liberty's store in London, responsible for some 400 different designs.

knuckle bow: Backward curving quillons on a sword or dagger, designed to protect the knuckles.

knuckle duster gun: Pepperpot pistol with a knuckle duster grip.

knuckle joint: Another name for a finger joint.

knurled foot: Another name for a Spanish foot.

ko kutani: "Old" Kutani ware, made in C17, as distinct from the products of C19 revival more commonly found.

Königsberg: Two factories, both short-lived, producing faience and creamware in Prussia, latter half C18.

Konya: Turkish centre of Kelim production.

Kornilov: Porcelain factory early C19 in St. Petersburg, producing high quality coloured and gilded wares but latterly mass-produced export wares.

kosta glass: From the Swedish glassworks, founded mid C18, noted especially for chandeliers.

kozuka: Japanese sword sheath, usually highly ornamented.

kraak porcelain: Dutch term for porcelain raided from Portuguese carracks (ships). Used to describe the earliest (C16 and C17) Chinese export porcelain.

krater: Ancient Greek bowl for mixing water and wine in which the mouth is always the widest part of the vessel. Variations refer to the shape of the two handles or of the vessel itself e.g. a volute-krater has handles shaped like the volutes on an Ionic capital, a columnkrater has columnar handles; a calyx and bell-krater are shaped like a flower bud and bell respectively.

Kreussen: Bavarian centre of stoneware production since the C17 noted for tankards with applied relief decoration.

kris: Malay or Indonesian dagger with a wavy blade.

Kruse, Käthe: Important German doll maker active from 1912, producing highly realistic imitations of babies, lifesize and filled with sand to imitate the true weight, usually numbered on the left sole of the foot.

ku: Chinese bronze winetasting vessel.

Kuan: Sung dynasty Chinese celadon ware, of greyer colour than usual, often crackle glazed.

kuang: Chinese bronze winetasting storage vessel.

Kuan Yin: Female Buddhist deity of compassion, a popular subject for Chinese potters.

kubachi: C16 and C17 flatware from Iran painted with naturalistic floral patterns, animals and human figures.

kuei: Chinese bronze ritual food-storage vessel.

kufic: Stylized form of Arabic script, often used for quotations from the Koran on Islamic ceramics and carpets.

kukri: Heavy curved Ghurka sword, broadening towards the point.

kula: Nomadic rugs from western Turkey, distinguishable from similar rugs by exclusive use of wool.

Kungsholm: Swedish glassworks, operating late C17 to early C19, noted for elaborate imitations of Venetian and German glass, often decorated with regal emblems or the monarch's initials.

Künnersberg: Bavarian faience wares, especially coffee jugs bearing hunting and sporting scenes, French rococo-style figures, noted for the quality of the draughtsmanship.

kurk: Finest wool, from the sheep's underbelly, used to make the softest carpets.

kutani: Japanese porcelain, similar to Arita ware, painted with blue and white underglaze motifs, first made C17 and revived C19.

Ku yueh hsuan: Chinese Qing dynasty enamelled cameo glass, named after a noted craftsman and imitating contemporary European techniques.

Kuznetzov: Huge Moscow-based ceramic enterprise, responsible for well over half the total Russian production before the Revolution.

kwaart: Clear lead-glaze used over tin-glaze in delftwares to provide the hard, glossy finish.

kwacho: Japanese prints illustrating birds, insects and flowers.

kylin: Mythical Chinese animal, symbol of goodness, with the head of a dragon, body of a deer and tail of a lion.

kylix/cylix: Ancient Greek pottery vessel consisting of a shallow cup on a tall stem.

Kyoto: Capital of Japan under the Shogunate, important centre of porcelain production in the C19.

L

labelled furniture: See trade label.

laburnum: Yellowish brown wood with darker brown streaks. Used as a veneer and particularly attractive when cut as an oyster.

lac burgauté: Chinese lacquer wares inlaid with mother-of-pearl and imported to the West in quantity from late C16.

lacche: Italian term describing painted or lacquered furniture.

lace bobbins: Used in the making of pillow-lace, one attached to each of the threads to hold the thread in place and identify it. From the C16 to the present day. Scores of regional types and names.

ladle: Silver serving spoon, with a deep bowl and long handle. Often made to match a tureen or bowl and used for serving punch, warmed brandy, etc.

Lafayette ware: Glass bottles and flasks, but also ceramics, celebrating the visit of the Marquis de Lafayette to the U.S.A. in 1824.

lair: Elaborately ornamented silver ewer.

Lalique, René (1860-1945): French designer of Art Nouveau jewellery in gold, silver and enamel, who founded his own workshop in Paris in 1885. After 1900 he turned to making figures in

niches, terminating in stylized tulip flowers.

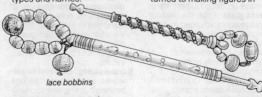

lace bobbins

lace glass: Speciality of Venetian glassmakers who formed a lace-like pattern of fine coloured or plain glass threads which was then enclosed between two layers of glass to form the body of the vessel.

lacework: Lace dipped in slip and applied to the porcelain which burns away in firing but leaves a lacy pattern.

Lacloche Frères: Leading firm of Parisian jewellers, noted for their Art Deco designs.

lacquerware: Oriental objects carved in wood and coated with successive layers of the sap of the lacquer tree which turns hard and black in colour on exposure to sunlight and air. It can then be carved and polished. The sap can also be coloured with various dyes and inlaid with powders, shell, etc.

lacy glass: Pressed glass, originally made early C19 by the Boston and Sandwich Glass Co., with a surface pattern of stippled dots resembling lacework.

ladder back: Descriptive of a country chair which has a series of horizontal bars between the two vertical uprights of the back.

ladik: Turkish prayer rugs ornamented with a pointed niche above three smaller

crystal and opalescent glass. From 1920 he emerged as the leading Art Deco glass maker, and his factory produced a huge range of designs.

Lambeth: Variously, the London factory producing delftware in the early C17 and C18; the factory in the same area established C19 producing stone and earthenwares; and a range of Doulton wares imitating early Italian maiolica, produced late C19.

lambing chair: Sturdy chair with a low seat traditionally used by shepherds at lambing time. It has tall enclosed sides for protection against draughts.

lambrequin (1): Wood or metal cut to imitate hanging drapery.

lambrequin (2): Ornate patterns resembling, or derived from, lacework, used as decorative motifs on ceramics, especially French C17/C18 faience and porcelain.

lamé: In armour, thin overlapping plates designed to allow freedom of movement.

lamellar armour: Armour made almost entirely of small overlapping metal plates to allow maximum freedom of movement.

lamina: Thin metal sheet cut into various human and animal shapes and used to decorate shields in antiquity.

lamp clock: Either a timepiece in which the hours are marked on a glass reservoir and the time is indicated by the falling level of oil as it is consumed by a lighted wick; or a lamp with a clockwork mechanism that pumps the oil from a reservoir to the wick.

Lancaster glass: Coloured glass jugs, bottles and flasks made by the Lancaster Glassworks, New York, established mid C18.

lance: Light cavalry spear with a wooden shaft and metal spike.

lands: Slight projections on the inside of a rifled gun barrel designed to rotate the bullet so that it spins on ejection.

Landsknecht: Swiss name for a professional soldier or mercenary. Often used to describe a C16 halberd, the Landsknecht's most effective weapon.

Lane Delph: C18 Staffordshire pottery, noted for its green-glazed wares, for which Wedgwood worked, and to which he later sent his early creamware products for glazing.

Lange Lijsen: Also known as Long Elizas; slender female figures on Chinese porcelain, copied on Dutch and English blue-painted porcelains.

langet: On a sword or sabre, a quillon, or crosspiece, which forms one continuous piece with the knuckle guard.

lang yao: Chinese name for sang-de-boeuf, or ox-blood glaze, so called for its rich red-brown colour.

lantern clock: Corruption of "latten", German for brass, perhaps because clocks of this form resemble a lantern; weight-driven wall clocks, often ornamented with brass fretwork, with only an hour hand, made from c1600.

lap dovetail: Dovetail joint which leaves the end grain showing on one side only, the other side being left clear for veneering. See also through dovetail.

lapis lazuli: Artificial stone or paste made by grinding silicates of bright ultramarine blue, much used by Ancient Egyptians for decorating jewellery.

lap joint: In silverware, the technique of joining a spoon finial to the stem, formed by cutting the two pieces to be joined into opposing L shapes.

lapped edge: Of Sheffield plate, the sheet silver turned over the edge or lip of the vessel to disguise the copper core, or an extra band of silver applied to the edge and fused to achieve the same effect.

lappet: Small projection or spur found at the top of some legs.

larch: Softwood with a colour that ranges from yellowish white to reddish brown. It was occasionally used as a carcase wood but tends to warp badly.

La Rochelle: Late C18 and C19 faience factory in France, producing wares decorated with historical and commemorative scenes and chinoiserie.

L'Art Nouveau Bing: Applied art commissioned by Samuel Bing for his Parisian shop opened in 1895 to sell the "new art"; later became the accepted name for the Art Nouveau movement.

latten: Archaic German term for brass, still used of older brass objects.

latticino: Glass, made in imitation of Venetian lace glass, containing thin threads of white, sometimes coloured, glass forming a lacy ornament.

lattimo: Opaque white glass; alternative name for milk glass.

lava ware: Purplish blue tableware of the latter half C19 made using iron slag.

laver: Large vessel, usually of metal, for washing the hands or the feet.

lay metal: Cheapest form of pewter, made of 3 parts tin to 1 of lead, used for the most utilitarian objects such as chamber pots.

Lazy Susan: Another name for a dumb waiter.

Leach, Bernard (1887-1979): Father of English craft pottery who studied in China and Japan in order to master oriental glazing techniques.

lead-crystal: Glass containing lead oxide which lends extra strength and brilliance; a formula developed by George Ravenscroft and used almost universally for high quality English glass from 1700.

lead glass: Earliest form of glaze used by early medieval potters, and continued well into C18; impurities, such as iron oxide, produce dull brown, green or yellow flecks and colouration, but the later refined glazes are colourless.

lead statuary: Garden statuary cast in lead, a cheaper alternative to stone, and superseded in the C18 by coade stone.

Le Bourgeoys: Leading French gunsmith, early C17.

Le Creusot: Late C18/early C19 glass from the factory near Sèvres.

Leeds: Yorkshire city producing earthenwares, especially creamware, from the C18, characterized by interlaced and lacy openwork handles.

left-hander: Shortsword or dagger with a large handguard, carried in the left hand to parry sword blows while the right hand carries the rapier.

Lehn ware: Turned and handpainted wooden boxes made C19 by Joseph Lehn of Lancaster County, Pennsylvania.

lekythos: Ancient Greek painted pottery vessels originally made as funeral objects; also used to describe a tall vessel with straight sides, sharp shoulder, tall handle and narrow neck.

Leleu, Jean (1729-1807): French cabinet maker who was taught his trade by Oeben. He was a very talented craftsman.

lemon squeezer: Two-handled implement with a saucer shaped clamp used for extracting the juice from lemons, oranges and limes, from early C19.

Lenci: Italian company manufacturing dolls with pressed felt faces in Turin in the 1920s, noted for the sideways glance of the painted eyes.

Lenzburg: Town in Switzerland producing French-style faience in the mid C18 and enamelled stoves in C19.

Léonard, Agathon: French Art Nouveau sculptor who created a famous gilt bronze series "Le jeu de l'écharpe" at the turn of the century, inspired by the dancer Löie Fuller whose movements were regarded as the epitome of fluidity, much admired by artists of the genre.

Lepage: Leading Parisian gunsmith, mid C19.

lesghistan: Brightly coloured woollen rugs from the eastern Caucasus, up to 10ft (3m) long but rarely more than 3ft (1m) wide.

Les Islettes: Factory in the Lorraine region of France producing traditional faience wares, late C18/C19.

letter rack: Originally, in the late C18, in silver, later of plate, wood or papier mâché, a stand like a toast-rack with vertical divisions for storing letters.

lever escapement: Mid C18 modification to the anchor escapement which made portable clocks and watches possible; the pallets which restrain the escape wheel are positioned either end of a lever which see-saws on a central pivot when rocked by a pin attached to the balance wheel.

Le Verrier, Max: French designer, famous for Art Deco figures in bronze and spelter.

Liao dynasty: Period in Chinese history AD 907-1125.

Libbey glass: Cut and pressed glass wares from the factory in Toledo, Ohio, established late C19.

Liberty & Co.: Principal outlet for Art Nouveau designs in England. Arthur Lasenby Liberty (1843-1917) founded his furniture and drapery shop in 1875. Later he commissioned designs exclusive to his store, including Cymric silver and Tudric pewter, which gave rise to a distinctive "Liberty style".

liberty glass: Cut and pressed glass wares made in New Jersey and the Mid West, late C19.

library chair: Another name for a reading chair.

library steps: Set of steps used as an aid when reaching books on a high shelf. Two main types; either fixed steps which may have a handrail, or folding

steps which usually form or fit into another piece of furniture.

library table: Name give to a particular type of rectangular table with frieze drawers, end supports and a central stretcher.

Liège glass: Made from the C16 onwards, often in imitation of Venetian forms.

lighthouse clock: Rare early C19 mantel clock in the form of a lighthouse, the dial enclosed in the glass lantern.

lignum vitae: Exceptionally dense wood which is dark brown with black streaks. Imported from the West Indies and used both solid and as a veneer.

Ligron: French factory producing lead glazed earthenwares and stonewares decorated with grotesque high relief human and animal figures.

Lilihan: Carpets from the Hamadan region of Western Iran, decorated with stylized flowers in bold colours.

Lille: French factory producing delftware from late C17 decorated with chinoiserie and baroque figures.

Lilliput range: Figures made by W. Britain Ltd to match the scale of OO and HO model railway gauges.

Limbach: Factory in Thuringia, Germany, founded late C18 and producing close imitations of Meissen figures.

lime: Whitish wood which is excellent for carving.

lime glass: Glass containing powdered limestone for strength and brilliance; lighter than lead glass and used from the mid C19 for cheaper glasswares.

Limoges: Variously used to describe late C18 porcelain in the Sèvres style, C19 wares imitating medieval Limoges enamel work and, in America, imported French, or domestically produced French-style porcelain.

Limoges enamel: Enamelled copper from the Central French town made from the early middle ages to the present.

line inlay: American term for stringing.

linen chest: Mix between a chest and a chest of drawers which typically has nine or twelve drawers and sometimes a lift-up top, in which case some or all of the drawers may be false.

linenfold: Carved decoration which resembles folded linen.

linen press (1): Frame which houses a wooden screw used to press linen between two boards.

linen press (2): Cupboard containing sliding shelves and raised above a series of drawers. Used for storing clothes and linen.

Lines Brothers: Manufacturers of mass-produced clockwork locomotives and other toys from c1910.

Ling zhi: Floral motif first found on C16 Chinese porcelain made during the reign of Jijing.

lining: Back and sides of a drawer.

lion mask: Carved decoration shaped as a lions' head. Also a type of brass ring handle in the form of a lions' head.

lion séjant: Seated lion, knop motif on early spoons, from C16.

lipp-work: Type of basketwork used to make chairs, cradles etc.

Lisbon: Portuguese maiolica, not necessarily produced in Lisbon, made from early C17 with Chinese-influenced designs painted in blue.

Li shui: Chinese name for Sung dynasty celadon wares.

lit de repos: Type of early French day bed which later developed into the sofa.

lit en bateau: Type of French bed with a canopy above and curtains around it.

lithyalin glass: Opaque coloured and marbled glass, invented by Egermann in Bohemia, 1828, in imitation of precious stones.

Liverpool: Important pottery production centre from the mid C18, noted for blue-painted delftware punch bowls, and early porcelain produced by several different factories, now eagerly collected.

livery cupboard: Three-tiered structure similar to a court cupboard except that the centre tier comprises an enclosed compartment, usually with canted sides.

loaded: In silverware, a hollow part of a vessel, usually a candlestick, filled with pitch or sand for weight and stability.

lobby chest: Small chest of drawers specifically designed for use in a small study or lobby.

lobster-tail helmet: C17 cavalry helmet; the neckpiece consists of flexible overlapping plates, like a lobster tail, and the face guard consists of a grill, like an American footballer's head piece.

lock: Firing mechanism of a gun.

locket: Item of jewellery made to enclose a lock of hair, used both as a love token and as mourning jewellery, from c1690.

locking plate: Alternative name for the countwheel, which controls the number of times a clock strikes on the hour.

lockplate (1): Plate which protects a keyhole.

lockplate (2): The base, or support, on a gun barrel to which the lock, or firing mechanism, is attached.

Loetz: German glassmakers based at Klöstermühle, Bohemia, which first produced iridescent glass in 1873.

London Armoury: Gunmakers from the mid C19.

long arm: Firearm with a long barrel, particularly common in early firearms where the length of the barrel assisted the aim and accuracy of the shot.

longcase clock: First made c1660 in England, a tall clock consisting of a case which houses the weights or pendulum and a hood housing the movement and dial. In U.S.A. also known as a tallcase clock.

Longqing (Lung Chinq): Chinese Ming dynasty emperor, 1567-1572.

Longton Hall: First porcelain factory in Staffordshire, founded 1749 but closed in 1760 so all products now rare and collectable, even though not especially refined.

loo table: Oval tilt-top table made during the Victorian period for playing "loo", a card game.

loper (1): Slide of wood which pulls out to support the fall front of a bureau when open. Also known as a bearer.

loper (2): Strengthening support typically found under the top of a small tea or occasional table. Also known as a bearer.

lotus ware: Thin-bodied porcelain with a mother-of-pearl sheen produced by the Knowles factory, East Liverpool, Ohio, late C19/C20.

Louis XIV: King of France 1643-1715. His long reign saw the growth of the Baroque style, exemplified by Versailles.

Louis XV: King of France 1715-74. The rococo style became popular in his reign.

Louis XVI: King of France 1774-93. The neo-classical style began to influence design.

Louisville: Coloured glasswares, flasks and bottles from the Kentucky factory, mid C19.

love seat: Settee formed as two seats side by side but facing in opposite directions. Also called a tête à tête seat.

lowboy: Name now given to a small dressing table, usually with either a single frieze drawer or a small central shallow drawer flanked on either side by a deep drawer.

lowdin ware: Soft-paste porcelain produced at Lowdin's factory, Bristol, c1750.

low dresser: See dresser.

Lowenthal & Co.: C19 German maker of papier mâché dolls.

Lowestoft: Suffolk town producing chinoiserie porcelain from the latter half C18; also a term used for Chinese export wares, imported through the port of Lowestoft, and re-exported to America.

low relief: Another name for bas relief.

lozenge: Carved decoration of diamond shape but with a horizontal axis.

Lucotte: French manufacturer of solid toy soldiers, 1790-1900.

lunette ornament: Carved decoration in the form of repeated semicircles which are usually embellished by floral or other decoration.

Lunéville: French factory in the Lorraine district producing faience-fine from the late C18.

Lung ch'uan: Sung dynasty celadon, characterized by its lustrous blue-green glaze.

luristan: High quality rugs patterned with abstract flower designs from southwest Iran.

lustre (1): Thin metallic film applied to the surface of

ceramics or glass to create a
metallic sheen.

lustre (2): C18 name for a
chandelier.

luting: Slip used to attach
applied ornamentation to a
ceramic body.

Lyman & Howe: Pittsfield
clockmakers, active 1785-
1800.

Lyons: French pottery centre,
noted for early tin-glazed wares
similar to Italian maiolica, blue
and white wares and yellow
painted decoration.

lyre: Descriptive of furniture
components, particularly some
chair backs and table supports,
which are shaped like the
musical instrument.

lyre clock: Early C19 American
pendulum clock, its shape
resembling that of a lyre.

M

Macbeth, Ann: Scottish Arts
and Crafts embroiderer.

**MacDonald, Frances (1874-
1921)**: Scottish artist and
designer of the Glasgow
School, specializing in enamel
and metalwork; also known as
Frances MacNair.

**MacDonald, Margaret (1865-
1933)**: Scottish artist and
designer of the Glasgow
School, married to Charles
Rennie Mackintosh.

mace: Originally a medieval club
or mallet used in battle, with a
round metal head, sometimes
spiked. Later a staff of office
resembling the weapon.

Macham, Samuel: London
maker of fine longcase clocks,
active 1700-15.

machete: Curving axe-type
weapon with a steel grip.

**Mackintosh, Charles Rennie
(1868-1928)**: Important
Scottish architect and designer
during the Arts and Crafts
period. He originally produced
graphic work and repoussé
metalwork in conventional Art
Nouveau style, but from the
1890s developed a distinctive,
simplified style highly
influential on Viennese
furniture and architecture.

**Mackmurdo, Arthur H. (1851-
1942)**: One of the fathers of
the Art Nouveau style. In 1882
he founded the Century Guild
of craftsmen and their
magazine, *The Hobby Horse*,
published from 1884, predates
the ornamental styles
developed by Morris & Co.

MacNair, Herbert (b.1870):
Scottish architect and
craftsman, associated with the
Glasgow School.

macramé: Form of lacework
consisting of threads knotted
together to form running
fringes or friezes.

maculated: Antique dealers'
term meaning spotted or
stained; usually used of books,
prints or textiles.

Madeley: Soft-paste porcelain
manufactured by Thomas
Randell in Shropshire, early
C19.

made up: Trade term to
describe a piece which has
been constructed from old
materials but which is not
genuine.

Madhen: Western Turkish
prayer rugs, principally made
for export.

Madras: Large Indian carpets
made late C19/early C20 for
export to Europe.

magascope: Alternative name
for a magic lantern.

Magdeburg: German city
producing brightly coloured
faience in C18.

magic lantern: Machine
equipped with a lamp and
lenses for projecting the image
present on a glass or
photographic slide.

magnum: Large glass for wine
and spirits, or a bottle designed
to hold two quarts.

mahal: Western Iranian carpets,
loosely woven but
characteristically soft,
decorated with floral and
geometrical motifs.

mahogany: Spanish mahogany
was first imported into Britain
in the 1720s and is hard and
dark with a slight grain. Cuban
mahogany was imported from
the mid C18. It is a richer and
lighter colour with a more
figured grain and is easier to
work. Honduras mahogany,
also known as baywood, was
imported during the second
half of the C18. It has an open
grain, is lighter in weight and
fades to a lighter tone.

maidenhead knop: Spoon finial
or knop in the shape of the
head and bust of a woman,
from the C16.

maiolica: Tin-glazed
earthenwares from Italy,
produced since the C14.

mainspring: In firearms, the
powerful spring that forces the
cock to strike the steel, or the
hammer to strike the firing pin.

91

maintaining power: Subsidiary spring which keeps a clock movement going while the mainspring is being wound.

Maison Cardeilhac: French silver company, established in 1804 to make cutlery and flatware, but under Ernest Cardeilhac (1851-1904) it became famous for Art Nouveau designs in gold and silver.

Maison Vever: French jeweller's founded by Ernest Vever whose sons, Paul and Henri, made it a leading outlet for Art Nouveau designs.

majolica: Often used, in error, as an alternative spelling for maiolica; correctly, a richly-enamelled stoneware with high relief decoration developed by Minton, mid C19.

Majorelle, Louis (1859-1926): French furniture designer who inherited his father's business in Nancy in 1879 and was, by 1900, the leading Art Nouveau furniture supplier in France.

makie-shi: Master craftsman in a Japanese lacquerware workshop.

Makkum: Dutch C18 factory in Friesland specializing in tin-glazed tiles and earthenware.

malaga work: Hispano-Moresque earthenwares with a gold lustre, produced in Valencia, Spain, from C14.

mallet decanter: Early C18 type with a hexagonal or octagonal body, squared shoulder and a long neck.

mamluk (1): Egyptian carpets of the C15 and C16, named after the ruling dynasty.

mamluk (2): Polychrome pottery produced in Egypt and Syria in the C13 and C15, exported to Europe in great quantity for storing spices and medicines.

Manardi maiolica: From Angarano, in the Veneto, north eastern Italy, made by the Manardi brothers C16/C17, decorated with very fine landscape paintings and flowers on a pearly white ground.

Mandarin china: Chinese porcelain exported to Europe late C18, and exceptionally ornate with painted figures framed in red, pink and gold panels.

manifer: In armour, an iron plated glove for the left hand, used in jousting.

Manises lustreware: Hispano-Moresque earthenwares with a golden lustre, made from C15 in the Manises region and in France by itinerant potters from that area of Spain.

manju: Netsuke of round flat shape carved in relief, named after similarly shaped sweetmeats.

mantel clock: Clock provided with feet to stand on the mantelpiece.

mantelpiece: Ornate frame surrounding a fireplace, incorporating a shelf and, in original examples, a matching mantel mirror (or chimney glass) or an overmantel.

mantling: In heraldry, the plumes of feathers or drapery on either side of a crest, or helmet, on a coat of arms.

mantua: Early C19 coloured glasswares from the factory at Mantua, Ohio.

manx foot: Chair or table foot which appears as a flatsoled shoe, complete with heel.

maple: Pale yellow wood with a close grain which is subject to a variety of markings. It is good for turning but was used mainly as a veneer.

Marieburg: Swedish factory founded 1758, noted for fine figures in tin-glazed earthenware, imitating porcelain.

marine chronometer: Timepiece of very great accuracy made for use at sea as a navigational aid.

Markham, Markwick: Noted London clockmaker active 1720-60.

Marlborough leg: Tapering leg of square section with a collar above a block foot. Used in C18.

Marot, Daniel (c1662-1752): Huguenot craftsman and designer who produced fine furniture in the Louis XIV style for the Royal households during the William and Mary period.

marotte: Doll on a stick which plays a tune when spun round.

marouflage: Scarlet coloured cloth backing to pierced lockplates.

marqueterie de verre: Marquetry in glass; a technique developed by Emile Gallé in which pieces of semi-molten coloured glass are set into the body of a glass vessel while the latter is still soft. Many pieces cracked in the process and examples are now rare. Most are signed by the artist.

marquetry: Design formed from different coloured woods veneered onto a carcase to give a decorative effect. Many early examples are Dutch.

marquise: Jewel cut into a pointed oval shape, especially for brooches and rings.

marquise chair: Wide French chair which can seat two people, much the same as a causeuse. They were made in C17 and early C18.

marriage: The joining together of two unrelated parts to form one piece of furniture.

marriage chest: Another name for a dower chest.

marriage cup: Venetian glass goblet, C15 and C16, decorated with enamel portraits of the bride and groom; later used of any vessel decorated to commemorate a wedding.

marriage plate: Pewter plates either made specifically to commemorate a marriage, with names, date and message; or one scratched or incised with a similar inscription.

marrow scoop: Mid C18 silver implement with a long narrow bowl for extracting the marrow from meat bones.

marrow spoon: Early C18 silver implement with an ordinary spoon bowl on one end but with a stem in the form of a marrow scoop.

Marseilles: French ceramic centre noted for colourful faience from the latter half C17.

Marseille, Armand: Prolific German maker of bisque head and composition dolls, 1865-1920.

martel de fer: Short-handled pickaxe, used in medieval warfare to pierce an opponent's armour.

martelé: Form of faceted glass, made to resemble hammered metal, invented by the Daum Brothers and used for their Art Nouveau glass.

Martin, Edmund: London maker of longcase clocks, active latter half C18.

Martin Brothers: Robert, Charles, Walter and Edwin. They founded the Fulham pottery in 1873, moved to Southall in 1877 and continued in production until 1914.

Martinware: Art pottery made by the Martin brothers between 1873 and 1914, characterized by grotesque human and animal figures in stoneware.

Mary Gregory: Inexpensive glassware painted with figures of children; late C19 European but also made at the Sandwich glassworks, Massachusetts and supposedly named after a female artist who, in fact, may never have existed.

Maryland pottery: Stoneware and earthenware made in Baltimore from c1800; Edwin Bennett's factory is the best known.

mascots: Figures made as trade marks for car radiators and bonnets, from c1900.

Mason, Charles James: Staffordshire potter who gave his name to the ironstone he patented in 1813.

Massachusetts clock: Early C19 form of wall clock associated with the Willard family of Massachusetts in which the case containing the movement sits on top of a box containing the weights or pendulum.

Massy: Noted family of London clockmakers, active mid C17 to early C18.

match: In early firearms, cord soaked in saltpetre and dried to provide a slow-burning material used to ignite the priming powder.

Matchbox toys: Die cast toys made by the Lesney Toys company from 1952, so called because they were originally sold in matchbox size packages. Now highly collectable.

matchlock: Earliest form of
firing mechanism, invented in
C14 and superseded by the
wheellock and flintlock in C17.
The serpentine holds a match
(cord saturated with saltpetre),
which pivots when the trigger
is depressed, bringing the
lighted match into contact with
the powder in the priming pan.

McIntire, Samuel (1757-1811):
American architect and wood
carver who worked in Salem.
His son Samuel was also a
carver.

Meakin ironstone: Made in the
factory of James and George
Meakin, in Staffordshire and
exported in quantity to
America, first half C19.

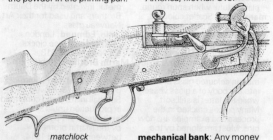

matchlock

matted silver: Either treated
with acid or covered in closely
spaced punched holes to give a
matt, non-shiny surface,
usually as the background to a
relief design.

mauchline ware: Souvenir or
commemorative boxes, needle
cases, napkin rings and eggs
made of varnished and transfer
printed wood, made by A & A
Smith in Mauchline, Ayrshire
(later Birmingham) from c1820
to the 1930s.

Maw: Factory in Broseley,
Shropshire, specializing in
reproduction maiolica tiles,
latter half C19.

Maximilian: Highly ornate
German Renaissance armour
named after Emperor
Maximilian I (1494-1519).
Often reproduced in C19.

Maya: Mesoamerican culture of
c200 BC-AD 900 based around
the Yucatan peninsula.

Mayhew, Thomas: See Ince,
William.

mazarine (1): Rich deep blue
colour, characteristic of Sèvres
porcelain; also found as a
background colour on English
soft-paste porcelain and bone
china.

mazarine (2): Dish liner, usually
silver, with pierced decorative
patterns, used as a stand for
either roast meat or fish, so
that the juices drain into the
larger dish below.

mazlaghan: Persian carpets
characterized by the zig-zag
edge to the field, in contrast to
the usual linear border.

mechanical bank: Any money
box which has moving parts
activated when the coin is
dropped.

medallion: Egg-shaped,
diamond-shaped or circular
framed design, usually the
centrepiece of Persian carpets.

medicine chest: Used by
itinerant medics from C17,
usually with compartments,
labelled bottles, spoons and
balances.

medieval: Period from the
decline of the Roman Empire in
the C4 to the beginning of the
Renaissance, early in C14.

medullary rays: Dense fibres
which radiate from the centre
of a piece of cut timber in the
form of lines or "rays".

meerschaum pipe: Tobacco
pipe with a bowl carved from
magnesium silicate, made
from c1800.

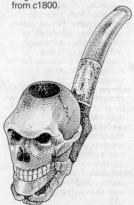

mehrschichtenglas: Inexpensive multi-layered glass, developed in Bohemia, early C19, and engraved to reveal one or more layers of colour.

Meigh pottery: From the Staffordshire pottery of the Meigh family, best known for Charles Meigh's gothic-style stoneware jugs, mid C19.

Meiji: Period in Japanese history, 1868 to 1912, when the nation's art was much influenced by contact with the West, and much was made specifically for export.

meillonas: Marseilles-influenced French faience from the Ain district, noted for the quality of the painted decoration, late C18.

Mei p'ing: Chinese for cherry blossom, used to describe a tall vase, with high shoulders, small neck and narrow mouth, used to display flowering branches.

Meissen: First European porcelain factory, founded 1710 and renowned for figures modelled in the 1730s and 1740s, widely imitated throughout Europe.

melon bulb: See Portuguese swell.

Mendlesham chair: Distinct type of country chair from the village in Suffolk of that name. Typically with a saddle seat and a squarish back which incorporates several small wooden balls in the design.

Mennecy: Porcelain factory at Mennecy-Villeroy, outside Paris, mid C18, noted for novelty items such as snuffboxes and walking-stick heads.

menuisier: Old French name for a craftsman who made furniture from plain or carved wood, as distinct from veneered items.

Mercury: Roman messenger of the gods, equivalent to the Greek deity Hermes.

mercury twist: Air twist of silvery colour or especial brightness.

merese: Glass discs used to join the bowl of a glass to the stem, the stem to the foot, or different parts of the stem.

meridienne: Regency name for a settee with scrolled ends, one higher than the other.

merryman plates: Sets of 6 to 8 delftware plates decorated with humorous verses and scenes from marital life, popular in England late C17.

Meshed: North-east Iranian centre of carpet production, noted for the use of deep pink; products usually have a central medallion and flower motifs.

Mesoamerican: Civilizations of middle-America, corresponding approximately to modern Mexico and noted for their artistic achievements: Aztec, Classic, Maya, Miztec, Teotihuacan, Toltec, Zapotec.

Mesopotamian wares: Rare and valuable polychromatic pottery produced in Mesopotamia in the C9 and C10 showing Oriental influence.

metropolitan slipware: From an untraced London pottery, lead glazed slipware of C17 often bearing Puritan mottoes.

meuble à hauteur d'appui: French term for a low cupboard or bookcase.

mezza-maiolica: Italian whiteslipped earthenware with sgraffito decoration, and sometimes green and orange dabs of colour, C14 to C17.

mezzotint: Prints made from engraved copper or steel plates treated so as to achieve subtle tonal gradations.

mianeh: Literally "half"; the term used to denote the size of a carpet.

Mies van der Rohe, Ludwig (1886-1969): German born modernist architect and furniture designer who moved to Illinois to escape Nazi persecution in 1938 and developed a form of architecture based on simple, functional cubic forms. He is best known for his 1929 "Barcelona" chair.

Mignot: French manufacturer of solid cast toy soldiers and other solid, flat and hollow figures, since 1830.

mihrab: Prayer niche with a pointed arch; the motif distinguishes a prayer rug from other types.

Milan: C18 centre of maiolica production, noted for chinoiserie flatware.

milas/melas/milis: Turkish prayer rugs; typically with a mihrab and tree-of-life on a terracotta ground with a yellow border.

mildner: Late C18 Bohemian glassware; double walled with internal decoration in gold, silver or enamel.

military chest: Chest of drawers designed for travelling. It has no protruding parts and has metal mounts to protect the corners. Made in strong woods such as teak and padouk.

milk glass: Glass made with tin oxide which makes it white and opaque like porcelain; developed C15 in Venice, much used by Bohemian glassmakers, who applied enamel designs, and for pressed glass in C19.

millefiori: Multi-coloured, or mosaic, glass, made since antiquity by fusing a number of coloured glass rods into a cane, and cutting off thin sections; much used to ornament paperweights.

Minerva: Roman goddess of wisdom and of war, equivalent to the Greek goddess Pallas Athene.

Ming dynasty: Period in Chinese history from 1368 to 1644.

miniature book: Those measuring less than 3 × 2in (7.5 × 5cm). From c1773 almanacs, church calendars, tide tables, etc. produced in this way for portability; most C19 examples produced as children's books or novelties.

Minoan: Art of the civilization which flourished in Crete from 3000 to 1400 BC, named after the royal line of legendary king Minos.

minster jug: Popular form in stoneware, decorated with figures of the apostles under gothic canopies, modelled in high relief; all in imitation of the original patented by Charles Meigh, latter half C19.

Minton: Pottery established by Thomas Minton, at Stoke-on-Trent, in late C18. Originally produced earthenwares and creamware; then, most famously, bone china. After 1850 the company produced fine copies of Renaissance maiolica and, in 1870, set up the Minton Art Pottery Studio in London as a training academy for young designers, producing fine Art Nouveau work.

miquelet lock: Early form of flintlock firing mechanism, developed primarily in the Mediterranean in early C17, and second only in popularity to the French lock. The distinguishing feature is that the mainspring is fitted on the outside, rather than within, the lockplate.

mir: Persian rug with an allover palm motif pattern, originally made in the village of Mirabad.

mira/miri: Palm-leaf motif used to decorate Oriental carpets.

mirror clock: One incorporating a looking-glass, an early C19 New England type.

mirror stand: Adjustable mirror on a pole with a tripod base.

Mirzapur: Town in India producing white carpets, usually with a very fluffy pile.

mitre joint: Rightangled joint where two surfaces are fitted together, each cut at 45°.

Miztec: Mesoamerican culture, of the period AD 900-1521.

mocha ware: Decoration on early C19 earthenware imitating Mocha stone, a chalcedony that often has inclusions of fossil ferns and mosses; dabs of colour are applied to wet slip so that the colour spreads.

Model Home Farm: Scale figures made by W. Britain Ltd from 1923.

Modelled Miniatures: Model cars produced by Meccano Ltd in 1933; in April 1934 the range was extended and the name changed to Dinky Toys.

Modernist: One of the most influential of the stylistic movements that arose after World War I in reaction to Art Nouveau, and one which emphasized the functional; its designers preferred modern materials, such as plastic and steel, and were influenced by Cubist art.

modillion: Series of brackets used to support a cornice.

Moko pottery: Inexpensive form of mocha ware; colour splashed or spattered onto the body before firing.

mokume: Japanese lacquerware made to imitate wood grain.

molinet: Stick used for mixing and stirring milk and chocolate in a chocolate pot: usually of precious hardwood with silver mounted ornaments.

moliquet: Alternative name for molinet.

momento mori spoons: Late C16 and C17 spoons, especially of Scottish origin, with a disc finial engraved with a skull, often with a motto associated with death on the handle.

Momoyama: Period of Japanese history 1573-1615 during which (c1598) Korean potters based at Kyushu introduced glazing techniques.

mon: Japanese heraldic emblem indicating the status or the family of the owner.

mondscheinglas: Moonshine glass; blue, semi-opaque glass developed by Emile Galllep´,, late C19.

monkey orchestra: Figures of monkeys playing musical instruments, first produced at Meissen, later much copied.

monk's bench: Incorrect term sometimes used to describe a table-chair or similar piece.

monopodium (1): Type of table support comprising a solid-looking three or four sided pillar, usually on paw feet and mainly found on drum and rent tables.

monopodium (2): Furniture leg carved as an animal's limb with a paw, and usually found on console or pier tables.

Montanari, Augusta and Richard: Mid C19 London makers of poured wax dolls.

monteith: Large silver bowl with a shallow, often detachable, rim with scalloped recesses from which wine glasses were suspended to cool over iced water.

montelupo maiolica: Produced in Tuscany, C15 to C17, characterized by bold painting covering the whole surface of the vessel.

Montereau: French factory producing earthenwares and faience-fine, C18 and C19.

month clock: One that will run for 32 days without rewinding.

montmorency: Curved, single edged blade with one shallow and one narrow fuller on each face.

Montpellier: Faience production centre near Marseilles, France, from the C16, noted for late C16/C17 pharmaceutical jars.

moonshine glass: Mondscheinglas; blue, semi-opaque glass developed by Emile Gallé, late C19.

moonstone glass: Alternative name for white milk glass.

moonwork: That part of some clock mechanisms that drives a display showing the phases of the moon.

Moorcroft, William (1872-1946): Staffordshire art potter, who worked for Macintyre & Co. from 1898, and set up independently in 1913. Known for colourful vases with floral designs and his "Florian" and "Aurelian" wares.

Moore, Bernard: Founder of art pottery based in Longton, Staffordshire, c1900 specializing in unusual glaze effects.

Moorfields: English carpets of the latter half C18 handmade in London, including some designed by Robert Adam.

moquette: Wool, linen or cotton cloth treated to resemble silk or velvet. Often used in modern carpet production instead of true knotting to give the appearance of a pile, and for upholstery materials.

mori (1): Carpet sellers' term indicating that a rug is made in Pakistan – usually in imitation of Persian styles.

Mori (2): Town in Afghanistan, centre for the production of some of that country's finest rugs.

morion: C16 and C17 infantry helmet, of tall domed shape with a rim and upturned peak at front and rear.

Morland barometer: One made by Sir Samuel Morland who patented the diagonal barometer, and made fine examples 1720-50.

morning star: Medieval club or flail with a heavy spiked head.

Morris, William (1834-96): Regarded as the progenitor of the Art Nouveau style. The company Morris, Marshall and Faulkner (later simply Morris & Co.) was founded in 1861 to produce wallpaper, stained glass, chintz carpets and tapestries. The origins of his style can be traced to medieval Gothic, but his organic flowers and bird motifs encouraged later artists to seek inspiration for their designs in nature.

mortar: Vessel for grinding foodstuffs and medicines.

mortar stand: Any small stand,

the top of which is designed to hold a small domestic mortar.

mortise and tenon: Type of joint. The mortise is a cavity, the tenon is a shaped end designed to fit into it exactly to form a joint. It is then held in place by dowels.

mortise lock: Lock which is set into the edge of the door and is concealed from view.

Mortlake: Long-established factory in south-west London producing household stoneware, delftware and earthenwares; an art pottery studio established c1900 in the same district specializing in glaze effects.

mortuary chair: Victorian term to describe those Yorkshire chairs which have a carved bearded head in their backs. This was popularly supposed to represent the severed head of Charles I.

mortuary sword: C17 straight-bladed longsword with a shell and basket hilt, so called because the hilt is often crudely carved with the head of Charles I.

Moser, Kolomann (1868-1918): Austrian graphic artist and influential figure in the Viennese Arts and Crafts movement; one of the founders of the Viennese Secession in 1897 and of the Wiener Werkstätte in 1901.

Moser, Ludwig (1833-1916): German glassmaker who founded a factory at Karlsbad in 1857 manufacturing engraved glass and later iridescent glass imitating Tiffany's "Favrile".

mote skimmer: Simple spoon with a perforated bowl designed for removing floating tea-leaves from tea-cups, C18.

mote skimmer

mother-of-pearl: Slices of shell which are used for inlay.

motif: Design element, usually repeated to create a complex pattern.

moton: In armour, a plate that protects the armpit.

moulded glass: Glassware produced in quantity to the same pattern by forcing glass into a mould using air pressure.

moulding (1): Shaped strip of wood applied either as decoration or to conceal a joint.

moulding (2): Originally any ornament cast in a mould. Now any shaped projection, carved in wood or stone or cast in plaster.

Moulins: Faience production centre in Central France, noted for elaborate rococo designs.

Mount Vernon: Blown-moulded glassware from the Mount Vernon works, New York, C19.

Mount Washington: C19 factory established in New Bedford, Massachusetts, producing art glass.

mourning jewellery: Black jewellery, usually of jet, but also made of the hair of the deceased, worn during the period of mourning.

Moustiers: One of Europe's chief faience production centres from C17. In southern France; noted for blue and white decoration based on the engravings of Jean Bérain, and for grotesques.

Moutesham Kashan: Antique Kashan rug, over 100 years old.

mouthpiece: Widest part of a scabbard into which the ricasso of a sword fits.

Mucha, Alphonso Maria (1861-1931): Czech-born artist and illustrator who worked in Paris and the U.S.A., best known for his posters publicizing Sarah Bernhardt but also a designer of jewellery, textiles, furniture and applied art.

mud: Pronounced *mood*; fine rugs from the Khorassan region of north-east Iran, often with colourful designs.

Mudge, Thomas: Important C18 clockmaker based in London and credited with the invention of the lever escapement.

mudjur: Turkish prayer rugs, characteristically with bright green, blue and yellow designs on a deep red ground.

muff pistol: Handgun for self-defence, carried inside a muff.

mulberry: Hard yellowish brown wood with dark streaks. Used as a veneer.

mule chest: Chest with one or two drawers in the lower part, a cross between a chest and a chest of drawers.

Müller & Strassberger: C19 German makers of papier mâché dolls.

muntin: Central upright connecting the top and bottom rails of a frame.

Muntz's metal: Early C19 copper and zinc alloy originally developed for ship's hulls but also used for decorative objects because of its resemblance to gold.

mural cupboard: Small hanging cupboard for storing salt and spices, etc. in the C17 and early C18.

Murano: Alternative name for Venetian glass.

Muromachi: Also known as Ahikaga era, the period of Japanese history AD 1338-1573.

murrhine glass: Ancient Roman glass containing murra, a type of fluorspar, often very delicate but strong. Revived as a trade-name for similar art glass in the late C19.

mushkabad: Small central Iranian rugs decorated with floral motifs.

musical clock: One with a cylinder and pins which drive a series of hammers that strike bells and play one or more tunes.

musician's chair: Distinct type of chair of elegant appearance with a low back and sides and usually on cabriole legs.

music stand: Tall stand for holding sheet music.

musket: Infantry soldiers' firearm whose essential form did not change from the C16 to the C19, though the length of the barrel was progressively reduced from 5ft (1.6m) to just over 3ft (1m) and the firing mechanism developed from the match, to the wheel and then to the flintlock. The bore was smooth (not rifled).

musketoon: Name sometimes given to a short barrelled musket, or to a blunderbuss.

Mycenaean: Ancient Greek objects, dating principally to the 2nd millennium BC.

myriopticon: Greek for "a thousand pictures". Mid C19 American mechanical peepshow in which pictures printed on a reel are wound from spool to spool.

mysterious/mystery clock: One usually of novel and ornate form in which the movement is ingeniously disguised or concealed.

N

nabeshima: Japanese porcelain of rich enamel colours and underglaze blue designs made only for the aristocracy.

nail-head decoration: Carved decoration resembling square heads of nails and found from the Middle Ages to the C17.

Nailsea: Factory near Bristol, established late C18, famous for novelty glass objects (rolling pins, walking sticks, etc.) decorated with bold, colourful twists. Subsequently any similar glass article, no matter where produced.

nain: Carpets from central Iran, densely woven with naturalistic allover flower decoration.

name chest: Term sometimes applied to chests which bear the name of the original owner either carved or painted on it.

Nankin: Generic name for Chinese wares exported through the port of Nanking in late C18/C19, especially willow-pattern.

Nankin yellow: Yellow glaze associated with Chinese Nankin export pottery of late C18/C19, often in association with blue and white wares.

Nantgarw: Factory near Cardiff specializing in brilliant white translucent soft-paste porcelain, founded by William Billingsley early C19.

napery drawer: Drawer in which it is particularly appropriate to keep table linen, such as might be found in a sideboard.

napier's bones: Simple calculator using sticks of ivory, wood or bone which are distributed into numbered compartments. Named after the mathematician John Napier (1550-1617).

napkin holder: Either a silver clip for attaching the napkin to a collar or shirt front, or a silver ring for tidying away a rolled napkin.

Naples: Porcelain factory founded in Naples under royal patronage, late C18, noted for classical figures in glassy soft-paste porcelain.

Neo-Greek: Term sometimes used to describe early C19 classical revival furniture in America, c1815-1840.

Neolithic: In Europe, the period c3000-1700 BC; leaf arrowheads, polished flint axes and crude pottery first produced at this time.

Neptune: Roman god of the sea, equivalent to the Greek god Poseidon.

nest of tables: Set of matching tables of graduating size, each one neatly storing beneath the next largest when not in use. There are either three or four tables in a set; if four they are also known as quartetto tables.

nest toys: Toys such as Russian dolls, eggs, houses or churches made in diminishing sizes so that each fits inside the next largest.

nest toys

Nara: Period of Japanese history AD 710-94.

nashiji: Japanese lacquerwork design incorporating strewn gold particles.

National Watch Company: Of Elgin, Illinois, makers of mass produced but fine quality watches from 1864 to the 1960s.

nautilus: Large sea-shell, with a mother-of-pearl interior, mounted on a silver stand and ornamented with nautical figures. Usually used as a drinking vessel.

neck ring: Ring around the neck of glass decanters whose form helps in dating.

needle gun: First gun in which the cartridge was fired by the impact of a needle; an early C19 German invention.

nef: Highly ornate silver salt container, usually of French or German origin.

Neo-classical: Style of architecture, furniture and ornamentation developed in late C18 by Robert Adam and others, using classical motifs but in an entirely new way.

netsuke: Japanese carved toggles made to secure sagemono ("hanging things") to the obi (waist belt) from a cord; usually of ivory, lacquer, silver or wood, from the C16.

netsuke-shi: Japanese master craftsman specializing in the carving of netsuke.

Neve, Henry: Noted Huguenot clockmaker, active in London 1700-20.

Nevers: French center of faience production since the C16. Gave its name to pottery decorated with pastoral scenes produced all over France in C18.

New Amsterdam: Glass from one of two C17 producers working in the Dutch colony that became New York. Collectible, even though most extant examples are now suspected to be later fakes.

New Bremen: Glass tableware from the works in Maryland, C18.

New Canton: Soft-paste porcelain made at Stratford-le-Bow, London, mid C18.

Newcastle: English center of glass production, noted for C18 enameled glassware; also a wine glass with a conical bowl and stem with multiple knops.

New Chelsea: Reproductions of Chelsea and other C18/C19 porcelain made at the factory in Longton, Staffordshire, founded early C20.

Newcomb: Art Nouveau earthenware from the pottery founded at Newcomb College, New Orleans, c1900.

newel staircase: Circular or winding staircase with a central post (the newel) which supports the narrow end of the steps. The newel is also the principal post supporting the banister at either end of a flight of stairs.

New England: Pressed and cut glass and paperweights from the early C19 glassworks of that name.

New Hall: Late C18 potters' co-operative in Staffordshire making porcelain and bone china wares.

New Jersey: Collective name for glass products in southern New Jersey, from the late C18.

Newry: Home of an Irish glassworks producing flint glass late C18/early C19.

new stone china: Spode stoneware containing potash feldspar, developed early C19.

nickel: Hard white metal, similar to silver and equally resistant to oxidation, much used as a substitute for silver in alloys.

nickel silver: Alloy of 25% nickel and 75% copper, white in color and used as an inexpensive alternative to silver for cutlery and coinage.

Niderviller: Mid C18 faience factory in Alsace-Lorraine noted for figures rivaling the finest porcelain, and for delicate floral decoration.

niello: Black metal alloy or enamel used for filling in engraved designs on silverware.

night clock: One designed for reading the time at night, usually fitted with a lamp behind a pierced dial.

night stool/chair: See close stool/chair.

night table: Small cupboard designed to stand near or next to a bed. They are sometimes fitted as a washstand and can be found with a drawer, a tambour slide or a tray top with carrying handles.

night watchman: Popular Toby jug in the form of a watchman holding a lantern.

nightwatchman's clock: One which records the time at which a nightwatchman visits each station on his rounds.

Nijushi Ko: Figures, twentyfour in total, representing aspects of filial devotion, often represented in netsuke.

nil: Pronounced neel; Persian for the indigo blue color used in carpets.

nim: Literally "half"; used to denote the size of a carpet as in "zaranim", one and a half zars, about 1½yd (1.5m).

nimcha: North African Muslim sword with a knuckle guard.

Ninsei: Japanese potter (1596-1666) credited with making the country's first porcelain in 1616.

nipple: In a percussion lock, the pointed cone onto which the firing cap was placed.

nitro-proof: Evidence that a firearm has been tested for firing with cordite, rather than gunpowder, usually consisting of the letters NP under a crown or cross keys marked on the barrel by a proving officer. Cordite, invented in 1880, is a more powerful explosive than gunpowder, and firearms of the time were often tested in this way to judge their suitability for conversion.

nodding figures: Porcelain figures with the head mounted on a pivot or spring which nods when touched; popular from the C19.

Noh drama: Japanese formal drama whose comic and serious characters were often represented in netsuke.

nomadic: Carpets and rugs made by nomadic people, often on simple looms, rather than in factory or workshop. Perhaps more primitive than factory carpets, but rarer and highly prized.

nonesuch inlay: Elaborate inlaid decoration dating from the second half of the C16 and representing the celebrated Palace of Nonesuch built by Henry VIII near Cheam.

non-flam celluloid: Nonflammable celluloid acetate which was discovered in 1926 and used widely in the 1930s and 1940s for electrical equipment, radios, telephones, boxes, etc.

northern celadon: Early Chinese gray-green glazed wares with a brown fabric or body, as distinct from the red fabric of southern celadon.

North pistols: Pistols made by Simeon North, of Middletown, Massachusetts, at the beginning of C19 and supplied in quantity to the American Navy.

Norway rug: Densely-woven upholstery material made in Norway in C19.

Nöstetangen glass: Made at the Norwegian glassworks, established C18.

Nottingham stoneware: Made by several potters, notably James Morley, from the early C17; principally salt-glazed mugs and storage vessels characterized by pierced and engraved decoration.

nulling: Decorative carving in the form of irregular fluting which is usually found on early oak furniture.

nunome: Japanese lacquerware made to imitate the appearance of cloth or textile.

Nuppenbecker: German glass claw beaker in medieval style, or any beaker decorated with prunts (nuppen).

Nuremberg egg: Early German watch worn as a neck pendant, so-named because Ohrchen – little clock – sounds like Eichen German for egg.

Nuremberg kitchen: C19 German toy designed to teach domestic virtues to young girls; often a perfect scale version of a contemporary kitchen with pots and pans.

Nuremberg pottery: C18 faience, noted for blue on white scenes based on engravings with crosshatched shading.

Nuremberg scale: Scale used for modeling German toy soldiers: 30mm high for foot soldiers, 40mm for cavalry.

Nuri-shi: The master craftsman in a Japanese lacquerware workshop, responsible for the preparatory work.

nutmeg grater: Cylindrical silver vessel with a lid containing a rasp for grating nutmeg and a container to catch the powder and store the nut. C18, used for grating nutmeg on warm beverages.

Nymphenburg porcelain: From the C18 factory near Munich, noted for the life-like figures modeled by Franz Anton Bustelli in a delicate, almost flawless porcelain.

Nyon porcelain: Late C18 factory near Geneva, noted for rococo decoration on a clear white body.

O

oak: Hard wood with a coarse grain much used for furniture because it is strong and durable. Early oak will often have darkened to a dark brown colour whereas later oak may be a lighter yellowish brown colour. See also bog oak and brown oak.

oar pattern spoon: One whose handle and finial resembles the shape of an oar.

obi: In Japanese costume, the waist sash from which sagemono ("hanging things") are hung, in lieu of pockets, secured by the netsuke (toggle).

obi-hasami: Netsuke with a hook which is designed to catch on the lower edge of the waist sash (obi).

objet d'art: Term used of decorative objects of such merit that they are entitled to be regarded as works of art; sometimes used much more loosely to mean simply "decorative pieces".

objet de vertu: Objects, usually very small, of particular beauty or rarity; precious and often displaying the finest skills of craftsmanship.

Obrist, Hermann (1863-1927): Leading artist of the German Art Nouveau movement, one of the creators of the Jugendstil.

obsidian: Extremely hard volcanic rock resembling glass, much used by ancient man for making axe and arrow heads.

obverse: Of a coin or medal, the front face, as opposed to the reverse; the monarch's or president's head usually appears on the obverse.

occasional table: Small table which is easily portable and can be moved about to suit the occasion.

Ochel: German manufacturer of flat cast toy soldiers, since 1925.

octant: Device for measuring angular distance, in the form of an eighth of a circle. Invented 1731.

Oeben, Jean (c1720-1763): Leading French cabinet maker much patronized by Royalty. After his death the business was continued by his widow until she married Riesener in 1767, the business then taking his name.

oeil de perdrix: French for "eye of the partridge", a pattern consisting of a small blue circle surrounded by darker dots, randomly scattered as a background decoration on porcelain.

oenochoe: From the Greek oinos, or wine, any ancient jug-shaped vessel of metal, glass or ceramic with a narrow neck, looped handle and wide lip used for pouring liquids.

O gauge: One of the gauges used for model railways at 1¼in (3.2cm) between the tracks; introduced c1900.

ogee: Double curved shape which is convex at the top and becomes concave at the bottom. It is often found on the feet of Georgian furniture. Also known as cyma reversa.

ogee clock: C19 New England mantel clock with ogee mouldings framing the case. Also known as an Og.

oignon: Onion watch; French type, common in late C17 and C18 so-named because of its shape.

oil gilding: See gilding.

ojime: Sliding bead threaded by a cord between the netsuke (toggle) and inro (medicine box); pushed down it keeps the inro closed; slid up it allows the inro to be opened.

Oibrich, Joseph Maria (1867-1908): Pupil of Otto Wagner at the Weiner Werkstatte and one of a group of young progressive artists working in Austria who produced fanciful but disciplined Art Nouveau designs.

Old English spoon: Term used to denote shape rather than date; one with an ovoid or sharply narrowing bowl and a handle that turns downward at the end; from the mid C18.

Oldfield ware: C19 salt-glazed stoneware from Brampton, Derbyshire.

old friend: Trade term for an antique that has been resold at auction many times.

Old Woman Who Lived In a Shoe: mid C19 sets of dolls, consisting of the old woman, the shoe, and numerous smaller wooden or rag doll children.

oleographs: Prints designed to resemble oil paintings, often made onto embossed paper, varnished and framed, from mid C19.

olive: Hard wood which is a dark greenish colour with black streaks. Used as a veneer.

omnium: Victorian name for a whatnot.

OO gauge: Also known as Double O, or Dublo; half the width of O gauge, i.e. ⅝in (1.6cm) between the tracks. Introduced mid-1930s.

opaque twist: White or multicoloured twist, popular in wine glass stems of the 3rd quarter C18.

open fret: Fretwork which is not carved into or applied to a solid surface but is left open so that it can be seen through.

open-mouth doll: Doll's mouth modelled in such a way that it appears to be open.

organ clock: One in which the hours are sounded by bellows operating on organ pipes instead of bells.

Oriental carpets: Term usually denotes carpets made in the Near East, rather than in China.

Oriental dolls: German bisque head character dolls made early C20 in the costumes of China, Japan, Burma, Polynesia, etc.

Orleans porcelain: Produced mid C18 to early C19 at Orleans in northern France.

ormolu: Strictly, gilded bronze or brass but sometimes used loosely of any yellow metal. Originally used for furniture handles and mounts but, from the C18, for ink stands, candlesticks, clock cases, etc.

orrery: Armillary sphere powered by clockwork, named after the 4th Earl of Orrery who commissioned the first example.

Orrery clock: Type of clock named after one first commissioned by the 4th Earl of Orrery showing the relative positions of the earth, moon and sun, sometimes the planets as well.

Orvieto maiolica: One of Italy's earliest production centres, dating back to C14; plates, jars and jugs of that period survive, decorated with gothic style ornamentation.

Osiris: Ancient Egyptian god of goodness and sunlight, god of the Nile and Judge of the Dead. Often depicted in Egyptian art carrying a scourge or in the form of the bull Apis.

ossuary: Pot with a lid, made in antiquity to contain the cremated bones of a deceased person.

Ottingen-Schrattenhofen faience: South German, C18, decorated with flowers in high temperature colours.

Ottweiler porcelain: German, established mid C18, producing figures and flatware.

Oude Loosdrecht: Dutch late C18 porcelain decorated with rural landscapes and peasant scenes.

outer stripe: Outermost band of a complex border on an oriental carpet.

over and under: Firearm with two barrels, one above the other.

overcoat pistol: Short barrelled pistol for the pocket, streamlined so as not to catch on clothes.

overcoil: In a clock mechanism, a second spring attached to the balance spring to ensure that it retains its concentric regular shape; invented late C18.

overglaze: Second glaze laid over a first and refired; also termed "enamelling".

overglaze printing: Earliest form of transfer printing, developed mid 1750s, in which the design is applied over the glaze and refired at a lower temperature.

overlay: In cased glass, the top layer, usually engraved to reveal a different coloured layer beneath.

overmantel: Area above the shelf on a mantelpiece, often consisting of a mirror in an ornate frame, or some architectural feature in wood or stone.

over stuffed: Descriptive of upholstered furniture where the covering extends over the frame of the seat.

ovolo: Moulding of convex quarter-circle section. Sometimes found around the edges of drawers to form a small overlap onto the carcase.

owl jug: From Eulenkrug, an owl-shaped jug, the head detachable and forming a cup, German, of faience from C16, later in stoneware.

oxbow: Reverse serpentine curve, the curve being exaggerated inwards.

Oxford flagon: Pewter flagon with convex sides, a spout, strainer and domed lid, from the early C18.

oyster veneer: Very decorative veneered pattern produced by the veneer being cut across the branch and then laid to create a geometric ringed effect.

P

pad foot: Rounded foot somewhat resembling the padded foot of an animal. Virtually the same as club foot, although this is perhaps a little more exaggerated and larger.

padouk: Hard and heavy reddish wood with darker figuring. Best known for its use in making military chests.

pagodes: Chinoiserie figures of elderly men; some with a pivotted nodding head, popular in C19.

paint: Used as one of the earliest methods of decorating furniture. Sometimes primitive furniture would be covered with cloth as a base for the paint but on the fashionable and sophisticated furniture of the later Georgian period delightful designs were applied directly to the surface of the wood. See also polychrome furniture.

pair-cased watches: Watches with a double case – standard from 1650 to c1800. The movement was itself encased

and this fitted, for protection, into another outer case, like a jewel box, and often ornate.

paktong: Cheap objects of copper, zinc and nickel alloy made in China for export to Europe, C18; especially candlesticks, fireside furniture and ornaments.

palace letters: Letters which can be found on French furniture made for the Royal households. Sometimes accompanied by an inventory number.

palas: Alternative name for a kelim or flat-woven rug.

Palladian: Influenced by the drawings, designs or architecture of Antonio Palladio (1518-80). He was influential in reviving Classical Roman motifs.

pallet: The arms either side of a clock linkage, which alternately engage and release the escapement wheel to regulate its movement.

palmette: Stylized palm-leaf motif, often used to decorate Oriental carpets, also furniture.

palstave: Bronze age axe head, cast to fit into a split wood handle, instead of having a socket for the handle.

pambe: Persian for cotton; used to denote carpets of that material.

pamuk: Turkish for cotton; used to denote carpets made of that material.

pan: In firearms, the receptacle which holds the priming powder.

panache: In military dress, the plume on a helmet.

panaches: The term that describes the plumes of feathers with which C17 tester beds were often embellished.

pan cover: In firearms, the lid over the pan which holds the priming powder, designed to protect the powder from rain and accidental firing. In early firearms, the cover had to be lifted manually. In the flintlock mechanism it moves aside automatically as the serpent descends.

Panderma: Western Turkish carpet production centre specializing in faithful reproductions of famous antique rugs.

pandora: Early C18 mannikin, made for displaying clothes and hairstyles rather than as a toy.

panel: An area which is either raised from or sunk into the surface of its framework.

panel cut: Decorations cut into glass using the face, rather than the edge, of a grinding wheel.

Pantin: Art glass made at Pantin, in France, second half C19.

pap dish: Cup or bowl with a spout for feeding infants or invalids.

paper doll: Dolls of lithographed paper or card, usually with a range of outfits which are suspended by tabs from the basic doll.

paperweight: Glass hemisphere encapsulating decorative coloured glass, sea shells, etc., highly popular C19.

paperweight clock: Small C19 clocks with a glass dome and a solid brass base.

paperweight eyes: Realistic doll's eyes in glass with pupils, made by enclosing coloured glass, similar to the technique of paperweight making.

papier-mâché: Paper pulp usually combined with a glue and moulded into boxes, trays and ornaments, painted or japanned. Also used to make furniture by building up layers of paper with pitch and oil over an iron frame. From early C18.

Pappenheimer: Large double-edged longsword used in the Thirty Years War of the C17 and named after a famous German commander.

parcel gilt: Term used to describe wood which is partly gilded.

parchemin: Decorative pattern in the form of an elaborate "X" used to infill panels, mainly in the C16.

Parian: Fine white biscuit porcelain, sometimes lightly glazed, resembling fine Parian marble, developed mid C19 by Copeland. Used mainly for miniature copies of classical statuary.

Parian doll: One with a head made of Parian stoneware or, more loosely, any doll with a white unpainted bisque head.

Paris: Products of a number of ceramics factories in the French capital, but principally late C18 porcelain in the Sèvres style.

Parisienne doll: French bisque head doll with a stuffed kid leather body, made by various manufacturers 1860s to 1880s.

Parkesine: Early form of plastic invented by Alexander Parkes and produced 1862-8. Principally toys, combs, buttons.

parquet: Hardwood flooring consisting of brick-sized blocks laid in various patterns, especially herring-bone and highly polished. Elaborate versions incorporate a veneer of coloured woods.

parquetry: Veneers laid in a geometric pattern for decorative effect.

partizan: C16 and C17 infantry spear with a long handle and blade with multiple sharp projections.

partridge wood: Brown and red wood, the colour mingled to suggest plumage. Imported from Central and South America and used as a veneer.

pasguard: In armour, especially in jousting, a plate to protect the vulnerable left elbow.

Passglas: German, originally C16, glassbeaker marked into sections, each showing the measure to be drunk as it was passed round during a toast.

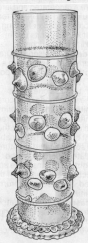

pastille burner: Ceramic object for burning pastilles of compressed herbs as an air freshener; numerous forms, but burners shaped like a cottage or castle (the smoke passing through the chimney or tower) popular in early C19.

patch box: Silver box, usually small and round, in which ladies – and in the C18, male beaux – carried the artificial beauty spots they applied to their faces for cosmetic reasons.

patchbox: Compartment in the butt of a gun used for storing accessories.

patch figures: Term for early English porcelain figures with an unglazed patch on the base where they were supported during firing.

patchwork quilt: Quilt made up of odd scraps of cloth sewn together to form a patterned surface. Numerous regional types with characterful names. Popular in New England from the late C17 but most that survive are C19.

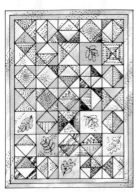

pate: Crown of a doll's head into which the hair is stitched, usually of cork in the better quality dolls.

pâte de verre: Technique reinvented by Art Nouveau glassmakers (originally used in ancient Egypt) whereby glass was ground up into a paste, moulded into the desired shape and then fired like pottery, producing a translucent, soft-edged glass.

patera: Small flat circular ornament, often in the form of an open flower or rosette, used as a ceiling or furniture ornament.

Paterson revolver: Progenitor of the Colt pistol, made at Paterson, New Jersey, in the first half of C19.

pâte-sur-pâte: C19 Sèvres porcelain technique, much copied, of applying slip decoration to the body before firing.

patina/patination: Surface colour of genuinely old wood resulting from the layers of grease, dirt and polish built up over the years, and the handling the piece of furniture has received in that time. Differs from wood to wood and is difficult to fake.

patinated: Noble and desirable dull green colour of ancient bronze, caused by oxidization of the metal, as distinct from the undesirable bright green verdigris which occurs when bronze is attacked by acid solution. Sometimes confused with patina, or patination, the colour of old wood.

pattern: Weapon officially approved and used as a standard service weapon, usually known by the year of introduction, e.g. 1822 pattern.

pattern-moulded glass: Glass produced by pressing the molten material into a mould to impress the pattern before blowing the vessel into its finished form.

pattern number: Introduced c1790 and used until superseded by the design registration marks of 1842. Useful for dating porcelain patterns and, occasionally, for identifying the porcelain factory which produced it – though few patterns were unique to one factory.

Paul, Bruno (b. 1874): German graphic artist who contributed to the Art Nouveau Movement's magazine, *Jugend*; founder in 1897, of the Vereinigte Werkstätten für Kunst, in Munich.

pauldron/pouldron: Armour plate to protect the shoulders.

Pauly, Johannes: Leading Swiss gunmaker, early C19.

pavis: Large convex shield, designed to protect the whole body against arrows, used especially during siege warfare.

paw foot: Foot which somewhat resembles a paw, usually with claws.

peach bloom: Pale red to brown glaze effect developed in

China, and imitated in late C19/early C20 in the West, with a silvery bloom like the skin of a peach.

peachblow: Late C19 art glass, first made by the New England Glass Co, in peachcoloured glass.

pear: Yellowish brown wood which sometimes has a pinkish tinge and was used to make country furniture.

pear drop: Descriptive of a drop handle which is pear-shaped.

pear drop moulding: Decorative moulding of inverted pear-shaped forms usually found below a cornice.

pearlware: Late C18 form of creamware, developed by Wedgwood, but much whiter and often transfer printed.

péché mortel: Type of French couch made up of a stool and an easy chair placed together.

Peck, Mrs Lucy: English maker of poured wax dolls, 1891-1921.

pedestal desk: Descriptive of a writing desk with two pedestals of drawers below the writing and working area.

pedestal stem: Early to mid C18 wine glass stem, thicker at the top than at the base and fluted.

pedestal table: Table raised upon a single central support.

pediment: Moulding or shape that tops a piece of furniture.

pediment barometer: Mid C18 to early C19 stick barometers, so-called because the top housing is carved in the shape of an architectural pediment. Elaborate examples incorporate other instruments e.g. thermometers, hygrometers, etc.

pedlar doll: Tableau, consisting of a doll in a bonnet and shawl standing at a market stall covered in a variety of wares.

peep-show: Box with a small front aperture and a series of painted glass or printed card scenes designed to create a 3-dimensional effect. Originally an architectural aid, but produced as a toy from early C19.

peg doll: Originally a doll made from a clothes peg, but now any small wooden dolls, especially those made for dolls' houses.

pegged furniture: Furniture held together by pegs or dowels, including pieces designed to be dismantled for storage by removing the pegs.

peg tankard: Late C17 form peculiar to northern England and Scotland with a series of internal peg markers, used for communal drinking.

pelican: Early and primitive tool for extracting teeth, with a screw clamp and handle, in use until c1830.

pellet moulding: Carved decoration in the form of repeated small dots.

Pembroke table: Small table with two short drop leaves along its length. Named after the Countess of Pembroke who is said to have been the first to order one. Also once known as a breakfast table.

pendant: General term to describe any form of suspended ornament.

pende: Tribal nomadic rugs from western Turkestan, noted for the richness of the natural colours.

pendulum clock: Any clock regulated by the swinging of a pendulum – a rod with a weight or bob attached to the end; made since the mid C17 and widely distributed.

penknife: Originally, as the name suggests, a knife used for cutting a point on a quill pen. Made from c1750, sometimes in novelty shapes, or with ornate handles.

pennanular: Describes the horse-shoe shape of ancient brooches and bracelets especially those of Celtic origin.

Pennington brothers: Liverpool potters of c1769 to 1799, noted for jugs and bowls painted with ships.

penny-farthing: One of the first forms of the bicycle to be produced in quantity, from c1870. So-called because of the relative sizes of the large front wheel (penny) and small back one (farthing).

pennyweight: Smallest measure in the Troy weight system of weighing silver, gold and precious stones; usually abbreviated "dwt".

Pennsylvania baby: Late C18 American doll of carved and painted pinewood.

penwork: Type of decoration whereby a piece is japanned black, then painted with designs in white japan and finally more clearly defined by detailed line work.

pepperbox: Repeating firearm with a revolving barrel with five or six chambers; an early C19 progenitor of the revolver.

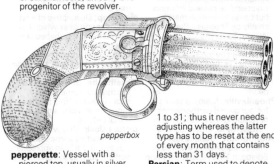

pepperbox

pepperette: Vessel with a pierced top, usually in silver, for sprinkling pepper.

percussion lock: Early C19 firearm, one of the first to be fired by the impact of a sharp-nosed hammer on the cartridge cap.

percussion weapons: Fast-firing weapons that superseded the flintlock in the early C19: the simple firing mechanism consists of a hammer which strikes a cap filled with fulminate; this explodes and the flash passes into the breech igniting the charge.

period: When used as an adjective (a period table) it means that the item was made at the time that the design etc. would suggest and is not, for example, a later copy.

periwig chair: Late C17 chair with a tall caned back with a carved arched cresting rail, and usually with a similarly carved arched stretcher between the front legs.

perpetual clock: Calendar clock with a dial marked with a one year (and sometimes a four year) calendar, as opposed to one marked with the numerals 1 to 31; thus it never needs adjusting whereas the latter type has to be reset at the end of every month that contains less than 31 days.

Persian: Term used to denote old and antique carpets made in the region broadly covered by modern Iran, distinguished by their complex floral designs.

Persian knot: Alternative name for the Sehna knot, characteristic of, but not exclusive to, Persian carpets as opposed to Turkish.

Pesaro maiolica: Made near Urbino, Italy, from C15.

petit feu: French for "little fire"; low temperature colours used in faience/maiolica decoration, allowing the use of a far wider range of colours and tones than was possible with high-temperature colours.

Petit porcelain: From the factory of Jacob Petit of Fontainbleau, near Paris; C19 revivals of rococo figure groups and ornate clock cases.

petronel: Short firearm, carried by C16 and C17 cavalrymen, and fired with the butt held against the chest.

petuntse: China stone; a granite used to make porcelain, and hard white porcelain glazes.

Petzold, Dr. Dora: Berlin maker of character dolls, 1919-1930.

pew group: English C18 group of two or three figures seated on a church pew. In earthenware and much reproduced in the C19/C20.

pewter: Alloy of tin and lead; the higher the tin content the higher the quality; sometimes with small quantities of antimony added to make it hard with a highly polished surface.

phenakistoscope: C19 form of magic lantern in which the pictures to be projected are mounted around the rim of a disc and spun to simulate movement.

Philadelphia Chippendale: American furniture of Chippendale era and influence, but being a variation made chiefly by Thomas Affleck and William Savery.

Phoenix glass: Made in Pittsburgh by the Phoenix glassworks, late C19, specializing in milk glass, known locally as mother of pearl.

Phoenixville: Majolica wares (colour glazed earthenwares resembling maiolica) made in Pennsylvania, latter half C19.

phonograph: Predecessor of the record player, patented by Edison in 1877, specifically one that plays a drum cylinder rather than a disc.

phrenological skull: Ivory or wood object in the form of a human skull mapped out with lines showing how variations in the shape, from one person to another, are supposed to determine character and fortune.

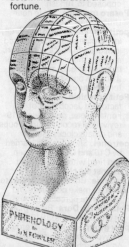

Phyfe, Duncan (1768-1854): Master cabinet maker who worked in New York. He was born in Scotland but moved to Albany at an early age. His furniture is both elegant and distinctive and often incorporates the lyre motif. He retired in 1847.

physionotrace: Late C18 and C19 projection machine which cast a silhouette; used by portrait artists.

piano lamp: Miniature version of a table lamp, made in pairs for fixing to a bracket on the piano front, popular from the mid C19.

piano-top: Descriptive of a type of Davenport desk which has a curved rising top shaped like that of a piano.

pichet: Small French pear-shaped tankard with a footring, C16 to C18.

Pickelhaube: German spiked-top military helmet, superseded in 1915 by the more functional basin-shaped metal helmet.

picture clock: One with a case painted with a scene that places the dial in an appropriate setting, such as in a church tower set in a rural landscape.

pie crust: Carved and scalloped edge found on some tripod tables. It resembles the rim of a crusty pie.

pier: Often used to describe a square column, as opposed to a round one; also the section of wall between two tall windows.

pier glass: Mirror designed to be fixed to the pier, or wall, between two tall window openings, often partnered by a matching pier table. Made from mid C17.

Pierotti family: London based makers of poured wax dolls, C19 and early C20.

pier table: Small table designed to stand against the pier, the area of wall between two windows.

pietre dure: Italian term for stones composed mainly of silicates, for example, the decorative inlaid marble table tops from Florence and Rome.

pigeonhole: Open compartment found amongst the internal fittings of a bureau.

pike: Long handled spear or spike used by C16 and C17 infantrymen.

pilaster: Flat-faced column projecting from a wall, used for decoration rather than support.

pile: Fine fibrous surface, or nap, of a carpet; created by looping yarn through the warp, so that the loops form a dense mat.

pilgrim furniture: Term sometimes used to describe early American furniture.

Pilkington: Associated with the Lancashire glass factory, this pottery produced Art Nouveau ceramics in the early C20, remarkable for its iridescent and colourful glazes.

pillar: Spacers whose job is to join together the backplate and dial-plate of a watch or clock movement; the number, position and shape are a useful guide to date and provenance.

pillar clock: One in which the hour hand moves up and down a vertical scale.

pillar rug: Chinese rug designed to wrap around a pillar.

pin-back badge: Circular, transfer printed badge often with a simple pin for attaching to clothing. Earliest and most collectable examples date to c1918.

pinchbeck: Early C18 copper and zinc alloy invented by Christopher Pinchbeck for use as a gold substitute especially for watch cases and jewellery.

pinched glass: Decorative motifs on glass made by pinching the glass with hand tools while it is still soft.

pincushion figures: Dolls heads, sometimes the arms and trunk as well, designed to be sewn into a pincushion: usually only the head was sold and the purchaser than made up the pincushion.

pine: See Scots pine.

pineapple wares: C18 yellow and green glazed pottery in the shape of the fruit.

pin hinge: Simple hinge of two linked loops. Found on early chests.

Pinten: Small German stoneware tankards made from the early C16.

Pinxton: Soft-paste porcelain imitating Derby, made in Nottingham by William Billingsley, from c1800.

pioneer sword: Sword issued to pioneers from the late C18, with a saw-edge, for use as a tool as well as a weapon.

pipe-backed blade: Blade with a solid cylindrical rib running down the back edge for two thirds of its length, early C19.

pipe stopper: Device for compacting tobacco in the bowl of a pipe, made since the early C18 in numerous forms, especially small cast figures.

pistol: Small firearm, made for hand-firing, with a stock at right angles to the barrel.

pitcher: Large jug of baluster form with tall narrow neck and lug handles.

pitkin glass: Small oval bottle or flask with moulded ribbing made in Connecticut from c1800.

pitting: Holes in the surface of a sword blade caused by rust.

Pittsburgh: High quality pressed glass from various glassworks operating around Pittsburgh from late C17.

Planck, Ernst: German company mass-producing toy locomotives from c1890.

plane: Close grained pale yellow wood occasionally used for inlay and marquetry in the early C18.

planished: Of silver or plate, the finishing of a vessel using a broad-faced convex hammer to achieve a smooth, polished surface.

planisphere: Scientific instrument for calculating distances in relation to points such as stars or planets.

plaster: Mixture of water and gypsum which can be poured into a mould and then rapidly sets to form a hard white concretion. Used since antiquity for statuary and architectural ornament, especially, in recent centuries, for decorative ceilings.

plasterware: Figure groups or sculpture cast in plaster of Paris from early C18.

plastic soldiers: Toy soldiers made of various plastics by injection moulding, introduced c1947.

plastiques: Articles made from early forms of plastic, such as Parkesine, Bakelite, etc.

plate: Old-fashioned term, still occasionally used, to describe gold and silver vessels; not to be confused with "Sheffield plate", or plated vessels generally, in which silver is fused to a base metal alloy.

plate handle: Handle with a protective backing plate.

plate pewter: Early form of pewter, made of tin and copper rather than tin and lead, used for flatware in the C16 and C17.

platform base: Flat base found below the column of a table.

playing cards: Produced since the C14 if not earlier, originally hand-painted, but printed from copper plates from the C17, often with satirical or propagandist themes.

playworn: Toy collectors' term for a piece that has suffered a considerable amount of damage and thus worth collecting only if a rare example.

plinth (1): Solid base around the bottom of a chest piece that is not raised on feet.

plinth (2): Square base of a column.

plinth (3): Block at the base of a fireplace or door architecture against which the skirting board abuts.

plug bayonet: Earliest form of bayonet, dating to the C17, designed to plug into a musket barrel after it had been fired.

plum: Yellowish red wood with a slight grain. Used to make country furniture.

plum pudding: Type of figuring in some veneers, produced by dark oval spots in the wood. It is found particularly in mahogany.

Plymouth: Short lived and early porcelain factory founded by William Cookworthy, who moved to Bristol in 1770; imperfect and crudely painted Chinese motifs in blue.

plywood: Composition of veneers which are glued together, each with the grain running at rightangles to the next to provide extra strength. It is mainly used for galleries and fretwork where extra strength may be needed.

pocket pistol: Small pistol for firing at short range in self-defence, carried in the pocket and streamlined so as not to catch in clothing.

Poertzel, Professor Otto (b.1876): Prominent German sculptor specializing in Art Deco figures of actors, dancers and mythological deities. Worked with Preiss, whose figures share many stylistic similarities.

pogmaggon: Slender rod with a heavy stone or bone head, used as a weapon by North American Indians.

poison bottles: Made of blue glass to a distinctive design to prevent confusion with other vessels. Often decorated.

poitrel: Armour to protect the breast of a horse.

poker work: Decoration on wooden objects achieved by placing the point of a hot poker on the wood to burn the surface; usually patterns made up of black dots, but sometimes pictorial scenes. C17 to C19.

pole: Linear motif in carpets linking a series of medallions along a single axis.

pole arms: Long handled weapons, such as spears and lances.

pole-axe: Short handled axe, sometimes with a hammer as well as blade, used in medieval warfare and in naval battles for boarding enemy vessels.

pole glass: German C16 to C17 tall beaker with a trailed spiral design, like a barber's pole.

pole screen: Small adjustable screen mounted on a pole and designed to stand in front of an open fire to shield a lady's face from the heat.

poleyn: In armour, plate to protect the knee joint.

policheh: Oriental rug measuring approximately 7ft x 4ft (2.1m x 1.2m), the "standard" size.

pollarding: Artificial production of knotty figuring in timber by removing the crown and top branches of a young tree and then trimming the new shoots which grow thereafter. A large club-shaped mass is produced which can be sliced through to provide a highly figured veneer.

pollard oak: Sought after variety of oak with a knotty figuring created by pollarding.

polonaise: Very fine C17 Persian silk carpet with free floral design: so named because many were commissioned by Polish aristocrats.

polychrome: Many coloured; often used of the broad range of colours found on low temperature maiolica/faience.

polychrome furniture: Furniture painted in many colours.

pomade: Bottle or jar, of glass or ceramic, made since the C16 to hold scented hair ointment.

pomander: Small spherical silver box, often with a pierced lid, sometimes with several internal compartments, originally made as a neck or wrist ornament and filled with sweet-smelling herbs.

pommel (1): Bolt which passes through a drawer front to secure a handle in place.

pommel (2): Terminal piece of a sword or dagger hilt, often spherical.

pomona: Late C19 frosted art glass of pale orange colour, mould blown and etched with floral designs, made by the New England Glass Co.

pompadour: Style associated with Mme de Pompadour, mistress of Louis XV; designs based on flowers, and idealized rural scenes, in pastel colours, especially pink and blue.

Pompeian: Objects decorated with motifs based on frescoes rediscovered when the city of Pompeii was excavated in the C18.

poniard: Small dagger, easily concealed, with a narrow blade.

pontil mark: Mark left on the base or foot of a blown glass vessel and made by the pontil, the rod used to remove the finished vessel from the blow pipe.

Pope, Joseph: Boston clockmaker, active 1790-1810.

poplar: Hard close-grained wood. It is whitish yellow in colour and was used for inlay and marquetry work.

poppy head: An ecclesiastical finial, decoratively carved as a figure, plant, bird, beast or human head etc.

porcelain: Ceramic fabric made of china clay (kaolin) and china stone (petuntse), fired at a very high temperature to produce a hard, white impermeable body.

porcellanous: Having some of the characteristics of true porcelain; sometimes used of ceramic fabrics developed before the discovery of porcelain ingredients, including various soft porcelains using frit or soapstone instead of china stone.

porringer: Two-handled dish, sometimes with a lid, originally for holding porridge or gruel. Usually silver or pewter and dating from C17 on.

porron: Drinking vessel of glass with a long spout used for pouring liquid down the throat, originally Spanish C17.

portable barometer: So called because instead of being wall mounted, it was free standing – mounted on a wooden pillar with three brass feet – late C17 and early C18.

portable lantern: Small and robust oil lamp designed to be carried by nightwatchmen, etc. Of brass or copper, sometimes with a lens, but often plain glass sides. From the early C19.

portable sundial: Made from the C16 onwards, usually of wood or ivory, with a hinged lid and rod and a compass to orient the dial in the correct direction so as to read the time.

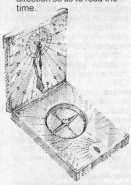

porter's chair: See hall porter's chair.

Portland vase: Jasperware vase made by Wedgwood and modelled on a celebrated Roman cameo glass vase in the British Museum.

portrait doll: One modelled on a well-known figure.

Portuguese swell: Bulging bulb-like part of a support or leg found on some C17 furniture. Sometimes referred to as bulb or melon bulb.

Poseidon: Greek god of the sea, renamed Neptune by the Romans.

posset: Pot with two handles, a domed lid and a spout used for making punch, or posset, in the C17 and C18. Often in delftware.

post bed: Bed with two or four posts supporting a tester.

potash glass: Made using wood ash as a flux; much used by German glassmakers;

produces a tough glass, ideal for engraving.

potato-flower: Fashionable motif on European pottery from the early C18, painted in cobalt blue and yellow.

pot belly stove: C19 stove of bombé shape, i.e. curving out to the waist and in again to the base.

pot board: Open shelf or board forming the lowest stage of a dresser or livery cupboard.

Potemkin: Late C18 Russian glass factory established to supply the Czar; briefly produced commercial wares in the C19.

potiche: General term for vases of oriental shape, i.e. high-shouldered and generally with a cover.

potichomania: C19 fashion for pasting printed paper designs, based on oriental motifs, onto the interior of plain glass vessels.

pot lids: Pictorial lids found on small pots made to contain paste or ointment, after the perfection of colour printed on ceramic in 1840; especially by the company of Felix Pratt. Much reproduced.

pot metal: Used both of a copper-lead alloy and cast-iron. Each of these was used for making large pots for suspending over an open fire.

pot pourri jar: Jar with a pierced lid, usually of porcelain but also of glass or silver, made to hold dried herb and flower mixtures.

Potsdam: Glass from the works near Berlin founded late C17, famous for engraved ruby-red glass and milk glass.

pottery: Collective name for earthenwares and stonewares, but not china or porcelain, and hand-made rather than cast.

pottery pig: Early money box, usually of tin glazed earthenware, mid C17 and C18.

pottle: Large earthenware pot made to hold half a gallon of beer.

Potts, T.H.: Leading London gunmaker, mid C19.

pounce box: Silver box or bottle with a pierced top for sprinkling pounce, a talcum powder used to soak up excess ink before the invention of blotting paper; C18.

pouncet: Pomander of box shape, rather than spherical, with pierced sides and top, filled with sweet-smelling herbs and worn as a wrist ornament or pendant.

pouncework: Decorative pattern on silver consisting of numerous small, closely spaced dots.

poupard: Doll without legs, often mounted on a stick; popular C19.

poured wax doll: One made by pouring molten wax onto a mould.

pouty doll: Generic term for character dolls with a pouting expression.

powder blue: Very fine specks of blue used as an underglaze decoration on porcelain, achieved by blowing powdered pigment onto the greased surface of the vessel.

powder clock: Series of hourglass flasks set in a frame, each one measuring a different duration such as the quarter, half, threequarter and full hour.

powder flask: Device for measuring out a precise quantity of priming powder, made to be suspended from a musketeer's belt or bandolier and often ornately decorated. Sporting flasks are often made of antler and carved with hunting scenes.

powder horn: Cow horn hollowed out, blocked at the wide end with a wooden plug and fitted with a measuring device at the narrow end, used by musketeers for dispensing a precise quantity of priming powder.

Powell, James and Sons: English glassmakers flourishing in the late C19, specializing in ecclesiastical and domestic stained glass of excellent quality.

practice sword: Sword with blunted edges and rounded tip used from the mid C19 for training cavalry soldiers.

prattware: Pictorial earthenware jugs, decorated in yellow, brown, blue and green, popularized by Felix Pratt of Fenton, Staffordshire, but widely produced late C18 and C19.

praxinoscope: Revolving peepshow, patented 1870, in which figures appear to move against a static background.

prayer rug: Islamic rug intended for kneeling on during prayers, with a design based on the mihrab or pointed prayer niche.

pre-Columbian: Art that predates the "discovery" of the New World by Columbus in 1492.

pre-Dynastic: Ancient Egyptian objects dating to the fourth or early third millennium BC, before the creation of the First Dynasty.

Preiss, Johan Philipp Ferdinand, known as Fritz (1882-1943): Leading Art Deco sculptor, producing ivory and bronze figures of children and athletes, including works for the Berlin Olympics of 1936. Figures embossed with a PK monogram were produced by the company he founded with Kassler in Berlin in 1906.

press bed: Bed that can be folded away so that it looks like a cupboard. First made in the C17.

press chest: See linen press (2).

press cupboard: Enclosed cupboard, usually in two parts, the upper part with either a recessed flat or canted front and the lower part entirely enclosed by doors.

pressed glass: Early C19 invention, exploited rapidly in America, whereby mechanical pressure was used to form glassware in a mould, instead of using compressed air.

preuning ware: C16 lead glazed jugs and flatware made in

Nuremberg of high quality, often painted with religious subjects.

Priapus: Greek and Roman god of fertility, gardens and vineyards.

pricker: Metal pin used to clean the touch hole of early firearms.

pricket: Silver, or other metal, candlestick with a spike to hold the candle rather than a socket.

prie-dieu: Chair with a low seat and a tall back. They were made during the C19 and were designed for prayer.

priming powder: Fine gunpowder, placed in the priming pan of a firing mechanism, which communicates fire to the main charge in the barrel.

primitive: Term sometimes used to describe very simplistic country furniture.

Prince of Wales feathers: Motif used by Hepplewhite on some chair backs. It comprises three feathers tied loosely at the base with a ribbon.

Prince's metal: Copper-tin alloy made to resemble gold, reputedly invented late C17 by Prince Rupert.

Princes wood: C17 name for what we now call kingwood.

print decoration: As distinct from hand decoration; introduced mid 1750s and used for the mass production of inexpensive tablewares.

printed doll: One made of fabric printed with facial and body features.

printies: Crater-like hollows cut into glass for decorative effect, especially on paperweights.

prism cutting: Zig-zag, or chevron, ornament found on the necks of decanters, late C18/early C19.

prisoner-of-war work: Collective name for objects made for sale or barter by soldiers and sailors held in prison camps, especially during the Napoleonic Wars (1792-1815). Subjects include model ships, toys of bone or wood, boxes and gaming pieces.

pristine: Term used to denote an object in near perfect condition; as new.

profile shaping: Cutting of flat boards into a decorative silhouette profile. Mainly used in the C17 on the seat rails and aprons of chairs, stools and tables.

projection clock: Night clock with a lamp behind the pierced dial. This casts a shadow of the hour numerals and the hands on the wall. Made since the early C18.

proof mark: Of firearms, an official mark made on the barrel to show that it had been tested for strength; usually using a greater quantity of powder and shot than would be needed in normal firing.

protector revolver: Patented 1888, a small firearm designed to be hidden in the palm and fired by clenching the fist.

proto porcelain: Chinese Han dynasty stoneware, so called because it resembles and is the predecessor to, true porcelain.

provenance: Authenticated history of an antique.

Providence glass: From a short-lived factory in Providence, Rhode Island, first half C19.

provincial: Term used to describe furniture made in the provinces, as distinct from the large cities, and usually given to pieces which look country-made and are of a lesser quality than their city-made counterparts.

provincial silver: English silver assayed at any office other than London.

Prunk Uhr: Name given to a type of Baroque German clock so ornate that the actual dial is almost obscured – often with moving figures and a complex chime.

prunts: Knobs of coloured glass applied for decorative effect and sometimes pinched or drawn into various shapes, especially on German glass beakers.

Prussian decanter: From 1800, heavily cut decanter with

mushroom stopper and tapering sides, narrowing to the base.

psyche: Regency term for what is now more commonly known as a cheval mirror.

ptolemaic: Ancient Egyptian objects dating from the C4 to C1 BC when Egypt was ruled by the Greek general Ptolemy I, and his successors. Objects of this period display a classical influence.

Pugin, Augustus (1812-52): Ecclesiastical architect whose writings on the Gothic style inspired the English neo-Gothic movement. He designed much stained glass, metalwork, furniture and other woodwork, all noted for its lavish ornamentation. Style much copied by other contemporary craftsmen whose work is often styled "Puginesque".

pull: In firearms, the pressure required to cause a trigger to release the firing mechanism, measured by means of a spring balance.

pull or push repeat: Clock fitted with a cord or a button which releases a mechanism that repeats the previous hour's strike. Invented 1676 as a means of hearing the approximate time in the dark.

pulse watch: Medical watch first made in the late C17 with a lever for stopping and starting the second hand.

pumpkin head: Alternative name for waxed doll; composition head coloured and dipped in wax.

punch bowl: Large silver bowl with two ring handles and a ring foot for mixing and serving punch, from C17. Often with a matching ladle or ladles.

punch pot: C18 china pot like an oversize teapot with a rounded base intended to sit over a heated stand. Used for mixing and warming punch.

purdonium: Form of coal box patented by a Mr. Purdon, with slots for matching shovels, often highly ornate, mid C19.

Purdy, James: Leading London gunsmith, mid C19.

Puritan: Term used to describe some of the more simple and unadorned C17 American furniture.

Puritan spoon: Mid C17 silver spoon with an unadorned stem, squared off end without a finial and a simple ovoid bowl.

Puritan watch: Early C17 English watch of oval shape so called because it was very plain.

purpleheart: See purplewood.

purple lustre: C19 Staffordshire wares, pink to purple and made by applying a mixture of tin and gold (purple of Cassius) over the glaze.

purplewood: Open-grained wood from Central and South America which is brown in its natural state but turns purple when exposed to the air. Used for marquetry and inlay. Also known as purpleheart.

pushti: Smallest rug size, typically 3ft x 2ft (1m x 0.66m).

Pu tai: Disciple of the Buddha, known as the laughing Buddha, a favourite subject in porcelain.

Putnam, Grace Storey: American doll maker, famous for the "Bye-Lo Baby", early C20.

putti: Cupids or cherubs used as decoration.

putto: Singular of putti; a nude boy or infant, portrayed in art and statuary from C15, often alongside female deities.

puzzle jug: Delftware form made from the C17 on with several spouts and a syphon system, none of which will pour unless the others are blocked.

Pyefinch: Notable maker of ornate stick barometers in London, 3rd quarter of C18.

pyrites: Crystalline mineral, sometimes called "Fool's Gold", used in early firearms. It gives off sparks when struck against steel and was used in the firing mechanism of wheellocks.

Q

Qian long (Ch'ien Lung): Chinese Qing dynasty emperor, 1736-95.

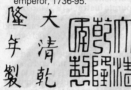

qilin: Mythical Chinese animal, symbol of goodness, with the head of a dragon, body of a deer and tail of a lion.

Qing: Alternative spelling of Ching – the dynasty that ruled China from 1644 to 1916.

quadrant: Quarter circle marked with degrees of a circle and with a weighted line or pointer used as a navigational aid.

quadrant drawer: Quarter-round drawer in the frieze of a table or desk which is pivoted and swings out.

quadrant stay: Quarter-round brass support for adjustable chair backs, etc.

quaiche: Silver drinking vessel with two flat handles based on medieval prototypes, probably then made of wood.

quality marks: Marks found on the best quality pewter: an X (for extraordinary ware) sometimes with a crown, or the legend "superfine" are the commonest marks.

Quare, Daniel: Celebrated clockmaker, active latter half C17 and early C18, credited with the invention of the repeating watch. He also made barometers.

Quare barometer: One made by the notable maker, Daniel Quare, late C17, early C18, of stick barometer type.

quarrel: Square-headed bolt shot from a crossbow or arbalest.

quarter clock: One which strikes the quarter and half hours as well as the full hours.

quarter veneered: Four consecutively cut, and therefore identical, pieces of veneer laid at opposites to each other to give a mirrored effect.

quartetto tables: Set of four matching tables of graduating size, each one neatly storing beneath the next largest when not in use. Also known as a nest of tables.

quatrefoil: Four-cusped figure which resembles a symmetrical four-lobed leaf or flower.

Queen Anne barrel: Firearm originally made in early C18 in the reign of Queen Anne, with a barrel that unscrewed for loading.

Queen Anne doll: Carved and jointed wooden doll made during the reign of Queen Anne, 1702-14.

Queen's ware: Wedgwood's improved and harder type of creamware, widely copied by C18 English potters for a variety of wares.

quilling: Trailed glass ornament made by pinching and pulling the glass while still soft.

quillon: Crosspiece of a sword, between the blade and the hilt, providing some protection for the knuckles.

quimper faience: From the factory in Brittany, France, established late C17 and closely modelled on Rouen wares.

Qum: Persian holy city, in central Iran, and a centre of carpet weaving famous for silk rugs often incorporating kufic inscriptions. Variant spellings include Qoom, Kum, Ghum and Ghom.

R

rabbet: Groove to hold a removable shelf.

rabinet: Small cannon with a pear-shaped barrel.

rack: Tall superstructure above a dresser.

rack strike: Also rack-and-snail strike. Clock refinement introduced c1676 whereby the movement of the hour hand regulates the strike mechanism.

raden: Japanese laquerware decorated with inlay of mother-of-pearl, shell, gold or silver foil.

Radiguet: French company massproducing toy locomotives from c1890.

raeren ware: Late C16 brown salt-glazed stoneware jugs and drinking vessels from the Rhineland.

rag doll: Cloth doll stuffed with rags.

rail: In furniture the horizontal piece of a joined frame or panelling.

raked: Inclined at a backwards angle.

raku: Japanese tea-ceremony bowls in stoneware with a black or earth-brown matt finish.

ramrod: In early firearms, when guns were loaded by pouring powder and shot down the muzzle end, an iron rod for ramming the firing mixture down the barrel; often carried as an attachment to the barrel.

ram's head: Decoration resembling the head of a ram which was used in mask form by Robert Adam.

range: Cast iron stove intended to fill a fireplace cavity. Had several cooking compartments and hotplates.

ranseur: In weaponry, a triple headed lance.

rapier: Sword with a pointed blade designed for piercing rather than cutting.

rapier chest: An essentially modern term to describe a long and narrow chest, the supposition being that such chests were specifically constructed for storing rapiers and similar weapons.

ratafia: Tall narrow drinking glass of the C18, in which the slender conical bowl forms one continuous line with the stem; said to have been used for drinking ratafia liqueur.

rating nut: Nut and screw at the base of the bob, or weight, of a clock pendulum allowing minor adjustments to its length and hence the rate of swing.

ratskanne: Early form of stoneware jug, made in the Rhineland, C16.

rat tail: Tapering support, often decorated, that joins the bowl to the handle of a spoon.

rattan: Stripped inner back of a palm grown in the Malay Peninsula. Used for caning.

Ravenscroft: Glass marked with a raven's head seal in honour of the inventor of lead crystal, George Ravenscroft (1618-81) and made from the late C17 by the London Glass Sellers' Co., Henley-on-Thames.

Ravenstein porcelain: From the German factory in Thuringia, late C18, imitating Meissen.

razor: Steel blades for removing facial hair; earliest surviving examples date to late C18, often with ornate handles and decorated blades, as well as boxed "seven day" sets.

reading chair: Chair of the same design as a cockfighting chair but fitted with candle holders and a bookrest in addition. Also known as a library chair.

récamier: Type of French daybed in the Grecian style with upwardly curved ends.

recessed carving: Carving in which the background is removed leaving the pattern exposed. Mainly used in C17.

red figure: Ancient Greek method of decorating pottery, revived in the C19, whereby the whole vessel is painted black and figures are then incised through the black slip to reveal the red-brown body of the clay beneath. Developed in C6 BC.

red gloss pottery: Preferred name for Roman "Samian" ware, noted for the brilliance of its gloss and made in various centres; also still reproduced in southern Italy.

red stoneware: Fabric of Chinese teaware sets imported from the C17 and copied at Meissen and Fulham before the development of true porcelain.

red walnut: Another name for black walnut.

redware: First specifically American earthenware pottery produced in quantity between the late C17 and C19. Early examples are rare.

reeding: Decorative carving of convex parallel lines.

re-entrant corner: Rounded corner which incorporates a cusp.

refectory table: Modern term for the long dining tables of the C17 and later.

regalia: Term used by collectors of militaria for Nazi insignia of the period 1924-45.

Regency: Strictly the period during which George, Prince of Wales, was Prince Regent i.e. 1811 to 1820; more generally used to cover the period from 1800 to the succession of William IV in 1830.

reggivato: Type of very decorative Italian vase stand.

regimental badge: British military badge worn on helmets, belts, buckles or shoulder belts and an important aid to dating military uniforms.

regimental buttons: Found on military tunics from 1767, of pewter embossed with the regimental number; of brass after the mid C19.

register plate: Inscribed plate on a barometer against which the level of mercury is read.

registration mark: A patent number and, on English porcelain from 1842 a diamond shaped mark with the letter R in the centre and coded numbers referring to the date the pattern was officially registered.

regulator: Clock of great accuracy, thus sometimes used for controlling or checking other time pieces.

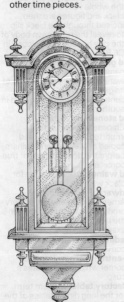

Reichsadlerhumpen: Late C16/C17 German glass beaker with a lid, enamelled with arms and double-headed eagle of the Habsburgs.

Reid, William: Liverpool potter operating from c1755 to 1761, producing crude blue and white painted porcelain.

Reinicke figures: Mid C18 Meissen figures modelled by Peter Reinicke.

relief: Term describing a design which is raised above the surrounding surface. See also bas relief.

religieuse: French for religious; a type of late C17 clock with a simple wooden case, though sometimes adorned with delicate inlay.

Remington: Mid C19 New York gunsmiths famous for Civil War revolvers, but also makers of rifles and pepperbox pistols.

remontoire: Device in clockwork designed to convert the power from the mainspring into a constant force, ironing out variations; usually in the form of a small ancillary spring which is continually rewound to maximum tension by the mainspring, and which acts as the power source rather than the mainspring itself.

Renaissance: Revival of classical ideas and styles, in rejection of the Gothic. It began in Florence c1400, and spread slowly throughout Europe; hence, in England, the Renaissance style does not influence art until early C17.

rendsborg: Blue painted wares from a pottery founded mid C18 in Denmark.

Rennes: French centre of faience production, C18 and C19, influenced by the Rouen style.

rent table: Table which usually takes the same form as a drum table but is traditionally used for keeping account of rents paid and owed. Some rent tables have initials on the drawers to help with this purpose.

repeater (1): Clock or watch which will repeat the strike of the preceding hour when a lever or button is pulled or pressed.

repeater (2): In firearms, a semi-automatic rifle.

repeating work: That part of a clock mechanism which enables the strike of the previous hour to be repeated.

Invented 1676 as a means of telling the time in the dark.

repoussé: French for "pushed out". Method of embossing silver or other metal by hammering into a mould from the reverse side.

reproduction: Piece which is a copy of an earlier design. Many reproduced items are now antique themselves.

reproduction armour: Made in quantity for antiquarians in the C19, particularly in Germany, France and Spain, and now sought after.

resist lustre: Lustrous pattern, often in silver, on ceramic applied by painting a pattern in wax or grease and dipping in pigment which coats the untreated areas.

restoration (1): Repairing of a piece, including the discreet replacement of any hopelessly damaged or missing parts.

Restoration (2): Term used to describe furniture made during the reigns of Charles II (1660-1685) and James II (1685-1689).

reticello: Rim or edge on a glass vessel ornamented with twisted strands of coloured glass.

reval faience: Rare late C18 wares from a short-lived factory in Estonia.

reveille-matin: Early form of alarm clock, made in quantity in the mid C19.

reversed areas: Parts of a ceramic body painted with grease or wax so that they repel glaze or lustre when dipped.

revolver: Firearm with a single barrel and a revolving chamber designed to hold a number of bullets.

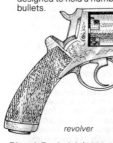

revolver

Rhead, Frederick (1856-1929): Pottery designer who worked for Wedgwood and several other potteries.

Rheinsberg: German faience factory, founded late C18.

Rhenish: Roman objects from the Rhineland region of south west Germany, including fine pottery which continued in production to the C7.

Rhineland stoneware: Jugs, jars and tankards of blue/grey and brown salt glazed stonewares, often with applied or relief moulded decoration, made from the C16 and much reproduced.

rhyton: Ancient drinking vessel of funnel shape, often in precious metal, sometimes in ceramic, and usually highly ornamented.

ricasso: Area of a sword nearest the hilt, parallel sided, unlike the rest of the blade which usually tapers.

rice grain: Common form of decoration on Chinese household wares from C16; the porcelain body is pierced at random intervals; the glaze fills over the perforations in firing but leaves a surface dimpled with shallow hollows the size of a rice grain, semi translucent when held up to the light.

Ricketts: Name of early C19 Bristol glass makers whose bottles are often stamped with the wine merchant's seal, usually on the neck.

Ridgeway: Factory in Hanley, Staffordshire, mass producing a great range of wares from C19.

Riesener, Jean (1734-1806): Most celebrated C18 cabinet maker in France, enjoying considerable Royal patronage. He was trained by Oeben, whose business he continued after the latter died and whose widow he married.

rifle: Gun with spiral grooving (rifling) inside the barrel, designed to aid the accuracy of the bullet's flight.

rifling: Spiral grooving in the inside of a gun barrel designed to spin the bullet and thereby counteract the bullet's tendency to veer in flight.

Rigby, John: Leading gunmaker, working in London and Dublin, late C19.

right: Antique dealers' term for an original and genuine piece, as opposed to "wrong", i.e. faked, altered or restored.

ring handle: Brass plate handle with a ring pull.

ring sundial: One consisting of a metal band pierced by a hole through which the sun shines onto a scale below.

ring trigger: Trigger in the form of a complete circle, found on early revolvers.

rising sun: See sunburst.

Rittenhouse, David: Philadelphia's maker of clocks and scientific instruments of outstanding quality, active 1750-90.

riving iron: Tool used for splitting wood into planks during medieval times. Also called a froe.

Robery & Delphieu: French makers of bébé dolls, late C19/ early C20.

robinia: Another name for acacia.

rocaille: Shell and rock motifs found in rococo work.

rocking chair: Chair which is mounted on bends of wood which act as rockers. An American invention that was made in various styles. See also Boston rocker and Salem rocker.

Rockingham: Yorkshire pottery, operating mid C18 to mid C19 which gave its name to a mottled purplish brown earthenware glaze used on utilitarian household wares; noted also for fine enamelled and gilded bone china.

rococo: Extravagant European style which developed out of the Baroque in the mid C18, essentially in interior decoration, and characterized by delicate curvaceous shapes and the use of Chinese and Indian motifs.

rod: Metal shaft of a clock pendulum, usually composed of brass and steel to equalize and cancel out variations in the length caused by temperature changes.

Roentgen, David (1743-1807): German cabinet maker who enjoyed Royal patronage in both Germany and France. His speciality was elaborately veneered pieces.

Rohmer, Marie: French doll maker, specializing in "Parisiennes", 1857-80.

Röhrken: German pewter tankards of slender cylindrical form, tapering out slightly towards the rim, with a hinged lid, C17 and C18.

roiro: In Japanese inro work, a highly polished and reflective black background.

rolling pin: Decorated and made of glass, sold as seaside souvenirs in great quantity from the late C18. Nailsea pins of coloured glass and commemorative pins are especially collectable.

roll top desk: Desk which has a curving slatted top enclosing the writing and working area.

Roman striking clock: Clock with two bells, one of which was used to strike the Roman numeral I, the other the numerals V and X. Thus the maximum number of strikes ever heard was four (IIII, VIII, VVII). Invented late C17.

romayne work: Term used to describe a decorative carving showing a head in profile within a roundel and with further embellishment such as scrollwork.

rond bosse: Earliest solid, three-dimensional toy soldiers, made in France from c1870, with round bases.

Rookwood: American pottery established 1880 by Maria Longworth Nichols Stoter in Cincinnati, Ohio. Produced high quality art pottery, influenced by Japanese designs.

rooted hair doll: One with tufts of real or synthetic hair, as opposed to modelled hair.

rope back: Descriptive of a chair made during the Regency period with a moulding of twisted rope appearance incorporated in the back. See also cable moulding.

Rörstrand: C18 Stockholm faience factory which pioneered transfer printing and specialized in ceramic vessels made to imitate silver.

Rose & Co.: Pottery founded in the early 1790s by John Rose at Coalbrookdale, known from the 1820s as Coalport and producing porcelain to rival the best of Sèvres and Minton in the mid C19.

rose bowl: Silver or glass bowl, varying in size from a finger bowl to a punch bowl, used from late C19 for flower arrangements, or for filling with water and scattering the surface with petals.

rose-cut: Jewel with a flat base and faceted upper surface; one with 24 facets is known as a Dutch Rose; one with 36 is Rose Recoupée.

rose-engine turned: Pottery decorated with flowing patterns of incised wavy lines or basket work designs, achieved by turning the leather-hard body on a rose-engine, or lathe.

rosehead nails: Name given to the old handmade nails used to secure iron fittings.

Rosenthal: Bavarian porcelain factory founded in 1879 and noted for its Art Nouveau and Art Deco wares.

rosette: Circular floral ornament.

rosewood: Purplish brown wood with distinctive black streaks and a coarse grain. Imported from South America and Honduras.

rosso antico: Burnished red stoneware vessels made by Wedgwood in imitation of ancient Greek black and red figure wares.

Roubilac figures: English porcelain figures based on sculptures by the great French sculptor Louis François Roubilac (1705-63).

Rouen: The most influential of all the French faience factories, founded in Normandy mid C16 and at its peak early C18. Renowned for its lacy painted designs, style rayonnant and bold use of iron-red glaze.

roundabout: Another name for a corner chair.

roundel: Circular ornament which may or may not incorporate additional decoration.

rout stool: Another name for a corridor stool.

rovine: Italian for "ruins"; ruined buildings in a romantic landscape were a popular type of motif on porcelain of the latter C18.

Royal Crown Derby: Factory founded in late C19 under royal patronage, noted for fine bone china; eventually absorbed all its surviving predecessors in the town.

Royal Doulton: Name given to Doulton products after 1900, notably handpainted vases and figures, and salt-glazed earthenware art pottery.

Royal Dux: Porcelain factory founded in 1860 in Dux, now Duchov, Czeckoslovakia, best known for Art Nouveau vases and Art Deco figures.

Royal Worcester: Products of the Worcester Porcelain Company after 1862.

Rozenburg: Pottery from The Hague, in Holland, made early C20, noted for Art Nouveau vases and vessels influenced by traditional Indonesian design and for wafer thin porcelain which contrasts with the bulkier pottery favoured by other producers of the era.

ruby glass: Glass containing copper, or more rarely gold, oxide to give it a rich, brilliant red colour. Invented C17.

Rudd's table: Distinct variation of the dressing table with three deep and fitted drawers, the central one containing a writing slope. The end drawers each have a swivelling mirror and can themselves be swung out to give the mirrors maximum versatility.

rug: Term used loosely to denote a small carpet, less than 40ft (12m) in area; sometimes used by specialists to describe all hand-made floor coverings, to distinguish them from machine-made carpeting.

rule hinge: Another name for an elbow hinge.

rule joint: Edging found on Pembroke and other drop leaf tables enabling the leaf to fold without leaving a gap.

Rummer/Roemer: Originally C16/C17 German wide-bowled wine glass on a thick stem, decorated with prunts, on a base of concentric glass coils, often in green glass (waldglas). Widely copied throughout Europe in many forms.

runner (1): Another term for the rocker of a rocking chair.

runner (2): Strip of wood on which a drawer slides in and out.

runner (3): Long narrow rug used in corridors or to flank the principal carpet used to cover the floor of a mosque or palace.

running footman: Another name for a dinner wagon.

rush seat: Seat made out of rushes which have been woven together. Also known as a flag seat.

russeting: Brown patination on sword blades caused by applying a corrosive solution to the metal which produces a rust-proof barrier.

Russia leather: Best quality leather used to cover seat furniture. It is made from calf or cowhide and known for its strength, aromatic odour and resistance to insect attack.

rutakali: Oriental rug made to serve as a horse blanket.

rya: Shaggy hand-woven Finnish carpets patterned with human and animal figures and religious symbols.

ryusa: Netsuke formed by joining two hollowed out sections each with a perforated or cut-out design.

S

sabaton: Armour plated shoes.

sabiji: Japanese lacquerware made to imitate the appearance of metal.

sabot: Metal foot to which castors are fixed.

sabre: Curved slashing sword, usually carried by cavalrymen.

sabre

sabre leg: Elegant curving leg associated with furniture of the Regency period but first appearing near the end of the C18. Also known as Trafalgar leg.

saddle seat (1): Seat which is cut away in a downwards direction from the centre. Often found on Windsor and other country chairs.

saddle seat (2): Seat shaped like a bicycle saddle, as found on cockfighting and reading chairs.

sadiron: Solid cast-iron smoothing iron, heated by placing on a stand over coals.

Sadler & Green: Liverpool pottery which pioneered the technique of transferprinting on earthenware and porcelain in the early C19.

Safavid: C16 to C18 Persian dynasty, under whose rule ceramics and carpet-making underwent a renaissance.

saff: Turkish silk prayer rugs characterized by multiple mihrabs. Also spelt saph, saaph, sarph.

saffron teapot: Miniature silver teapot used for making saffron tea in C18.

sagemono: Japanese for "hanging things"; items suspended from the obi (waist) and secured by the netsuke (toggle).

St. Amand-les-Eaux: C18 faience factory in northern France, noted for lacy patterning on pale grey glaze.

St. Clement: Late C18 factory in Lorraine, France, specializing in faience-fine.

St. Cloud: Factory near Paris, famous for soft-paste porcelain in the first half C18, decorated in Kakiemon style and imitation blanc-de-chine.

St. Ives: Pottery in Cornwall founded in 1920 by Bernard Leach and Shoji Hamada. Renowned for its hand-made pieces.

St. Louis Glass Factory: Founded late C18 in Lorraine, France, pioneer of pressed glass and famous for coloured glass vessels and paperweights.

St. Omer: Late C18 faience factory near Calais, northern France, noted for lively rococo style decoration.

St. Petersburg: Porcelain factory in the former Russian capital operating late C18/C19 and noted for large ornamented pieces painted with copies of famous oil paintings and Russian peasant figures.

Saint-Vérain stoneware: Dark blue glazed vessels and especially tiles, decorated with Renaissance relief motifs, from the Nièvre region of France, made from C16 and as late as C18.

saku: Japanese term meaning "made by" e.g. Kajikawa saku – made by Kajikawa.

Salem rocker: American variation of the Windsor chair from Salem, Massachusetts.

Salem secretary: Variation of a Sheraton style secretaire bookcase from Salem, Massachusetts.

Salem snowflake: Carved decoration in the form of a sixpointed snowflake found on some furniture from Salem, Massachusetts.

sallet: Renaissance soldier's helmet protecting all of the rear of the head and neck, but coming down only to the nose in front.

salon chair: General term to describe a French or French style armchair.

salt: An especially large dish or cellar designed for holding salt is sometimes termed "a salt".

salt glaze: Hard translucent glaze used on stoneware and achieved by throwing common salt into the kiln at high temperatures; produces a silky, pitted appearance, sometimes compared to orange peel.

salver: Flat plate, often with feet, made for placing underneath other dishes. Usually of silver or silver plate.

Samadet: Faience factory in south-west France, mid C18 to C19, noted for green painted wares and chinoisiere grotesques.

samarkand: Chinese carpets from Sinkiang, formerly distributed through Samarkand, now in Soviet Central Asia. Loosely knotted of wool pile on cotton warp and notable for subtle colours (especially creams and yellows) and fine floral designs, including the flowering pomegranate tree.

Samarra: Fine pottery of the C6 to C4 BC painted with geometric designs on a white background, named after Samarra in Mesopotamia, the possible production centre for these wares.

sambo bank: Late C19 mechanical money box, introduced 1882, in the form of a negro whose eyes roll when a coin is dropped into the mouth.

sambo clock: C19 American clock in the form of a banjo-playing negro.

Samhammer, Philip: German wax doll maker, late C19/early C20.

Samian: General term for fine Roman pottery with a high red gloss, made in imitation of silverware and decorated with impressed or applied designs. See red gloss pottery.

samovar: Urn used for providing a constant supply of hot water for tea making, with a brazier below, or a tube that could be filled with coals and immersed in the water. Russian, of silver or copper.

sampler: Needlework pictures designed to teach children the different types of stitch, rare before the mid C17, relatively common in the C19 when nearly every schoolgirl produced one; this practice virtually ended with the First World War.

Samson & Co.: Paris factory, established 1845, specializing in reproductions of Meissen, Chinese porcelain, Delft and old maiolica; sometimes passed off as genuine C18 pieces by unscrupulous sellers.

sandblasting: Technique of decorating glass by blasting sand through a stencil to etch a superficial pattern.

sand cast figures: Toy soldiers sand cast in aluminium, as distinct from lead, relatively common since the 1950s.

Sanderson silver: Rare C17 silver made by Robert Sanderson in Boston, U.S.A.

Sandwich glass: From the Boston & Sandwich Glass Co., founded 1825 in Cape Cod,

Massachusetts; famous for
early pressed glass.

sang de boeuf: French for bull's
blood; a rich, deep red glaze
made using copper oxide, first
developed in China in the
early C18 and not successfully
imitated in the West until late
C19.

Sarab: North western Iranian
carpetmaking centre, noted
especially for runners.

sarcophagus (1): Coffin of
stone, lead or wood decorated
with sculpture, painting or
inscriptions. Rarely found
complete, but fragments of
ancient Egyptian, Etruscan,
Roman and early Christian
sarcophagi are relatively
common.

sarcophagus (2): Descriptive of
the shape of an item, usually a
cellaret or tea caddy, which is
shaped somewhat like a stone
coffin of the same name.

sari: Colourful Persian pottery of
the C10 and C11, often in the
form of large dishes painted
with birds and flowers.

Sarreguemines: French factory
in the Lorraine region
specializing in reproductions of
old maiolica from 1800.

saruk: High quality carpets from
south west Teheran, in
traditional Persian floral
designs but more recently
harshly coloured Western
influenced designs made for
export.

sashi: Netsuke of elongated,
rather than rounded, form.

sashka/sashqua: Slightly
curved Cossack sword without
quillons.

satin glass: Late C19 art glass
heated with hydrofluoric acid
fumes to give a lustrous, satin-
like finish.

satinwood: Yellow wood with a
very close grain. It is tolerably
hard and was used both as a
veneer and solid. It was much
favoured in England in the late
C18.

satsuma: Early Japanese
ceramics, influenced by Korean
designs, from the port of
Satsuma in southern Japan,
often crackle-glazed.

satyrs: Woodland deities, half
human and half animal, the
companions of Bacchus, used
to represent lustfulness in
classical art.

sauceboat: Long, narrow boat
shaped silver vessel with a
wide spout, foot and handle
sometimes with a matching

spoon, from the late C17. For
serving sauces or gravy.

Savery, William (1721-1787):
American cabinet maker who
worked in Philadelphia. He
produced Chippendale style
furniture.

Savona ware: C17 and C18
maiolica from the Italian town
near Genoa, distinguished
from most traditional maiolica
by its blue painted chinoiserie
designs.

savonnerie: Very fine French
carpets and tapestries made by
a company founded in 1627
and operating from a soap
factory (savonnerie); originally
hand knotted in oriental style,
but later cut pile.

sawbuck table: American table
with either a plain or scrolled
X-shaped frame. Made in New
England.

sax: Roman or early medieval
sword with a short, wide,
tapering blade.

sayling hance: Original term for
an overhanging canopy, as
found on high dressers, etc.

scabbard: Any sheath for a
sharp-edged weapon.

scagliola: Imitation marble used
for table tops from C18. It is a
mixture of marble chips and
plaster. Also a mixture of
plaster and glue painted to
resemble marble which was
used in C19 for fireplace
surrounds.

scale armour: Another name for
lamellar armour; made of
overlapping plates like fish
scales.

scalloped: Decorated with a
series of depressions
resembling the shape of a
scallop shell — usually of rims
on silver or earthenware
vessels. Also any shell-shaped
ornament.

scarab: Originally a beetle with
iridescent wings revered by
the Ancient Egyptians and
frequently portrayed in their
art. Now also used of antique
gemstones cut in the shape of
a beetle, with an intaglio
design cut into the flat
underside and used as a seal.

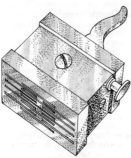

scarifier: Early medical instrument with a sprung set of knives in a cube-shaped box, used in blood letting.

Sceaux faience: Produced near Paris in the late C18, distinguished for brilliantly coloured rococo style flower and bird decoration in close imitation of Sèvres porcelain.

scent bottle: Small, portable flask of flattened pear shape, made of silver, rock crystal, porcelain or glass.

Schaper: C17 German glass ornamented with black enamel; Johan Schaper was a prominent practitioner of the art, specializing in landscapes, usually painted on beakers.

schiavona: C17 Italian straight two-edged sword with an ornate basket hilt of interwoven metal strips.

Schilling, Barbara & Ferdinand Max: Doll makers specializing in papier mâché and wax dolls, German, late C19/early C20.

schist: Fine-grained crystalline sandstone which can be carved in fine detail. Much used by ancient Indian cultures for statues of the Hindu deities.

Schläger: German ritual duelling sabre.

Schleswig faience: Fine wares from a late C18 Danish factory noted for rococo style figures and manganese-purple decoration.

Schmelzglas: Marbled glass, predominantly white, made to imitate precious minerals such as opal and onyx.

Schmidt, Bruno: German doll maker specializing in character dolls, 1900-25.

Schnabelkanne: C16 stoneware jug from the Rhineland with a long spout, decorated in carved relief.

Schnelle: Rhineland stoneware tankard, tall and tapering

inward to the top, often with relief decoration and a pewter lid; made from C16.

Schoenau & Hoffmeister: German doll maker, active from 1901.

Schoenhut Co.: Philadelphia doll maker, early C20, specializing in dolls with spring-jointed limbs.

Schrezheim faience: Mid C18 products of a Bavarian factory noted for large figures modelled by J. M. Mutschele.

Schwanhardt: Strictly, glass engraved by Georg Schwanhardt and his sons in Nuremberg in C17, but generally of any fine glass engraving of similar style and quality.

Schwarzhafner: Black ironstone made in the C15/C16 in southern Germany and Austria.

Schwarzlot: Painting or enamelwork on glass or porcelain in black, similar in appearance to an engraving.

scimitar: Eastern curved sword used for hacking and chopping, not thrusting.

scissor toys: Traditional wooden toys from Saxony consisting of soldiers, or a girl driving a flock of geese, mounted on the cross pieces of a criss-cross concertina which simulates movement.

sconce: Strictly a plate or a bracket on the wall to which lights or candle-holders could be attached; now used to refer to the candlesticks as well; silver or other metal, C18.

scoop pattern: Repeated band of carved decoration in the form of round-ended gouges which have been scooped from the wood. Where two pieces are gouged out one above the other it is known as double scoop.

scotia: Type of classical moulding of concave semi-circular profile.

Scots pine: Rather plain light yellowish wood with a straight grain. It is much used for carcases and drawer linings. Normally referred to simply as pine. Also known as deal.

Scottish pistols: Made at Doune, in Stirling, during C18. Distinctive features are the all-metal stock and the lack of a trigger guard. Contemporary replicas abound, often made in Birmingham with pseudo Scottish names, now collectable in their own right.

scramasax: Early broadsword with a short single edged blade, used from the Bronze age through to early medieval times.

scratch blue: Incised decoration overpainted in blue, typical of C18 saltglazed stonewares.

scratch carving: Simple and cheap form of decoration on C16 and C17 joined furniture whereby a design is formed by a simple outline scratched into the surface of the wood.

screen: Series of tall hinged frames, each filled with silk, tapestry or other decoration and used to form a division or private section within a room. However, see also banner screen, cheval screen and pole screen.

screw pistol: Has a barrel which unscrews for loading.

scribing line: Inscribed mark made by a cabinet maker when preparing to cut joints. Often seen with the dovetail joints of drawer linings.

scrimshaw: Objects of whale and walrus tusk, whalebone and teeth, engraved by sailors using a knife and needle, from late C17.

scripophily: Love of scrip – short for subscription receipt, i.e. bonds and share certificates.

scripopolist: Collector of bonds and share certificates.

scroll: Curving decoration. Often found shaped as an ornate "C" in which case it may be called a C-scroll.

scroll foot: Term used to describe a foot that curves outwards and back onto itself.

scroll top: Another name for a broken pediment.

scrutoire: American term for an escritoire; also sometimes used for other types of writing furniture.

scutcheon: Shield-shaped ornament or fitment.

seal bottle: Wine bottles with an applied glass medallion or seal personalized with the owner's name, initials, coat of arms or a date. Produced from the early C17 to the mid C19 when bottles were relatively expensive.

seal spoon: Spoon with a finial shaped like a wax seal – sometimes even engraved like one – a mid C16 to late C17 form.

sear: The pin which, in a firing mechanism, holds the hammer at full or half cock.

sear spring: Spring which holds the sear under tension, causing it to hold the hammer at half or full cock on a firiing mechanism. The strength of the seár spring determines the pull of the trigger.

seat rails: Horizontal rails which form the seat of a chair.

seaweed marquetry: Distinct, highly decorative marquetry in the form of flowing and curling thin leafy patterns which usually cover most of the visible parts of the piece to which it is applied. Generally associated with the William and Mary period.

Secession: Austrian Art Nouveau movement dominated by the architect Josef Hoffmann and greatly influenced by Mackintosh and the Glasgow School. Objects of this style, not necessarily made in Austria, are described as secessionist.

sechiello: Italian name for a silver wine bucket, from C17.

secretaire: Piece of writing furniture which often resembles a chest of drawers but with the top drawer fitted as a writing desk. The drawer pulls forward and the front drops down to form a writing surface and reveal the fitted interior. Known in America as a secretary.

secretaire à abattant: Type of French writing desk with a fall front.

secretaire bookcase: Secretaire with a bookcase fitted above it.

secretary: American name for a secretaire or bureau.

sedan clock: Carriage clock resembling a large watch, designed to be suspended from the bow-shaped handle.

Seddon, George (1727-1801): Prominent English cabinet maker who had a large-scale business producing fine quality furniture.

sedjadeh: Alternative name for the "standard" size of Oriental carpet, measuring about 5ft x 8ft (1.5m x 2.5m).

Sehna carpets: From the town of Kurdistan, on the Iran/Iraq border, which gave its name to the Sehna knot, and produces very fine, dense, short-pile rugs with repeated small floral designs; paradoxically often made using the Ghiordes knot.

Sehna knot: Also senneh, sinneh; one of the two knotting techniques used in rug making, typical of Persian, as opposed to Turkish, rugs. The weft is looped under and over one warp thread and under the adjacent one.

seichur: Caucasian rugs characterized by a repeated diagonal cross motif.

self-cocking: Firing mechanism which cocks automatically when the trigger is pulled, as opposed to one which is cocked manually.

Selig, Conrad: Clockmaker active 1800-25 in Reading, Pennsylvania.

seljuk/seljuq: Very fine ceramics produced in Asia Minor in C12 and C13, noted for the use of turquoise glaze and deep lustre.

selvedge: Strip of flat material, made by weaving the warp threads, at the short edges of a carpet. Designed to prevent fraying.

semi-flat figures: Toy soldiers produced in quantity from the 1930s, intermediate between flats and solids, regarded as inferior because they lack fine detail.

serapi: Alternative name for rugs from the Herez region of north-western Iran; large with bold geometric designs.

Sereband: Town in central Iran, near Teheran, producing rugs with an allover boteh design; any similar style of rug, no matter where made.

serpent: S-shaped armature in a firing mechanism that pivots when the trigger is released. It incorporates the jaws holding the flint which strikes the steel and causes a spark which ignites the powder.

serpentine: Double-curved outline.

serre-papier: Another name for a cartonnier.

serving table: Long rectangular table designed for use in the dining room. They were intended to stand against a wall and sometimes have a raised edge on three sides.

settee: Long seat with an upholstered back and sides. It generally has a square-ended appearance and may have a space between the seat and the back and sides, all of which help to make it quite distinct from, say, the sofa.

setting sun: See sunburst.

settle: Long wooden seat with a back and either with a box seat or on legs. At each end are arms or side-pieces.

Sèvres: Europe's leading porcelain factory, founded in Vincennes in 1738 but relocated to Sèvres in 1756; dominated ceramic fashion from then on until 1815; noted for richly painted and gilded rococo style vases but also highly ornate clock cases, tea, coffee and chocolate services and boxes.

sextant: Navigational device based on an arc representing one sixth of a circle, invented 1757.

SFBJ: Société de Fabrication de Bébés et Jouets; doll maker founded 1899 by merging the businesses of Jumeau, Bru and others. Products regarded as inferior to those of the original makers.

sgrafitto decoration: Literally scratched or incised, usually through the slip to reveal a contrasting body colour beneath.

shagreen: Skin of shark or ray fish used on sword grips and scabbards.

Shah Abbas: Bold, sweeping floral design on Persian carpets named in honour of the famous ruler.

Shaker furniture: Simplistic furniture made by the Shakers, an early C19 American sect. They made a wide range of furniture in pine, maple and fruitwoods, much prized today.

shako: C19 military cap, conical or cylindrical in shape, with a peak and either a plume or a ball crest.

shakudo: Gold bronze alloy used by Japanese makers of inro.

sham drawer: False drawer, but especially one which actually opens only to reveal some kind of fully fitted interior instead of the expected open space.

shamsir/shamshir: Eastern sword with a curved blade, short quillons and a pommel set at right angles to the grip.

Shang yin: In Chinese history, the period c1532-1027 BC.

share certificate: Certificates issued to owners of shares in commercial enterprises, especially road and railway schemes, canal works, mining or foreign investments. Very rare examples date to the C17, but most of those now collected date to mid C19.

Sharps, Christian: Leading American gunmaker, mid C19.

shaving stand: Made in various designs but basically a stand with an adjustable mirror and probably incorporating one or more boxed compartments for shaving equipment.

Shaw, Joshua: Leading American gunmaker, early C19.

Shearer, Thomas: English cabinet maker working in C18. His designs are similar to those of Sheraton and, to this day, his contemporaries Hepplewhite and Sheraton are given much of the credit due to him.

sheep's head clock: Late C17 type with an outsize dial which hides the case from view.

Sheffield plate: Process, invented in Sheffield, Yorkshire, whereby two rolled sheets of silver are fused to a core of copper. Made from the 1760s on, but hallmarking did not begin until 1784. Cheaper than silver, but often used for same types of vessel and decorated in similar ways, except that deep-engraving was avoided.

shell: Decorative motif used in C18 and revived again during the Edwardian era. Also known as scallop, which is the type of shell usually represented.

shellac (1): Polish used in the process of French polishing. It is made from the shell of the lac beetle and was produced in France, although most now comes from India.

shellac (2): Early form of plastic, invented 1868 and used principally for gramophone records, but also, more rarely, for moulded ornaments.

Shelley Potteries Ltd: The name, after 1925, of the Foley pottery, founded in Staffordshire by H. Wileman in 1860. The Shelley pottery produced fine Art Deco dinner services.

shellguard: Disc between the quillon and the blade of a sword to protect the hand.

shelves: Oak hanging shelves for books and china, etc. were in existence during Tudor times and the vogue for displaying china in this way continued until early C18 when it became the fashion to put china in a cabinet. See also book stand, glass case and trencher case.

Shenendoah Valley: Simple earthenwares and slip-decorated redwares produced by several valley towns from 1800, of which the Bell family's products are the best known.

shen-lung: Chinese dragon motif found on carpets and porcelain.

shepherd's crook arm: Curving chair or settee arm which is shaped somewhat like a shepherd's crook. They were fashionable throughout most of the C18.

shepherd's sundial: Small portable sundial with a complex scale designed for year round use, taking into account the sun's seasonal movement.

Sheraton, Thomas (1751-1806): English furniture designer. He recommended light, delicate furniture and was particularly fond of satinwood for his finest pieces.

Sheraton barometer: One with a case made by the celebrated cabinet maker or in the Sheraton style.

Sheraton revival: Descriptive of furniture produced in the style of Sheraton when his designs gained revived interest during the Edwardian period.

Sherrebek: Tapestry weavers established in Schleswig-Holstein to revive an ancient industry; producer of Art Nouveau textiles designed by Otto Eckmann amongst others.

shibayama: Decorative inlaid work named after Shibayama Dosho, a Japanese artist. It usually comprises ivory, mother-of-pearl, coral, gold or silver inlaid into a lacquered ground.

shibuichi: Silver-bronze alloy used by Japanese makers of inro.

shield: Any defensive plate of wood, metal, etc., used to protect the body in battle and parry blows.

shield back: Descriptive of a type of chair designed in C18 which has a back shaped like a shield. Mainly associated with Hepplewhite.

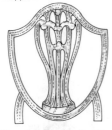

shino: Japanese medieval tea-ceremony bowls with designs painted in red-brown slip.

shipping furniture: General term which is usually applied to lesser quality furniture intended for export.

ship's barometer: From late C18, often bound in brass, a wheel barometer of great accuracy made for use on board ships.

ships in bottles: Made by sailors from c1870 to 1920, but mass-produced from 1900.

Shiraz: Distribution centre in central-southern Iran for nomadic rugs, decorated with simple geometric motifs.

shirvan: Caucasian rugs from the shores of the Caspian Sea, often decorated with a mixture of typically Caucasian geometric designs and Persian floral motifs.

shishi: Japanese name for "Dog of Fo", the mythical lion-dog, guardian of the temples of Buddha.

shoe brace: Bar at the bottom of a chair back into which the central splat is fitted.

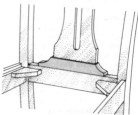

shoe tree: Wooden implement for stretching leather shoes and boots and keeping them in shape.

shoo-fly: American rocking horse patented 1859 consisting of two horse-shaped cut out boards on rockers joined by a seat.

shoot: Securing part of a lock which protrudes when the key is turned.

shooting plate: Pewter plate awarded as a prize in shooting contests and suitably decorated, German, late C18.

shoulder head doll: One with head, neck and collar made to be inserted into the body.

shovelboard table: Table used for playing shovelboard, a game more commonly known nowadays as shove ha'penny. The table top is marked with a series of grooves and the object of the game is to slide a coin or counter to rest entirely within one of the sections.

show bottle: Decorative glass containers, sometimes also of porcelain, made for retailers to store and show candy, pharmaceuticals, novelties, etc.

show wood: Visible wood on an upholstered piece of furniture.

Shunzhi (Shun Chih): Chinese Qing dynasty emperor, 1644-61.

sideboard: Piece of dining room furniture with cupboards and drawers for holding plates, cutlery, wine and table linen, etc.

sidelock: Any firearm in which the firing mechanism is attached to the side of the breech.

side rails: Two outer vertical members which form the back of a chair. Also known as uprights.

side table: Small table designed to stand at the side of a room next to a wall.

Siegburg: Earliest Rhineland stoneware, usually simple cylindrical vessels, produced before AD 1400.

Siena: Tuscan town noted for its Renaissance maiolica, often with Moorish-influenced designs and using burnt siena – the orangebrown colour named after the town.

sigillata: Relief decorated pottery cast in a mould, in imitation of ancient Roman Samian or red gloss wares.

signpost barometer: Alternative name for an angle barometer; one with a tube bent, towards the top, almost to the horizontal for greater accuracy of measurement.

sileh: S-shaped motif found on Caucasian rugs.

silent striking clock: One with a device to shut off the strike at will, during the night, for example.

Silesian stem: Early C18 wine glass stem; hexagonal or octagonal, flaring up to a pronounced shoulder.

silhouette: Portrait made by tracing the outline of a figure, either painted or cut out of paper and mounted on card. Popular 1770 to 1840.

silicon ware: Colourful vitreous, or enamel-like, stoneware produced by the Doulton factory in the 1880s and 90s and widely imitated by other potteries.

silver lustre: Silvery, iridescent lustre on ceramics achieved by painting the vessel with platinum-based pigment.

silver table: Small rectangular table designed for use in the dining room. They usually have a fretwork gallery.

silverwood: C18 name for harewood.

Simon & Halbig: German porcelain company making high quality bisque heads which were supplied to doll makers. From 1870.

Sincency: Early C18 to mid C19 faience factory near Paris, noted for muted colours and chinoiserie scenes.

singing doll: Large C19 doll containing a music box.

single action: Firing mechanism which automatically cocks and fires as the trigger is depressed, or one which fires without cocking.

singletrain movement: One in which all the functions of the clock – moving the hands and striking the chime – are performed by one mechanism.

Sinkiang: Very fine antique carpets made in the Persian style but with Chinese influenced motifs and originally marketed through Samarkand. Now mass-produced Chinese carpets.

siphon barometer: Generic term for barometers with a vertical column of mercury and a vertical scale, as distinct from the wheel barometer which has a dial and indicator hand.

sivas: Persian-influenced carpets from central Turkey, noted for delicate colours.

six-character mark: Marks found on the base of imperial Chinese ceramics, supposedly naming the reigning emperor, dynasty and the date, from the early C15 to the early C18. However, not all such marks are what they purport to be and independent verification is advisable.

sleeper: Antique dealers' term for a piece that has been stored away for years and has escaped use or restoration.

sleeve vase: Oriental vase of narrow tubular form.

sleigh bed: Type of American bed made in the French Empire style and resembling a sleigh.

sleigh bed

Six Dynasties: Period in Chinese history AD 265-589.

six-hour dial: One with only six divisions instead of twelve, often with the hours 1 – 6 in Roman numerals and 7 – 12 superimposed in Arabic numerals.

Skånska: Glassware from the Swedish works founded in the late C17, noted for its simple forms.

skean-dhu: Short Highland Scottish dagger normally carried in the stocking top.

skeleton clock: Deliberately made to expose the workings by cutting the plates to the minimum required to support the movement. Usually encased in glass.

skeleton escutcheon: Simplest form of lock escutcheon which merely outlines the shape of the keyhole.

skirmisher: Shortsword carried by foot soldiers from C16.

skiver: Thin skin of leather used as a writing surface on writing tables, desks etc.

skull: In armour, the upperpart of a helmet, reinforced to provide extra strength over the cranium.

skyphos: Ancient Greek pottery form; a deep cup or basin with nearly vertical sides and two horizontal handles situated at the rim.

slat back: Descriptive of a type of country chair with a back formed of curved vertical strips or slats of wood.

slice: Silver knife with a broad, trowel-shaped blade, sometimes pierced or engraved, from C18.

slide: See brushing slide and candle slide.

slip: Clay mixed with water and paint for decorating pottery.

slip cast: Pottery made by pouring slip into a plaster mould which absorbs the water leaving the moulded clay; a technique for producing very varied forms.

slipper chair: Type of C19 upholstered drawing room chair with a back that is more reclined than usual and continuous through the seat in a curving line.

slipware: Earthenware decorated with slip (fire clay and water); variously trailed, combed or incised.

slit heads: Wax dolls with a slit running across the pate into which hair was inserted to fall either side and simulate a parting.

smallsword: Any short sword, under 30in (75cm) in length designed for hand to hand fighting, duelling, thrusting, or fencing.

Smith & Wesson: Leading gun manufacturers, established mid C19 in the U.S.A.

Smith, George (fl.1790-1826): English cabinet maker and furniture designer who was among those who revived both the neoclassical and Egyptian styles.

smoker's bow: Variation of the Windsor chair but with a low back, and arms formed from a continuous hoop, above spindles.

Smyrna: Turkish carpets formerly marketed through Smyrna (modern Izmir); often of inferior quality made for export to Europe.

snakewood: Deep reddish brown wood with dark spots, imported from South America. It is hard and is used as a veneer.

snapes: Thin metal strips used for fixing pear drop handles and early bail handles to the drawer front. The snape was bent back on the inside of the drawer front and secured.

snaphaunce: Derived from the Dutch "snap hann" meaning snapping hen, a C16 and C17 firing mechanism developed in Northern Europe at the same time as the flintlock, often dated on the lockplate interior. A major difference from the flintlock was the lack of a half-cock safety catch.

snaplock: Collective term for both flintlock and snaphaunce firearms.

snowman figures: Early English porcelain figures, of the 1750s, associated with Longton Hall, so-called because of the very thick glaze which smooths out and obscures modelling details.

snuffbox: Box made to contain snuff in silver, or any other material; early examples have an integral rasp and spoon; from C17.

snuffer: Cone-shaped metal implement with a socket and handle used for extinguishing candles.

snuff grater: Rasp used for grating compacted dried tobacco leaf to provide the snuff powder. Sometimes incorporated in the snuff box.

snuff horn: C18 vessel of sheep's horn, sometimes of hoof, used for storing tobacco or snuff, often with ornate silver mounting.

snuff mull: Horn snuff container, from the Scottish Highlands, ornately chased or mounted with silver, often with accoutrements such as rasper and spoon.

soap box: Silver sphere, from the C18, with a cover and a foot, often with pierced or fretted ornament.

socket bayonet: Late C17 French invention, enabling the musket to be fired while the bayonet was in place. In use until the C19.

soda glass: Glass containing soda as a flux, light and easily worked; the earliest form of glass, much used by Venetian craftsmen.

sofa: Long seat which developed from the French day bed. It is generally fully upholstered and of a more rounded appearance than, say, a settee.

sofa table: Type of drop leaf table which developed from the Pembroke table. It was designed to stand behind a sofa, so is long and thin with two short drop leaves at the ends and two drawers in the frieze.

soft-paste porcelain: Developed by English potters in the mid C18 as a by-product of the search for true porcelain; ground frit, soapstone (or steatite) and bone-ash are used instead of the petuntse of true porcelain; difficult to make because precise temperatures in firing are critical. Generally superseded by hard-paste by the late C18.

softwood: One of two basic categories in which all timbers are classified. The softwoods are conifers which generally have leaves in the form of evergreen needles. See also hardwood.

solids: Collectors' term for three-dimensional toy soldiers, introduced c1890 as distinct from "flats" or "cut-out" figures. Now the most popular and collected form.

soumak: Very fine flat-woven Caucasian carpets, richly coloured and decorated with abstract designs formed by both the warp and the weft (instead of the warp only); the pattern formed by the weft thread resembles chainstitch.

South Boston glass: Early C19 wares, made by an unrecorded Massachusetts factory, showing the influence of the Boston Glass Co.

southern celadon: Early Chinese wares with a distinctive deep red fabric and grey-green glaze, from the southern province of Chekiang.

South Jersey glass: Simple, free-blown glassware made by numerous factories in South Jersey, late C18/early C19, often in coloured glass.

Southwark: South London pottery centre noted for the earliest English delftware, C17.

souvenir figure: Dolls made from the mid C19 for sale as souvenirs, often dressed in national costume.

soy frame: Silver or plated frame designed to hold a number of small cut-glass sauce bottles.

spade foot: Tapering foot of square section usually found on tables, chairs and sideboards of the late C18.

spandrel: Decoration usually associated with clocks, where either brass or painted spandrels decorate the four corners of the dial.

spangled: Glass coated in a mineral, such as mica, to create a glittering effect.

Spanish foot: Chair or table foot which appears a little like a hand resting on its finger knuckles when seen in its most elegant form. At its simplest it is merely a sliced off outward curving end to a square section leg.

Spanish mahogany: See mahogany.

spanner: Winding key used to tension the springs in a wheellock firing mechanism.

sparrow beak: Usually of a silver jug with a simple triangular spout.

sparta: Turkish carpets intended for European export, made and marketed chiefly in Smyrna, but generally of better quality and finer colours than Smyrna carpets.

sparver bed: Another name for a tent bed.

spatterware: Cheap pottery, much of it made in England for export to America, decorated with simple designs on a spattered background, early C19.

specimen chest: Small chest of many small drawers, sometimes with enclosing doors, designed for housing a collection.

specular: Meaning "mirrorlike". A carpet design in which the two halves, top and bottom or left and right, are symmetrical.

spelter: Zinc treated to look like bronze and much used as an inexpensive substitute in Art Nouveau appliqué ornament and Art Deco figures.

spice box: Silver casket with numerous internal divisions for storing precious spices, the lid often in the form of a shell. From late C16.

spice-box spoon: Spoons designed for dipping into spice boxes, usually with a broad bowl and a short curved "swan" handle.

spice cupboard: Small, squarish wall hanging cupboard, which is often fitted with small drawers for storing spices and elaborately decorated. Made C17 and C18.

spill vase: Porcelain vase, often with a flat back for hanging on a wall, made to contain spills for lighting candles.

splat: Central upright of a chair back.

splint seat: Seat made of interlaced strips of wood, usually oak or hickory, and found mainly in C18 American country furniture.

split baluster: Turned baluster which has been split vertically in half to provide two flat surfaces.

split baluster gateleg: Type of table leg in which the gate is part of the end leg. The leg splits in half down its length when the gate opens.

Spode: Important factory founded in Stoke-on-Trent, Staffordshire, by the first Josiah Spode (1733-97) who pioneered cheap, transfer printed bone-china. More recently noted for its reproductions of fine porcelain figures.

sponged/spongeware: Akin to spatterware; decoration on cheap china produced for export to America in C19, made by dabbing a slipsoaked sponge at random over the surface of the vessel.

spontoon: Or espontoon; an early C18 pole weapon, a cross between a pike and a halberd.

Spool furniture: Form of decoration introduced in America in the 1850s, based on bobbin-turning, which had been popular in the C17. It was used on many types of furniture, including chairs, beds, and tables.

spoon: Apart from knives, the earliest form of eating implement; silver spoons can usually be dated to within a decade or so by the bowl shape and finial type.

spoon back: Term used to describe the back of a chair which has a central splat shaped somewhat like the handle of a spoon.

spoon hands: Wooden dolls with very simple hands, with only the thumb articulated.

spoon tray: Early C18 small silver tray, used to hold teaspoons before the saucer came into general use.

sporting guns: Highly accurate guns, often more finely made than military equivalents. Produced in quantity from early C18.

spout cup: Covered cup with a spout and two handles, used for feeding invalids, early C18.

sprigging: Applied decoration on pottery, generally of a repeated foliage motif; sections were cast and applied to the body, and the stems modelled by hand.

Spring and Autumn Annals: In Chinese history, the period 770 to 480 BC.

spring driven: Clockwork movements powered by the tension in the mainspring, rather than by weights or a pendulum.

Springfield type: Dolls with moveable limbs, similar to Ellis dolls, but manufactured by other companies in the region of Springfield, Vermont.

spring-loaded bayonet: Early C20 bayonet, with a release button to allow its swift removal from the gun barrel, and a hooked quillon, enabling it to be used as a hand weapon.

spruce: Wood of the fir family. It is soft and white in colour.

spur mark: Rough mark or discolouration occasionally found on the base of pottery where the vessel was supported during firing.

squab stool: Joined stool with a seat with a slightly raised rim designed to hold a loose cushion. C16/C17.

squeezer: Late C19 small firearm designed to be concealed in the hand and fired by clenching the fist.

staartklok: Dutch for "tail clock", a wall-clock made from c1800 with a pendulum (tail) and anchor escapement.

stackfreed: Early German clock device, the predecessor of the fusee, consisting of a counterspring which exerted a diminishing amount of pressure on the mainspring as the latter unwound, thus making the power relatively constant.

Staffordshire: Centre of the English pottery industry since C18; the term itself usually denotes late C18 and C19 blue transfer-printed wares, and cheap earthenware figures produced in great quantity in C19.

Staffordshire bank: Early ceramic money box or "piggy bank", of various forms. Made by numerous Staffordshire potteries mid C18 to late C19.

stain: Colouring applied to wood to enrich or transform its natural colour.

stairs: Each stair consists of a riser (the vertical face) and the tread (the horizontal surface). The shaped edge of a tread is called a nosing. A winder is a wedge shaped head, wider at one end than the other. The skirting board which disguises the cut ends of the risers and treads is called a string.

staked leg: Simple and primitive way of fitting a leg to a seatboard. The top of the leg is pushed through a hole in the seatboard and secured by a wedge.

Stalker and Parker: Firm which greatly popularized the art of japanning during the late C17 and early C18.

stamp box: Cases made from 1845 onwards for storing and dispensing postage stamps, often in silver but also in Tunbridge ware.

stamped: Design impressed into the body of a ceramic while it is still soft.

stamps: After 1751 the makers of French furniture had to stamp their name on every piece they made. This can prove useful as a means of identifying makers of individual pieces, although sometimes they refer only to the repairer of a piece and not to its original maker.

standard (1): Large dometopped iron bound travelling chest with carrying handles.

standard (2): Dining chair without arms is often referred to as a standard chair.

Standard Time Company: Founded 1876, specializing in electric clocks of great accuracy supplied principally to business firms.

standing cup: Usually a purely ornamental and highly elaborate silver or gold vessel, used as a display piece.

standing salt: Large, ornate, salt-storage vessel, from the C17 when salt was a precious commodity and a symbol of wealth.

standing screen: Screen of hinged panels, originally lacquered and imported from the Orient for use as room dividers or draught excluders; from early C19 many variants.

standish: Common term for a silver ink stand before C18.

Stangenglas: German C16/C17 tall cyclindrical glass beaker decorated with prunts.

stannary: Tinware, named after the Cornish tin-mining district.

stater: Ancient Greek coinage of gold or silver.

statuary porcelain: Alternative name for mid C19 Parian wares, so called because of its resemblance to marble.

Staudenmayer: Leading London gunmaker, early C19.

Staunton, Edward (also Stanton): Noted London maker of longcase and bracket clocks, latter half C17.

steeple clock: Early Gothic clock case with pinnacles resembling a church tower; also C19 clock cases of similar form.

Steiff, Margarete: Maker of dolls and highly prized Teddy Bears, she first exhibited at Leipzig, 1903, but died 1909. The company she founded continued to mass produce toys, dolls and bears for export. Products can be identified by the "Steiff" button trademark, usually in the ear.

Steiner, Hermann: German maker of character dolls, active at Sonneberg, 1921-25.

Steiner, Jules Nicholas: French doll maker, active 1855-91, specializing in clockwork walking and crying dolls.

Steingut: German creamwares produced from late C18.

stele: Ancient Egyptian standing stone or slab, carved with hieroglyphs or a sculptured design.

stem: Shank joining the bowl to the foot of a wine glass; of many forms which can be diagnostic of date or place of manufacture.

step-cut: Foot of a glass bowl or wine glass cut in a rising series of concentric circles of diminishing radius.

stephane: In classical and Egyptian sculpture, an elaborate wreath or crown worn by a deity or ruler.

stereoscope: Binoculars used for viewing two slightly different versions of the same picture so as to achieve a three-dimensional effect.

sterling silver: Silver of at least 925 parts per 1000 pure silver; the minimum standard for English silver since 1300; metal of this quality is stamped with a lion passant (walking to the left) in England.

stethoscope: Instrument for listening to internal chest sounds, such as breathing and heartbeat; early examples have silver and ivory mounts.

Stevens Company: Manufacturers of early American mechanical money banks, late C19.

stick barometer: One with a vertical scale and register plate, rather than a circular one as in the wheel barometer.

Stickley, Gustav (1857-1942): American furniture maker who espoused the ideals of William Morris and developed, from 1898, a famous range in the "Craftsman" style.

stick screen: See pole screen.

Stiegel glass: Pre-revolutionary American glass made in the Pennsylvania glassworks of Henry William Stiegel.

stiff-jointed doll: One with limbs hinged so that they only move backwards and forwards in one direction, as opposed to ball-jointed.

stile: Outermost vertical part of a panelled construction.

stiletto: C16 or later dagger, designed for easy concealment, with a short, thick blade.

stone china: Stoneware containing china stone (petuntse), developed C19 by Spode; resembles porcelain but heavier.

stoneware: Ceramic made of clays that vitrify in the temperature range 1200-1400°C; impervious to liquid even without glazing; coarser than porcelain and not translucent.

stool: Small backless seat which has several variations.

stool table: Joined stool which is fitted with falling leaves that can be raised for use as a table.

Store Kongensgade faience: Leading Danish factory, producing blue-painted wares from mid C18, noted for large trays and bowls made in the shape of a bishop's mitre.

Storr silver: Made by the celebrated English silver and goldsmith, Paul Storr (1771-1844).

Stoter, Maria Longworth Nichols: Founder, in 1880, of the Rookwood pottery in Cincinnati, Ohio. Strongly influenced by Japanese designs.

Stourbridge: Glass making centre in Worcestershire, England, noted for imitations of Venetian and C19 art glass.

stove tile: Tin glazed earthenware tiles with scenes painted in blue, made principally in the Netherlands and Germany from C16 to the C18 for decorating the walls of a stove recess.

straining spoon: One with a bowl pierced with fine holes, often forming a pattern, and a long handle – used for straining tea, etc. From early C18.

straining spoon

stirrup cup: Silver cup, without handles, so-called because it was served, containing a suitable beverage, to huntsmen in the saddle, prior to their moving off. Often made in the shape of an animal's head.

stock: Wooden part of a firearm, to which the metal barrel and firing mechanism are attached.

Stockelsdorff faience: From a late C18 factory in Schleswig-Holstein, noted for large vases, stove tiles and trays.

Stralsund faience: Factory in the once-Swedish (now East German) town, producing very large vases and trays, latter half C18.

strapwork: Repeated carved decoration suggesting plaited straps. Originally used from mid C16 to mid C17 but revived again in the later C18.

Strasbourg: In the Alsace region, long an important centre of ceramic production; noted for fine naturalistic flower painting on C18 faience animal-form dishes and imaginative chinoiserie designs.

strass: Term used of the very finest glass paste used in jewellery, after C18 jeweller Georgeo Stras.

Strawberry Hill: House built in Twickenham in the mid-C18 in the neo-gothic style for the author Horace Walpole. Its design and furnishings were much admired.

straw work: Type of furniture decoration. Small strips of coloured straws are arranged to form geometric patterns or pictures.

stretcher: Horizontal strut connecting table or chair legs.

style rayonnant: Decorative pattern common on late C17 and C18 French ceramics, consisting of a pattern of lines radiating from the central point of a circle, terminating in ornate designs derived from lacework, wrought ironwork or baroque flower swags.

stylized: Pattern based on an object – often a flower – reduced to a geometric pattern.

stylograph: Earliest form of the fountain pen, with an integral ink reservoir, patented 1879.

subsidiary dial: Smaller dial on a clock or watch face which shows, for example, the seconds or phases of the moon, etc.

sucket fork/spoon: Implement with a spoon bowl at one end and a two-pronged fork at the other, from late C17.

sucket fork/spoon

strike: Of clocks; sounding the hours or quarters on only one bell, as opposed to a multiple chime.

strike ring: Dial or ring on a clock which turns the striking mechanism on or off.

stringing: Decorative, thin inlaid line of wood or brass.

stripped: Furniture which has had the old surface removed and has been reduced to bare wood.

strut table clock: C19 table clock provided with a back strut for stability.

Stuart: Period 1603 to 1689 including the Commonwealth interregnum.

stucco: Plaster that contains powdered stone used for ceiling ornaments and statuary.

stuffed over: See over stuffed.

stump bedstead: Bed of simple construction comprising a wooden framework on four short legs and no headboard. If it has a headboard it is known as a stump-end bedstead.

stump doll: One carved from a single piece of wood, with fixed head and limbs.

stump-end bedstead: See stump bedstead.

stump leg: Plain, slightly curved rear leg found on some Queen Anne and Chippendale chairs.

stumpwork: Form of decorative embroidery found on some seat furniture. It dates from C17.

sue: Early Japanese ceramics, with grey-green mottled glaze.

suf: Persian for "embossed"; the technique of cutting the pile of a carpet to create a design in shallow relief.

Suffolk chair: See ball back and Mendlesham chair.

sugar tongs: Sprung silver tongs for lifting pieces of lump sugar, the earliest shaped like fire-tongs, later of scissor form, with claw or spoon ends. From late C17.

Sui dynasty: Period in Chinese history AD 589-617.

sumack: Rich mauve-blue colour in carpets, named after the plant from which the dye is obtained.

sumpter chest: Type of chest made specifically as a baggage pack from a lightweight material such as leather or wicker. Usually made in pairs to strap either side of a transport mule.

sunburst: Characteristic decorative motif of the late Art Deco, especially used on mass produced items as late as the 1950s, and consisting of a linear stylized version of the sun's rays. Known in America as rising sun.

Sunday fresh: Term used by toy collectors to denote minimum damage, as if the toy was only played with on Sunday under supervision.

Sunderland: Cheap earthenwares produced from late C18 in County Durham, and creamwares decorated with purple-pink mottles.

Sung dynasty: Ruling Chinese dynasty from AD 960 to 1279.

sunray clock: Clock with a dial in the form of a stylized sun, often with gilded radiating rays in relief, popular under Louis XIV.

supper canterbury: Another name for a cutlery stand.

supper table: Circular table on a tripod base, the top of which displays a circle of eight dished areas around its edge, each about the size of a plate. Introduced in the C18.

supporter: In heraldry, the figures either side of a shield, e.g. lion, unicorn, griffin, etc.

surcoat: Cloth coat worn over armour; aids identification.

surgical instruments: Ivory or wood handled up to 1872 when Lister discovered the value of sterilization. Thereafter boilable instruments all of metal were the norm.

Sutherland table: Drop leaf table which typically has end columns joined by a central stretcher and a distinctive narrow centre section when not in use. Introduced in the C19 and named after Harriet, Duchess of Sutherland.

Swadlincote: C19 Derbyshire factory noted for toby jugs.

swag: Decoration of hanging chains of flowers or husks.

swagged: Of silver, applied strips of ornament made in mould, not necessarily of swag or garland shape.

swan neck (1): Another name for a broken pediment.

swan neck (2): Type of brass cabinet handle in vogue late C18.

Swansea porcelain: Much prized soft-paste porcelain of the early C19 noted for William Billingsley's flower painting.

Swatow ware: Chinese Ming dynasty porcelain decorated with bright enamel colours, made specifically for export from C16.

sweet chestnut: See chestnut.

sweet gum: Reddish brown American wood with a close grain. It is sometimes used as a substitute for mahogany which it can easily be stained to resemble.

swept hilt: Sword hilt with a metal loop designed to protect the hand.

Swinton: Factory near Leeds noted for creamwares, late C18.

swirl: Millefiori glass which has been twisted in firing so that the colours form a spiral.

swivel gun: Heavy musket fitted with a spike designed to fit into the socket of a stand for ease of turning.

sword: Long-bladed weapon with quillons and hilt, designed for both cutting and thrusting.

sword-breaker: Dagger with a series of teeth along the blade intended for left hand use, to catch an opponent's blade and immobilize him.

sword knot: Loop of cord used to attach the sword to the hand to prevent the user from being disarmed.

swordstick: Thin-bladed sword in a sheath disguised to look like a walking stick.

sycamore: Close grained white wood with a slight fleck. It was used mainly as a veneer, but was also stained to a greenish colour and called harewood.

syllabub dish: Silver cup, like a caudle cup, with handles for mixing cream, egg and wine syllabub. From early C18.

sympiesometer: In barometers a device that uses gas instead of mercury to measure air pressure.

T

tabachi: Poorest quality wool, taken off dead animals and producing relatively coarse carpets.

taba-tabriz: Term used to denote recently-made Tabriz rugs as distinct from old ones.

tabernacle clock: Type of C16 clock case of elaborate open or fretwork, often in the shape of

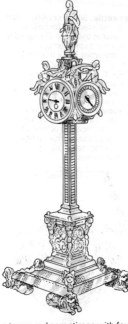

Talavera maiolica: Considered the finest early Spanish pottery, C17, produced in Castile.

Talbotype: Mid C19 early form of photographic print named after Fox Talbot, inventor of photographic papers and film.

tale glass: Poor quality glass, made from the first metal from the melting pot and containing most of the scum and impurities.

talish: Caucasian carpets, typically with a deep pile and with simple geometric designs on a plain ground.

tallboy: Chest of drawers raised upon another chest of drawers. Also known as a chest on chest.

a tower and sometimes with four dials.

table à ouvrage: Another name for étagère.

table-chair: C17 armchair which can be converted to a table by means of a pivoted back that drops across the arms of the chair. Also known as a chair-table.

table clock: Early type of domestic clock, some say the predecessor of the watch, in which the dial is set vertically: often of drum shape.

table plateau: Circular glass tray with a pedestal foot, used to support the centrepiece on a table.

tabouret: Low, upholstered French stool made in the C17 and C18.

Tabriz: Carpets from the old capital of Persia, often very fine and the first to be exported to Europe.

tachi: Long, gently curved, single-edged Japanese Samurai sword.

taille d'épergne: Linear decoration filled with coloured enamel on silverware.

taka-makie: Japanese lacquerware decorated with low-relief designs.

take: Buddhist sacred jewel, an emblem found in Oriental art.

tallcase/longcase clock: First made in England c1660 and subsequently introduced into colonial America. Either term is correct.

talwar/tulwar: Hindi word for sword, especially Indian swords with disc-shaped pommels.

tambour: Flexible sliding shutter made of strips of wood stuck side by side onto a canvas backing.

Tammany Hall bank: Late C19 mechanical money box in the form of a fat man who swallows coins.

tang: End of a sword blade that fits into the socket of the hilt.

T'ang dynasty: Period in Chinese history AD 618-906 during which porcelain was first developed.

tankard: Straight sided pewter beer mug with handle, lid and thumbpiece.

Tanner, John: Newport clockmaker, active 1740-60.

tansu: Japanese for a cabinet of wood, often made specifically for storing inro and netsuke, with velvet or silk-lined compartments.

tanto: Japanese Samurai dagger used with the tachi.

tanzaku: Japanese verses in fine calligraphy painted on strips of silk for hanging on the wall.

tape twist: Broad, white spiral band in the stem of a wine glass.

tappit hen: Pewter measure from Scotland, lidded ("tappit") and in various sizes.

tapul: In armour, the ridge down the centre of a breastplate which becomes more pronounced from C16 on.

target pistols: Distinguished from other firearms by the spurred trigger guard, which freed the trigger finger from having to steady the weapon, hence enabling more accurate marksmanship.

tarsia: Type of Italian marquetry which usually represents a pattern of flowers or ribbons. Mainly used on tables and chairs.

tasset: In armour, a plate or skirt of plates to protect thigh.

tastevin: Small flat silver bowl, usually of French or German origin, used for tasting wines – about 3in (8cm) in diameter, with a simple ring handle.

tavern clock: Alternative name for an Act of Parliament clock.

tavern table: Small rectangular four-legged table which usually has one or two drawers and was used in taverns in C18.

taxidermy: Art of stuffing and mounting animals, birds and sporting trophies.

tazza: Wide but shallow bowl on a stem with a foot; ceramic and metal tazzas were made in antiquity and the form was revived by Venetian glassmakers in C15. Also made in silver from C16.

teak: Heavy brown wood which is strong and durable. Consequently much used for military chests and ships' furniture etc.

tea kettle: Silver, or other metal, vessel intended for boiling water at the table. Designed to sit over a spirit lamp, it sometimes had a rounded base instead of flat.

teapot: Silver or china vessel with a handle, spout and lid made in numerous forms since the late C17.

teapoy: Piece of furniture in the form of a tea caddy on legs, with a hinged lid opening to reveal caddies, mixing bowl and other tea drinking accessories.

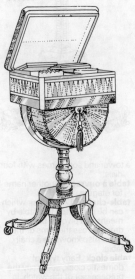

tear: Tear-drop shaped air bubble in the stem of an early C18 wine glass, from which the air-twist evolved.

Tebo figures: French rococo style figures produced at Bow and Chelsea mid C18, so-called after the modeller's mark.

Teco: Short for Terra Cotta, Illinois, the home of a pottery celebrated for Art Nouveau vessels and green-glazed wares.

teddy bears: Stuffed toy bears named after President Theodore (Teddy) Roosevelt who refused to shoot a bear cub on a hunting trip in 1902. Examples pre-date that event but it was Morris Michtom who capitalized on the event by producing toy bears which he originally called "Teddy's bear".

Teheran: Now the capital of Iran, noted for very fine and now rare carpets decorated with animals set against intricate floral and foliage designs.

Te Hua: Region of Fukien province in southern China famous for its blanc-de-chine figures in white glazed porcelain.

Tekke: Nomadic tribe of the Soviet/Iranian border region noted for their deep-red carpets decorated with gul motifs.

telephone covers: Dolls with very long wired skirts designed to cover a telephone; especially popular in the 1920s when the type of instrument then in use was regarded as ugly.

telescope: Series of tubes, of wood, parchment or brass, containing lenses designed to magnify distant objects.

tell-tale clock: One used to check that a nightwatchman was doing his rounds; the commonest type has a series of pins around the dial which can only be depressed at a precise time. Common in banks, etc. in early C19.

tent bed: Bed with a domed canopy which resembles a tent when covered with drapes. Made in C18 and C19 and also known as a sparver bed.

Teotihuacan: Influential Mesoamerican civilization, flourishing c200 BC-AD 900 based on the Valley of Mexico.

term: Pillar or pedestal terminating in a human head and torso, usually armless.

terminal: End of a chair arm where the hand rests.

terra cotta: Italian for "baked earth". Unglazed biscuit-fired clay, orange red, usually used for tiling but also for garden statuary and pots.

terra sigillita: Fine Roman pottery of the C1 BC to the C3 AD, covered in red slip somewhat like Samian, and decorated with designs in relief.

terret: Horse brass hinged to a frame, used to decorate the horse's head or the peak of the collar.

Terry clock: Strictly one made by Terry of Plymouth, Connecticut, active 1792-1852. Also those of the same general type: a mantel clock with architectural side pillars and

pediment, with a painted glass panel below the dial.

tester: Wooden canopy over a bedstead which is supported on either two or four posts. It may extend fully over the bed and be known as a full tester, or only over the bedhead half and be known as a half tester.

tête à tête seat: Another name for a love seat.

theodolite: Surveying instrument for measuring and mapping heights above sea level, first made in the 1730s.

thermoluminescence: Scientific method of authenticating antiquities, often abbreviated to "TL dating".

thimble: Small cap for protecting the finger tips whilst sewing. Can be of silver, hand-painted porcelain, ivory, etc. Rare before the C18.

thirty hour movement: Clock which requires rewinding every thirty hours.

thistle bowl: Glass bowl resembling the shape of a thistle flower, with tapering upper section and rounded base.

Thomas clock: Similar in form to a Terry clock but made by Terry's former apprentice, Seth Thomas, active 1810-30, in Connecticut.

threading: Decoration in glass consisting of fine threads of metal, used around the neck or rim of a vessel.

three faced doll: Doll with a revolving head and three distinct faces, late C19.

Three Kingdoms: Period in Chinese history AD 221-265.

three piece glass: Vessel made of three parts welded together; e.g. the bowl, stem and foot of a wine glass.

three train movement: One with three separate sets of mechanisms, one for turning the hands, one for striking the hours and another either for an alarm or for the quarter hours.

through dovetail: Dovetail joint which has the end grain showing on both sides of the angle.

thrown chair: Old name for a turner's chair.

thumb mould: Rounded projecting edge to a table top.

tiller

thumbpiece: Concave depression on the flange of a hinged vessel lid, or on the handle, which either helps in lifting the vessel, or is pressed to raise the lid.

thuya: Reddish brown wood imported from Africa and used as a veneer.

Tianqi (Tien Chi): Chinese Ming dynasty emperor, 1621-27.

tidal-dial: Clock face showing the state of the tide at a particular port, from C16.

Tiefschnitt: Intaglio design cut into the glass as distinct from Hochschnitt, or high relief decoration.

t'ien lung: Dragon of the skies; motif on Chinese carpets and porcelain.

tie-pin: In use from the early C19 when cravats succeeded stocks as male neckwear.

Tiffany, Charles Louis: Father of the famous Art Nouveau designer, Louis Comfort. American goldsmith for whom his son designed jewellery at the beginning of the C20.

Tiffany, Louis Comfort (1848-1933): America's most influential Art Nouveau designer. He founded Associated Artists in the 1880s, specializing in interior decoration, and the Tiffany Glass Company in 1885, originally to produce stained glass and later developing into the manufacture of Favrile glass, ceramics, lamps, jewellery, furniture and textiles.

tigerware: Rhineland saltglazed earthenware jugs with a glaze-pattern resembling a tiger's stripes; sometimes also used to describe trailed white slip decoration on a coloured body, similar in appearance.

tikh: Knife with a curved end used in carpet making to loop and compact the knots.

till (1): Original name for what we now call a drawer.

till (2): Old name for the small lidded compartment found in some chests, now commonly known as a candle box.

tiller: Central arm of a cross-bow; also used to describe the similarly shaped stock of early firearms.

tilt top table: Any table with a hinged top that can be tilted over in one piece for easier storage when not in use.

ti-lung: Earth dragon; motif on Chinese rugs and ceramics.

tin: Silvery white metal, normally used in alloys, such as pewter, or as a coating (tin-plate) for other metals.

tinderlighter: C17 and C18 pistol-shaped tinder box with a flintlock mechanism.

tine: One of the prongs of a fork – early forks have two tines, later ones three.

tin glaze: Glassy white glaze of tin oxide; re-introduced to Europe in C14 by Moorish potters; the characteristic glaze of delftware, faience and maiolica.

ting-tang: Onomatopeic name for the quarter chime on C19 Black Forest clocks.

Ting yao: Chinese Sung dynasty porcelain with a thick white glaze and incised floral patterns.

tinned: Interior of a base metal or plated vessel, treated with a flux of tin to give a silvery appearance and to prevent liquids being tainted by contact with the metal itself.

tin-plate: Metal objects, usually flatware of iron or steel, covered in molten tin to give them a silvery coating.

tinware: Cheap household items made of beaten and soldered tin, similar in appearance to pewter but less durable.

tipstave: Solid staff or truncheon carried by law enforcement officers from the Middle Ages.

tired: Used of objects which show signs of use or wear.

to: Japanese for "carved".

toasting fork: Long-handled fork designed for toasting bread or muffins at the fireside, relatively common after c1720, telescopic from c1800.

toastmaster's glass: Glass with a thick-walled bowl which appears to hold more liquid than is actually the case.

tobacco box: Silver or ceramic box or jar made in many forms since C17.

tobreh: Nomadic carpet bag of hammock shape.

toby jug: Originally a jug in the form of a man in a tricorn hat, first made by Ralph Wood of Burslem, mid C18; since produced in great quantity in many different forms.

Toft ware: C17 slip-trailed dishes made in Staffordshire by Thomas and Ralph Toft, often portraying a mermaid, a pelican or the head of King Charles II.

togi-dashi: In Japanese lacquerwork, pictures resembling water-colour painting covered with a thin layer of translucent lacquer.

Tokugawa: Better known as the Edo era, the period in Japanese history, 1615-1867, when Tokyo became the capital.

tôle peinte: French C18 method of varnishing sheet iron vessels so that the surface could be painted upon. And by derivation, painted metal panels applied to furniture.

Toltec: Mesoamerican civilization of the period AD 900-1521.

tomahawk: Axe with a hammer head and short shaft, originally used as a weapon by North American Indians.

Tompion & Banger: Company co-founded by Thomas Tompion, noted for fine watches, early C18.

Tompion, Thomas: Prolific and perhaps the best known London clock and watchmaker, active 1671-1710.

Tongzhi (T'ung Chih): Chinese Qing dynasty emperor, 1862-74.

tonkotsu: Small carved Japanese tobacco pouch made for suspending from the waist sash (obi).

tooling: Working of a pattern onto a leather skiver.

topsy-turvy doll: Has two heads and two trunks, joined at the waist. A reversible skirt covers one or the other as required.

torbas: Nomadic carpet bags, usually made in pairs as a saddlebag and carried by goats.

torchère: See candlestand.

Torelli maiolica: C19 factory in Florence producing reproductions of Renaissance wares.

torpedo bottle: One with a pointed base, intended to be laid on its side; used by Jacob Schweppe from late 1790s for the sale of soda water. The water, in contact with the cork, helped keep it airtight.

torque/torc: Necklace of woven silver or gold, originally worn by the pre-Roman Belgic and Celtic tribes of Europe.

Torricellian tube: Simple early form of barometer, named after its inventor, Evangelista Torricelli (1608-47).

torso: Sculpture representing the human body without head or limbs.

tortoise shell: Mottled brown glaze on late C18/early C19 ceramics, especially Whieldon ware, resembling real tortoiseshell.

torus: Type of classical moulding of convex semi-circular profile.

touch hole: Hole in a firing mechanism that carries the combustion from the priming powder to the main charge.

touch mark: Maker's mark stamped on much, but not all, early English pewter. Their use was strictly controlled by the Pewterers' Company of London: early examples consist of initials, later ones are more elaborate and pictorial, sometimes including the maker's address.

touch pin: Protrusions on the dial of a clock which enable the time to be felt in the dark.

Toulouse faience: Now extremely rare early C18 pieces from the southern French town.

Tournai wares: Town in Belgium producing faience from C17, soft-paste porcelain mid C18 and noted for white biscuit figures. Made mostly earthenware in C19.

tou t'sai: Alternative spelling of "doucai", Chinese for "contrasting colours".

tracery: Carved Gothic decoration which resembles the stone openwork typically found above Gothic windows.

tracheid: Fibres which produce the grain in timber.

trade label: Label placed on an item by maker or retailer.

trade token: Coins produced by shopkeepers, innkeepers and factory owners from mid C17 and used instead of the legal coinage for the exchange of goods.

Trafalgar chair: Type of dining chair made during the Regency period. It has sabre legs and a rope back.

Trafalgar leg: Another name for the sabre leg.

trailed decoration: Slipware decoration on ceramics resembling piped icing sugar.

train: Set of cog wheels and pinions in a clock mechanism, usually dedicated to a specific function, such as moving the hands or regulating the strike.

trajectory: Path taken by a projectile after firing.

transfer-printed: Ceramic decoration technique perfected mid C18 and used widely thereafter for mass-produced wares. An engraved design is printed onto paper (the bat) using an ink consisting of glaze mixed with oil; the paper is then laid over the body of the vessel and burns off in firing, leaving an outline, usually in blue. Sometimes the outline was coloured in by hand.

Transylvania: Antique Turkish carpets, so-called because many were used to decorate churches in Transylvania from C16.

travelling clock: One designed to operate despite the jolts and motion of travelling.

travelling pistols: Usually boxed pairs of pistols with accoutrements, carried for self-defence by C18 coachmen.

tray top: Term used to describe the top of a night table which has the appearance of a tray, complete with carrying handles incorporated into the sides.

treasury notes: Paper money first issued in the U.K. during the First World War.

Tree of Life: Symbol of immortality used as a stylized motif on Oriental carpets.

treen: Small wooden objects associated with domestic, trade or rural life.

trefid: C17 spoon form with a finial cleft into three: a central stem and two sidelobes.

trefoil: Three-cusped figure which resembles a symmetrical three-lobed leaf or flower.

trek: Of Delft, the blue, purple or black design outline.

trembleuse: Silver stand with feet designed to support a cup.

trencher case: Small decorative display shelf for the storage and display of glassware, treen, pewter, etc. Made in C17.

trennail: Old name for a dowel.

trephines: Early surgical instruments used for removing a portion of the skull.

trespolo: Elegant three-legged Italian table which was designed to stand against a wall and carry a candlestick or small objet d'art.

trestle: Horizontal beam with diverging legs used as a support for some early table tops. Also known as a dormant.

triads: Owner's initials sometimes found on old pewter, so-called because they usually consist of just three letters.

trial marks: In armour, small dents in the breast plate caused by pistol shot, fired at close range to prove the strength of the armour. Often faked.

trial piece: Vessel or slab of

ceramic used for experimental purposes; usually to test that the glaze mixture has been properly prepared. Highly prized if they relate to a specific factory and product.

Trichterkannen: Rhineland salt-glazed stoneware jug with a bulbous body and a tall cylindrical neck.

tricoteuse: Small French galleried sewing table.

tridarn: Welsh variety of the press cupboard with three tiers. The full name is cwpwrdd tridarn.

trifle pewter: Pewter of 79% tin, 15% antimony and 6% lead; the best quality until the development of higher grade "hard metal" c1700.

triple top table: Another name for a harlequin table.

tripod table: Descriptive of any table with a three-legged base but generally used to describe only small tables of this kind.

triton: Sea-deity, half human and half fish portrayed in antique sculpture.

trompe l'oeil: Any flat decorative motif intended to deceive the eye into seeing the third dimension of depth.

trophy: Ornamental device used in plasterwork and on overmantels and wood panelling, consisting of a group of objects such as weapons of war, fruits, musical instruments or game birds.

troy weight: System of weights used for quantifying gold, silver and precious stones.

truckle bed: Early bedstead which can be moved by means

of wooden wheels under the uprights. Also known as a trundle bed.

trumpeter clock: Like a cuckoo clock but with a model military bugler that sounds the hours.

trundle bed: See truckle bed.

trunk: See coffer.

trussing coffer: Type of early coffer which is equipped with shackles or lifting rings for transportation purposes.

tschinke/teschner: C16 to C17 wheellock gun designed for hunting. Originated in Silesia.

tsuba: Guard of a Japanese sword, usually consisting of an ornamented plate.

tsuge: Japanese for "boxwood", one of the commonest materials used for carving netsuke.

tsuikoku: Carved black Japanese lacquerware, the natural colour, as opposed to tsuishu, which is coloured red.

tsuishu: Japanese carved lacquerware in red.

tsun: Chinese bronze wine-storage vessel.

Tucker porcelain: Highly prized wares made by William Ellis Tucker of Philadelphia, C19, similar to Sèvres and noted for fine painting and gilding.

Tudor: Tudor period is from 1485 to 1603 and furniture made during that time may be referred to as Tudor. However, furniture made during the reign of Elizabeth I (1558-1603) is more likely to be called Elizabethan.

Tudric: Range of Celtic-inspired Art Nouveau pewter of high quality, designed for mass-production by Archibald Knox and retailed through Liberty & Co.

tulip ornament: In vogue from c1650 to c1700.

tulip tankard: C18 pewter resembling the cup of a tulip flower.

tulipwood: Yellow brown wood with a reddish stripe imported from Central and South America and used as a veneer and for inlay and crossbanding. It is related to rosewood and kingwood.

tumbler (1): Notched wheel inside a firing mechanism which controls the sear and hammer, causing the hammer to rest at half or fullcock or to fall and strike the steel or cap.

tumbler (2): Flat bottomed stemless glass, with parallel or tapering sides, from late C18.

tumblers (1): Parts of a lock mechanism which retain the bolt until the correct key raises them to release it.

tumblers (2): Toys with a weighted and rounded bottom which oscillates when pushed but always returns to the upright.

Tunbridge ware: Objects decorated with wooden inlay made of bundles of coloured wood cut into sections; usually simple geometric designs, but sometimes whole scenes; mid C17 to late C19.

tureen: Very large bowl on a foot, often with two side handles, used for serving soup from early C18.

turkey red: Dye obtained from the root of madder plants and used in carpet making; dark red but with an orange tint, as distinct from the brownish-red of Turkoman carpets.

turkeywork: European-made imitations of Turkish carpets, often made by stitching wool to a canvas background and used for furniture covering and upholstery from C16.

Turkish carpets: Traditionally of deeper pile than Persian carpets and decorated with geometric or stylized motifs rather than floral.

Turkish knot: Alternative name for the Ghiordes knot, typical of – but not exclusive to – Turkish-made carpets as distinct from Persian.

Turkoman carpets: Woven by the nomadic tribes of the region that stretches from the Caspian Sea to Sinkiang in southern China. Carpets predominantly decorated with gul motifs.

turnabout doll: Rag doll with two faces, one on the front, one on the back, either of which could be covered by a reversible bonnet.

turned furniture: Furniture constructed from turned parts and without a joined frame.

Turner blackware: Late C18 and C19 black porcelain made by John Turner of Staffordshire in imitation of Wedgwood's Basaltes.

turner's chair: Chair made entirely from turned parts.

turnery: Production of an item by turning on a lathe.

turnip foot: American furniture foot similar to a bun foot but narrower and with a ringed moulding around the top.

turn-off pistol: One with a barrel that unscrews for loading.

turnover: In glass, a rim that is folded back on itself.

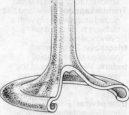

turnover doll: See topsy-turvy doll.

turn-up bed: Chair or sofa that can be converted into a bed.

turret clock: Strictly, the type of clock installed, since the Middle Ages, in towers and driven by a weight suspended from a rope wound round a drum; but also smaller clocks with a similar drive, usually suspended on a wall.

turtle back: C16 decorative ornament resembling the shell of a turtle.

Tuscan: Plainest of the classical orders. Tuscan columns are undecorated and the capitals consist of a simple cushion.

tutenag: Silver-like alloy of copper, zinc and nickel.

twist: Spiral grooving inside the barrel of a rifle.

twist-over: Revolver with a twist action to align each of the chambers in succession with the firing mechanism and barrel.

two-faced doll: One with a revolving head and two different faces.

two-stage barrel: In firearms, a gun barrel made in two parts.

two-train movement: One with two separate mechanisms, one for turning the clock hands, the other for the strike.

U

umoregi: Japanese for jet, the black semi-precious stone formed of fossil wood.

underglaze printing: Technique which superseded overglaze transfer printing in the early 1760s, using high temperature glaze applied to the biscuit-fired body before glazing and thus eliminating the additional low-temperature firing involved in the earlier technique.

underhammer gun: Gun in which the percussion hammer is seated below the breech.

Underweissbach: White glazed porcelain figures based on sculptures by Ernest Barlach and produced at the Schwarzburger Werkstätten early C20.

Undine: In classical mythology, a water-nymph, hence any statue of a nude girl or woman pouring water from a jar.

undress sword: One used in action, rather than for ceremonial.

upholder: C18 name for an upholsterer.

uprights: Another name for side rails.

Ur: Ancient city state in Mesopotamia. Archaeologists divide its development into three chronological stages: Ur I, Ur II and Ur III, and these terms are used to provide an approximate date for all early Near Eastern objects.

Urbino maiolica: Important Italian production centre, noted for istoriato (narrative) and Raphaelesque painting in bright colours in C16.

urn stand: Stand designed to carry a jardinière or small objet d'art. They usually incorporate a candle slide.

urushi: Japanese for raw lacquer, a sap obtained from several varieties of the ash tree.

ushabti: Also known as ushibdi or shabti; small objects, usually of glazed earthenware, in the form of a mummified human figure, found in great quantities in Ancient Egyptian tombs and burial chambers.

ushak: Long-pile, loosely woven carpets from Turkish Anatolia, usually with a central medallion on a plain ground.

Usk ware: Japanned tin wares made in the town of Usk, latter half C18.

V

valais flagon: C17 pewter tankard said to derive from the Swiss Valais region. Has a bulbous body, narrow neck and heart-shaped flat lid.

Valencia: Important centre of maiolica production in Spain from C14, through which Moorish potters introduced tin-glazed earthenware techniques and from where

itinerant potters took the techniques to all parts of Europe.

vambrace: In armour, flexible plates protect the arms.

varguéno: See barguéno.

vase: Any tall vessel whose use is primarily ornamental.

vase carpets: Generally Persian with a vase of flowers as the central motif.

vaseline glass: Greenish-yellow glass, developed late C19. Also known as yellow opaline.

Vaucanson, Jacques: Early C18 maker of mechanical toys.

Vauxhall glass: Products of the Duke of Buckingham's glassworks at Vauxhall, founded in the third quarter C17, chiefly producing plate glass and silvered glass for mirrors.

velocipede: Earliest form of bicycle (name means "fast feet"). Invented c1760.

veneer: Thin sheet of wood applied to a surface for decorative effect and to improve the appearance of a piece. Veneers can be cut in several different ways; burr, oyster, straight-grained or figured.

Venetian glass: Fine soda glass and coloured glass blown and pinched into highly ornamented vessels of intricate form, made in Venice, and widely copied from C15.

Venetian porcelain: Now rare early soft-paste porcelain produced in Venice in early C18.

vent: In firearms, the alternative name for the touch hole.

ventail: In armour, a piece of metal protecting the neck, onto which the helmet fits.

Venus: In Roman mythology the goddess of love and beauty (equivalent to the Greek goddess Aphrodite). A popular subject in decoration.

veramin: Very fine carpets from the region south of Teheran in Iran, decorated with floral motifs around a central vase or diamond, and sometimes including animal figures.

verge escapement: Oldest form of escapement, found on clocks as early as AD 1300 and still in use 1900. Consisting of a bar (the verge) with two flag shaped pallets that rock in and out of the teeth of the crown or escape wheel to regulate the movement.

vernier: Sliding scale, used in conjunction with the fixed scale on a barometer, for taking accurate pressure readings.

Vernis Martin: Term used generically to describe lacquers and varnishes used in France for interior decoration and on clocks and furniture during the C18. It takes its name from the Martin brothers who were permitted to copy Japanese lacquer. It is found in many colours, but especially green.

verre de fougère: French term meaning "fern glass", describing the limpid green colour.

verre de nevers: Glass toys and figures made from heating and manipulating rods of coloured glass, originally made c1600 at Nevers in France, but widely copied elsewhere.

verre double: Early form of cameo glass, developed by Emile Gallé, and first shown in 1899. Coloured glass is sandwiched between two layers of plain glass, and areas carved or etched to reveal the colour underneath.

vesta case: Ornate flat case of silver or other metal for carrying vestas, an early form of match. From mid C19.

vestibule lamp: Oil lamps similar in form to table lamps but fitted with chains for suspension from the ceiling; from early C19.

Veuve Perrin: Highly prized and colourful faience from the Marseilles factory made in the latter half C18 under the management of the widow of Claude Perrin.

Vicar and Moses: Staffordshire figure group produced in quantity late C18/early C19. Depicts a parson preaching while his clerk sleeps.

Victorian: Term used to describe furniture and other items made during the reign of Queen Victoria (1837-1901).

Usually divided into early Victorian (1837-1860) and late Victorian (1860-1901).

Vienna: Porcelain factory founded 1719 and noted for extensive use of trelliswork patterns, scrollwork and gilding; and, between 1747 and 1784, for the figures modelled by J. J. Niedermayer.

Vienna regulator: Early C19 Austrian pendulum clock with a glass-fronted case which reveals the fast-swinging pendulum.

viewmark: Official mark stamped on the barrel of a firearm, consisting of a V under a crown or crossed keys, denoting that it has been examined for defects.

Vile and Cobb: Prominent English cabinetmakers and upholsterers to George III in the early years of his reign.

vinaigrette: Portable and ornamental container, often of glass with silver mounting, containing a small sponge on a stick and sweet, scented vinegar, the C18 equivalent of smelling salts. More recently, a vinegar flask as part of a condiment set.

Vincennes: Rare soft-paste porcelain produced by the Sèvres factory between its foundation in Vincennes in 1738 and its relocation to Sèvres in 1756.

vinegar stick: Small silver or other metal box, pierced and mounted on a stick. Designed to hold a vinegar-soaked sponge, which was used as an air freshener.

vine trail: Repeated band of carved decoration in the form of leaves, flowers and grapes.

Vinovo porcelain: From a short lived factory near Milan, late C18.

violet wood: Another name for kingwood.

virgin spoon: Spoon with a finial depicting the Virgin Mary.

Virginian walnut: Another name for black walnut.

visor: In armour, the hinged front piece of the helmet that protects the face.

Visscher glass: Dutch glass, early C17, engraved by the Visscher sisters. Now extremely rare.

vitrine: French display cabinet which is often of bombé or serpentine outline and ornately decorated with marquetry and ormolu.

vitrine table: Another name for a bijouterie table.

vitro a reticelli: Italian name for the most ornate and complex forms of Venetian lace glass.

vitro di trina: Italian name for Venetian lace glass.

vitro porcelain: Alternative name for milk glass; also a late C19 form of English art glass made from slag and having a streaked, marbled appearance, somewhat like a ceramic material.

vitruvian scroll: A repeated border ornament of scrolls that resemble waves. Used during C18.

V-joint: Technique of joining the terminal of a silver spoon to the stem, by cutting the two ends to form opposing V shapes.

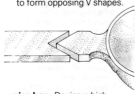

voice box: Device which enables a doll to make noises, such as crying.

voider: See voyder.

voisinlieu: French art pottery, from mid C19, made near Beauvais.

Volkstedt: German centre of porcelain production, late C18 and C19, noted for Meissen-style tableware.

volute: Decorative spiral scroll, especially on an Ionic capital.

votive: Any small bronze or ceramic figure of a deity.

voulge: Early form of halberd with axe blade and spike.

voyder: Butler's tray or plate bucket used for clearing, or "voiding" a table.

Voysey, Charles Francis Annesley (1857-1941): Highly influential English architect who, as a young man, designed furniture and textiles in the Arts and Crafts tradition.

Vulliamy: Important Swiss family of clockmakers working in London from c1750 to 1854 making very fine time pieces, under royal patronage. Also noted for clocks with porcelain cases.

W

Waals, Peter van de: Dutch cabinet maker who worked with Gimson and the Barnsleys, designing simple Arts and Crafts furniture from 1901 until 1937.

wag-on-the-wall: Popular name for a pendulum clock without a case, so that the pendulum is visible.

wainscot (1): Timber panelling used to line the internal walls of a house or a piece of furniture with a noticeable amount of panelled work.

wainscot (2): European oak imported into England in C16 and C17.

waisted: Shape of a wine glass bowl that tapers into a well defined waist and flares outwards to form a rounded base.

waiter: Term generally denoting a salver less than 6in (15cm) in diameter.

wake table: Long, thin table, which may or may not have drop leaves, on which a coffin rested prior to the funeral. The table was then used by the mourners to eat and drink at after the funeral.

wakisashi: Longer sword of a Japanese Samurai warrior's daisho.

Waldenburg: Stoneware jug from the Rhineland characterized by a chevron pattern around the rim and base.

Waldglas: Literally "forest glass"; German glass made in the Black Forest region using potash as a flux and tinged green, brown or yellow.

Walker, Izannah: American dollmaker who patented the first mass-produced rag dolls in 1873.

Walker Colt: Colt revolver of the mid C19 with a barrel over 15in (37.5cm) in length, as designed by Captain Samuel Walker.

wall clock: Clocks designed to be hung on the wall in order to accommodate the length of the driving weight and chain mechanism.

Wallendorf: Late C18 porcelain factory in Thuringia, Germany, producing Meissen imitations, re-founded late C19.

Wall period: Period during which Dr. John Wall, founding partner in the Worcester Porcelain factory, managed the enterprise; i.e. 1751-1774.

wall pocket: Popular Staffordshire ornament; flat-backed half-cone for hanging from the wall to contain flowers, spills or letters.

walnut: English walnut is a hard golden brown with a range of figuring. It is good for carving, turning or veneering. See also black walnut and white walnut.

Waltham clocks: Made by the company of that name, in Boston. Noted for simple elegance and fine quality.

Waltham Watch Co.: Founded 1850 in Boston, Massachusetts. The first American company to begin mass production of watches.

Walton figure: Staffordshire bocage figures modelled by John Walton of Burslem, early C19.

wandering hour clock or watch: One in which the hour numeral, revealed through an aperture and engraved on a revolving disc, moves around the perimeter of the dial, pointing to the minute divisions marked around the fixed edge of the dial.

wanfried: German slipware, made at Wanfried-an-der-Werra, Hesse, C16 and C17.

Wanli (Wan Li): Chinese Ming dynasty emperor, 1573-1620.

Warburton: Principally creamwares made by Wedgwood and decorated by members of the Warburton family, C18.

ward: Fixed projection from the inside plate of a lock which prevents the passage of a key unless correctly shaped.

wardian case: Glass case for growing indoor plants, especially tropical ones, intended for fixing against a window pane.

warming pan: Predecessor of the hot-water bottle, a metal pan on the end of a long handle filled with glowing coals and used to warm the bed; produced from mid C17 until mid C19.

warp: Long threads of yarn used to make a carpet or textile, the first to be stretched across the loom and into which the weft is woven: the warp is rarely visible on the surface of the design.

Warrant Holder's Plaque: Signs displayed by tradesmen patronized by the monarch and royal family.

Warring States: Period in Chinese history 484-221 BC.

Warsaw: Faience wares produced C18 in Warsaw, decorated in Imari and chinoiserie style, and some pieces with Kufic inscriptions made for the court of the Ottoman Sultan.

washed carpets: Term normally used to denote that a modern carpet has been treated in a chemical wash to reduce the brilliance of the colours and achieve an aged appearance that may deceive the unwary.

washing stand: Stand designed to hold a basin for washing in the bedroom. Generally of two types. Either three or four uprights supporting a circular top to hold the basin and with a triangular shelf with a drawer. Or as a cupboard raised on four legs with a basin let into the top, sometimes with enclosing flaps. Also known as a basin stand.

wassail: Bowl, often of wood with silver mounting, used for drinking hot spiced ale.

watchcock: Or watchbridge; the metal plate which protects the balance wheel of a watch, often highly ornate of gilt brass and usually engraved with a maker's name.

watch keys: Used for winding watches and now collectable in their own right.

watchman's chair: Another name for a hall porter's chair.

watch paper: Circular advertisement placed inside the case of a watch.

watch stand: Designed to hold a pocket watch so as to convert it into a miniature clock for standing on a table.

Waterbury Watch Company: New York company, one of the first to produce inexpensive watches in the 1880s and 1890s.

watered steel: Used of Islamic swords with a high carbon content to the steel, producing a surface appearance of wavy lines.

Waterford: Production centre in Ireland for very fine cut glass lead crystal wares, especially decanters, since the late C18; also a glassworks of the same name in New Jersey.

water gilding: See gilding.

water leaf: Decorative carved motif representing a narrow leaf with a central stem and horizontal undulations.

Waterloo glass: Products of a short-lived early C19 glassworks in Ireland.

Waterloo teeth: Early dentures consisting of real teeth set into ivory plates, so called because battle fields were a frequent source of the teeth used.

Waters pottery: Produced at the Lambeth factory of Richard Waters, early C19. Gaily decorated earthenwares.

waxed doll: Composition doll dipped in wax to give a surface finish that could be modelled or painted.

waywiser: Wheel-based instrument for measuring distance between two points.

Wear Bridge jugs: Late C18 and C19 jugs produced in Sunderland and decorated with views of the Wear Bridge.

Webb glass: Either stained glass or tableware designed by Philip Webb, friend and partner of William Morris, in England in the latter half of C19; or table glass produced by the Stourbridge glassworks of that name.

web foot: Another name for duck foot.

Webley, Philip and John: Leading C19 gunmakers working in Birmingham, U.K.

Webster: Noted family of London clockmakers – Robert active 1680-99, William 1730-50.

Webster, William: Leading English gunmaker, early/mid C19.

wedge: Either a triangular thumb piece on the hinged lid of a pewter or silver tankard, or a stand of silver designed for resting a dish at an angle for decorative purposes.

Wedgwood: Pottery founded by Josiah Wedgwood (1730-95) at Stoke-on-Trent and noted for numerous innovations; especially creamware, basaltes, and pearlware; perhaps best known for jasperware, the blue stonewares decorated with white relief scenes from late C18.

Wedgwood-arbeit: German for Wedgwood-work; blue porcelain with applied white relief decoration made in imitation of Wedgwood's famous jasperware from late C18.

Weesp: Dutch porcelain factory, founded C18 but which moved shortly after to Oude Loosdrecht.

weft: Crosswise threads that are interwoven between the long threads, or warp, in carpet making or textile weaving. The weft is predominantly responsible for the design.

Wei dynasty: Period in Chinese history AD 386-557.

Weisweiler, Adam (b.1750): German cabinet maker, born at Neuwied. He was trained as a cabinet maker by Roentgen and was in business in Paris before 1777. He was employed by Royalty and the aristocracy.

welcome cup: Silver goblet, usually for ceremonial use, often inscribed with a message expressing comradeship and designed for communal drinking.

153

welded armour: Armour made by gas welding rather than rivetted. Diagnostic of modern reproduction armour, or modern repairs.

well: Hollow or interior of a bowl or dish.

Wellington chest: Distinct type of tall, narrow chest of drawers. They usually have either six or seven thin drawers one above the other and a hinged and lockable flap over one side to prevent them from opening. Made in the C19.

Welsh ware: Late C18 and C19, rustic flatware, decorated with trailed and combed slip.

Wemyss ware: Hand painted, lead-glazed earthenware figures first produced in Fife, Scotland, in 1880s. Production transferred, using the original moulds, to Bovey Tracy from 1930 to 1952.

Wesley figures: Highly popular late C18/early C19 Staffordshire figures of the founder of Methodism, notably those based on the bust sculpted by Enoch Wood.

Western Han: Period in Chinese history from 206BC-AD24.

Western Zhou (Chou): In Chinese history, the period 1027 to 770 BC.

Westerwald: Blue-glazed Rhineland stoneware jugs with impressed and incised decoration.

Westley Richards, William: Leading London gunmaker, C19.

Westmoreland Glass Company: Established late C19 in Grapeville, Pennsylvania, specializing in reproductions of early American glassware.

wet plate camera: Earliest form of camera, made 1840-80, often of brass-bound mahogany and with bellows.

whatnot: Tall stand of four or five shelves and sometimes a drawer in addition. Some were made to stand in corner. Used for the display of ornaments and known in Victorian times as an omnium.

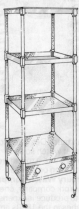

wheat ears: Carved decorative ornament suggesting ears of wheat. Mainly associated with Hepplewhite.

Wheaton, Caleb: Clockmaker active 1785-1822 in Providence, R.I.

wheel barometer: One with a circular register plate; a weight floating on the mercury surface is attached to a pulley and wheel mechanism. The vertical motion is used to turn the pointer round the arc of the circular dial.

wheel engraving: Designs cut in glass using small revolving metal wheels and an abrasive paste.

wheeling glass: Made by one of several early C19 factories in Wheeling, West Virginia.

wheellock: Early C16 firing mechanism superseded by the flint lock but still made as late as the C18 for hunting weapons, highly prized for their ornamented stocks. The action of pulling the trigger caused a steel wheel to spin against a piece of mineral pyrites; the friction produced sparks which ignited the priming powder.

Whieldon ware: Various innovative products made by Thomas Whieldon (1719-95), especially tortoiseshell and cauliflower ware; noted also for marbled glazes.

whimsies: Small glass objects (hats, shoes, animals, etc) originally made in the craftsman's spare time, but then mass produced in C19/C20 as commercial trinkets.

whistle tankard: Silver tankard with a hole in the handle: this permitted air to escape from the hollow formed during manufacture, but traditionally drinkers blew on it to "whistle" for a refill.

Whitefriars: Long-established glassworks in London, making imitations of Venetian glass as early as the C17; noted, in the C19, for fine art glass designed by Philip Webb.

white metal: Nickel or tin based alloy intended to imitate silver.

white walnut: American variety of walnut which is light brown in colour and open grained. It is also known as butternut and is less highly regarded than black walnut.

Whitney: Firearms made by Eli Whitney in New Haven, Connecticut from the end of the C18; among the first to be made with standard, interchangeable parts.

Whitney glass: From the factory established late C18 in Glassboro, New Jersey; principally bottles and flasks.

whorl: Decorative circular ornament, the distinctive characteristic being that the enclosed carving radiates from a central point in a curve.

wickerwork: Weaving of boiled and dried willowshoots, called withies, to make items such as cradles, chairs etc.

Wiener Werkstätte: The Vienna Workshop, founded in 1901 by Hoffmann and Moser, and a leading producer, until 1932, of Art Nouveau furniture, textiles, metalwork, glass and ceramics.

wig stand: Name sometimes erroneously given to a tripod washing stand.

Wilkinson, A. J. Ltd: Pottery at Newport, Staffordshire, that employed Clarice Cliff and other leading artists of the 1930s, and produced Cliff's "Bizarre" and "Fantasque" ranges of household china.

Willard clocks: Made by the Massachusetts family of clockmakers: Simon, active late C18 to mid C19 is credited with inventing the banjo clock and his nephew with that of the lyre clock.

Williamite: Late C18 decanters and wine glasses, decorated with symbols and portraits of William III, as somewhat belated counter-propaganda to Jacobite glass.

Williamsburg style: Reproduction furniture and objects which were based on those used in the restoration of the colonial town of Williamsburg, Virginia.

Williamson, Joseph: English clockmaker credited with inventing the equation clock, active late C17/early C18.

willow: Whitish wood occasionally used for inlay.

willow-pattern: Garden scene, based on an actual garden in Shanghai, painted in blue on Chinese export porcelain and copied by numerous English potters, with slight variations, from late C18.

Wilton: Carpet-making centre in Wiltshire established c1740, producing moquette cut-pile carpets until the early C19 when taken over by Axminster and production of machine-knotted carpets began.

Wiltshaw & Robinson: Stoke-on-Trent pottery, founded in 1897, makers of Art Nouveau Carlton Ware.

Wincanton: C18 delftwares produced at Wincanton, similar to the products of nearby Bristol.

Winchester, Oliver F.: Leading American gunsmith, active mid C19.

Winchester rifle: Twelve-shot semi-automatic rifle invented by B. Henry Taylor and manufactured at New Haven, Connecticut, after the American Civil War.

Windmills, Joseph: Noted London maker of clocks and watches, active late C17/early C18.

window seat: Upholstered stool with raised ends, wide enough to seat two people.

Windsor chair: Country chair of various designs, characteristically having a saddle seat, a hoop back and simple turned legs.

wine cellar: See cellaret.

wine cooler: Container designed to hold wine bottles and water or ice with a lining of lead for this purpose. They do not have lids.

wine funnel: Cone with a spout and often a matching dish for filtering or decanting wine, of silver, from C17.

wing chair: Upholstered chair with a high back with winglike side projections at head level. From early C18.

winged stem: Wing or ear shaped ornamental mouldings of fine glass, attached to the stems of wine glasses and bowls and typical of the Venetian style.

Winterthur wares: Delftware from the Swiss town, noted especially for decorative stove tiles.

wirework: Any metal object, such as a fruit basket or toast rack, made of strands of wire.

Wistar glass: Early American glass made by Caspar Wistar who founded a glassworks in Salem county in 1739.

witch balls: Hollow glass balls, sometimes coloured, often silvered internally; their original use unknown, but used as Christmas tree ornaments in the C19.

withdrawing table: Table with two additional leaves, usually hidden within the carcase, which can be pulled or drawn out to increase its length. Also known as a draw leaf table.

WMF: Short for the Austrian Württembergishe Metallwarenfabrik, one of the principal producers of Art Nouveau silver and silverplated objects, early C20.

Wolfe & Co.: Liverpool porcelain factory of c1795 to 1800, noted for attractively painted polychrome wares. Now sought after.

Wood: Famous family of Staffordshire potters; Ralph (1715-72) and his nephew Enoch (1759-1840) were noted especially for fine porcelain figures and for toby jugs.

Wood, David: Newburyport clockmaker, active 1765-90.

Wood, John: Philadelphia clockmaker active 1770-93.

Wooden clock: One with a wooden movement, usually pendulum driven.

woodworm: See common furniture beetle.

Worcester: Important porcelain factory, founded 1751; its designs variously influenced by silverware, Qing dynasty Chinese wares and the products of Meissen and Sèvres; noted especially for outstanding painted decoration; figures produced since the late C19 equally fine and collectable.

work table: Name generally given to a table designed for needlework or sewing.

wrigglework: Wavy engraved designs on silver or pewter.

Wright, Frank Lloyd (1869-1959): Influential and accomplished American architect who also designed fresh and classic furniture.

Wright and Mansfield: Victorian cabinetmakers who made fine reproduction furniture in the styles of Adam and Sheraton.

writing chair: Another name for a corner chair.

writing table: Any table designed for writing at, usually with an inset leather top. First appeared late C17.

Wrockwardine: C18 glassworks in Shropshire making Nailsea glass.

wrong: Antique dealers' term for a piece that has been faked, altered or restored.

Wucai/Wu ts'ai: Chinese for "five colours; although in practice, more than five colours were often used.

wych elm: Variety of elm.

X

X-frame: Term describing the X-shaped construction of some chairs and stools.

Xianfeng (Hsien Feng): Chinese Qing dynasty emperor, 1851-61.

Xuande (Hsuan Te): Chinese Ming dynasty emperor, 1426-35.

Xuantong (Hsuan T'ung): Chinese Qing dynasty emperor, 1909-11.

Xylonite: Early and rare form of plastic made from 1868, simulating wood.

Y

yallameh: Brightly coloured rugs from the Isfahan region of Iran with geometric decoration.

yami-makie: Japanese lacquerwork in which black designs are made on a subtly contrasting black background.

yao: Chinese for "kiln", hence the wares of a specific region or province e.g. Jian yao – pottery from the Jian region of Fukien province.

yastik: Turkish for a small rug.

yataghan: Turkish sword with a short hilt and no guard.

yayoi: Early Japanese bronze and ceramics, dating from c300 BC to AD C1.

year clock: Clock that goes for a year without rewinding.

yellow metal: Copper and zinc alloy developed early C19 in imitation of gold.

yen yen: European term, perhaps derived from Chinese "yen" or "beautiful", for a baluster vase with a broad flaring neck.

yew: Hard, deep reddish brown wood used both as a veneer and solid. It is very resistant to woodworm and turns well.

yezd: Modern hand-made carpets from the village of that name in the Kirman region of central Iran.

yi hsing: Chinese tea-ceremony vessels in unglazed stoneware.

ying ching: Chinese Sung and Yuan dynasty porcelain decorated with carved or moulded floral patterns and covered with pale blue-green translucent glaze.

yin-yang: Chinese motif found on carpets, bronzes and ceramics. Consists of a circle divided into two comma shaped portions in contrasting colours symbolizing the unity of opposites.

yomud: Carpets from the Soviet/Iranian border region; diamond patterns on a deep red or blue ground.

Yongle (Yung Lo): Chinese Ming dynasty emperor, 1403-24.

Yongzheng (Yung Cheng): Chinese Qing dynasty emperor, 1723-35.

Yorkshire chair: Type of mid C17 chair with a tall back which features ornately carved arched rails. Also known as a Derbyshire chair.

Yorkshire clock: General term for bulky, grandiose longcase clocks of the late C18 and early C19, not necessarily from Yorkshire.

Yorkshire pottery: C18 and C19 lead glazed earthenwares decorated with cream slip, produced by many factories in England's largest county.

yu: Chinese bronze ritual food-storage vessel.

Yuan dynasty: Period in Chinese history AD 1280-1368 during which the art of underglaze painting was developed.

yueh: Chinese stoneware with a green glaze and delicate low relief decoration from the Yueh district of Chekiang province.

yuruk: Carpets made by south east Turkish nomads, loosely woven, brightly coloured with geometric designs.

Z

zaanclock: C17 Dutch wallclock with a case extending above as well as below the dial to accommodate a pendulum pivoted above the movement rather than below.

Zanesville: Range of coloured glasswares made early C19 in Zanesville, Ohio.

zanzibar chest: Type of Eastern chest, usually made in India, and shipped via Zanzibar. Elaborately decorated.

Zapotec: Mesoamerican culture, flourishing c200 BC-AD 900 in the Valley of Oaxaca.

zar: Unit of measurement in carpet making. One zar is approximately one yard/one metre in length.

zaranim: One and a half zars, or about 5ft (1.5m), the typical width of many Oriental rugs.

zebrawood: Brown wood from South America. It has distinctive black stripes and was used as a veneer.

Zechlin: C18 glass producing centre in Silesia, specializing in glass ornamented with applied portrait medallions, often gilded.

Zeikhur: A type of rug from the Caucasus.

Zerbst faience: Short-lived C18 factory near Leipzig.

Zeus: Supreme deity of the ancient Greeks, equivalent to the Roman Jupiter.

Zhengde (Cheng Te): Chinese Ming dynasty emperor, 1506-21.

Ziegler: Persian carpets imported by the Manchester-based firm of that name in the latter half C19.

Zinnsoldaten: Toy soldiers of lead or tin alloy manufactured in the Nuremberg area from the C16 and widely exported C18 and C19. Also known as "flats" because they are two-dimensional, with a narrow base.

zoëtrope: Revolving cylinder into which a circular strip of pictures is placed; when spun, the figures in the picture seem to move.

Zurich porcelain: Latter half C18, figures and tableware decorated with Swiss mountain scenes.

Zwischen goldglas: Doublewalled glass made by fitting one vessel inside another and fusing them together: the outer surface of the interior vessel is decorated with gold leaf ornamentation (sometimes also of silver – Zwischen Silberglas).

Zwischen goldglas